19|1

Dispatches from the Front Line of Popular Culture

Tony Parsons

Virgin

For Yuriko

First published in Great Britain in 1994 by
Virgin Books
an imprint of Virgin Publishing Ltd
332 Ladbroke Grove
London W10 5AH

The extract from *Class* by Jilly Cooper on p. 233 is reproduced by kind permission of Methuen London

A catalogue record for this book is available from the British Library

ISBN 1 85227 449 2

Typeset by TW Typesetting, Plymouth Devon
Printed and bound in Great Britain by
Mackays of Chatham, Chatham, Kent

Contents

Travel

Polemic

Culture

Introduction and Acknowledgements

VERY FEW professions pay you good money to spend time in the company of people like Muhammad Ali, Morrissey and Jung Chang. And there are very few jobs that pack you off to places like Texas, Japan, Chicago, Manila and West Africa with the instructions – wander around for a while, tell us what you think. And there are a very, *very* small number of gigs that invite you to mouth off on subjects as diverse as music, sex, love, *A Clockwork Orange* and the decline of the working class. But journalism does all of these things. It's a beautiful job – why would anyone ever want to give it up?

And yet they do! Most journalists dream of writing fiction. They all dream in different ways, of course. Some might pine for a two-book shopping-and-fucking deal. Others might fancy a big fat John Grisham-sized thriller perched at the top of the *New York Times* bestseller list. Still others might yearn for literary credibility – critical kudos, a Booker nomination, snooker once a fortnight with Martin and Julian. But I never felt like that.

I published my first novel, a bad book (no, I insist) that sold well, when my day job was a night shift in an Islington gin distillery. The fiction came first. So I never dreamed of the self-imposed agoraphobia of writing novels – I wanted the mad, hold-the-front-page adrenal fever of working for newspapers.

'Chicago, 1928, that was the general idea,' wrote Tom Wolfe, describing his own newspaperman fantasy. 'Drunken reporters out on the ledge of the News peeing into the Chicago River at dawn. Nights down at the detective bureau – it was always night time in my daydreams of newspaper life.'

My bad novel got me a wonderful job – at the *New Musical Express*, covering the punk rock goldrush. These days the music press seems rather like the Civil Service – you sign on for life and grimly serve out your thirty years, and no pale nineteen-year-old dressed in black can ever dislodge you. Some of them are over *thirty* – can you believe that?

But in the second half of the '70s the music press was wild and all-consuming and you were considered an old man at 24. We were callow and cruel and selling 250,000 copies a week. We were so successful that our owners left us alone to merrily run amok. And if you were lucky enough to work up there, it commandeered your life.

The *NME* took over your life because you quite literally did not need anything else. Good times, bad times, hard liquor, soft women, weird sex, exotic cocktails, good friends, bitter enemies, creative fulfilment, a punch in the cakehole – you could get absolutely everything you wanted without ever stepping out of the office. Apart from a sandwich.

It was never meant to last. Not one of my contemporaries ever considered making the music press a lifetime's work. By your first grey hair you were either gone or you were dead. It was like doing your National Service – a couple of years and you were out. You went in a boy and came out a man. Or, in some cases, a basket case.

Before I joined the *NME* I thought that the music business would be an endless round of discovering great young bands, sharing the rites of wanton gratification with rock stars and flying off to America. And when I joined the *NME*, I discovered that's exactly what it was like. The late '70s was the perfect time to work for a weekly music paper. You could go out seven nights a week in London and see a different great unsigned band every night – and still have change for a pair of bondage trousers. It was a great place for a young journalist to learn his craft because it felt like every young person in the country who could read without moving their lips was buying the paper. I was at the *NME* for three years and every day I walked into the office with a shiver of excitement, wondering what was going to happen that day. Then it wore off. Then it was the '80s.

I could never buy the notion of the '80s as a superficial, trivial, another-spritzer-over-here-garçon kind of decade. My father died in the '80s. My son was born in the '80s. And I can't think of anything more important than that.

Anyway, I left the *NME* and wrote a few more novels. 'The old dream, The Novel, has never died,' said Tom Wolfe. The books did well – especially the first one, *Platinum Logic*, a blockbuster about the music business. But I missed journalism. I know that there are a lot of timeservers and hacks and downright dirty liars in the racket but to me it is a noble profession and I have never stopped loving it.

I missed getting out of the flat. I missed the deadlines. The fraternity. The gut-level thrill of turning a piece around quickly, seeing it appear in print and watching the hate mail roll in. But I think that most of all I missed the free air travel. I published four novels before my thirtieth birthday. I was ready to get back to the world.

Music is where I started and for anyone of my jammy-git generation – a baby when Elvis had a thirty-inch waist, a child during Beatlemania, an adolescent when Bowie was breaking, a young man during punk – music will always be important. Born at the right time. If I had been born ten years earlier or later then no doubt I would have been begging to be allowed on to the motoring pages by now. But to find things that excited me as much as punk did, I had to look outside music. By now Nick Logan had quit as editor of the *NME* to start up his own magazines. Nick drove me to the airport.

The first story in this collection is from the *New Musical Express* in late 1976 – a report on the opening date of the Sex Pistols' Anarchy In The UK tour. The penultimate story appeared in *The Daily Telegraph* in early 1994 – an interview with Jung Chang about her book *Wild Swans*. What a long, strange trip it's been -- from the inky outrage of the *NME* to writing columns in *The Daily Telegraph*, from working alongside the great Nick Kent to occasional columns in *The Sunday Telegraph* that appear with the punchline, 'Peregrine Worsthorne is on holiday.'

But perhaps the trip has not really been so strange. One of the things I loved about the *NME* was that it sold to what felt like every nineteen-year-old in the country. And I love it that *The Daily Telegraph* is read by eight million people every day. I have always been excited by mass-circulation newspapers. I was never much interested in flogging fanzines from the top of the stairs in the Roxy. Even when punk rock was just a few dozen people in London, we dreamed of conquering the mainstream. The underground is for losers.

The stories here are collected from around a dozen different sources. But mostly they are from the *NME* in the '70s, *Arena* in the '80s and *The Daily Telegraph* in the '90s. Nick Logan (now publisher of *The Face*, *Arena* and *Arena Homme Plus*) was my editor at *NME* in the Seventies. Dylan Jones (now at *The Sunday Times*) was my editor at *Arena* in the '80s. And Max Hastings is my editor-in-chief at *The Daily Telegraph* today.

Nick, Dylan and Max are all great editors because they are all ready to stand back-to-back with you in a rat-infested alley facing down a gang of crack-crazed street toughs. Better still, they make sure you get paid on time. I am lucky to have had them on my side.

Love and thanks also go to the journalists who asked me to write these stories – Nigel Reynolds, Christena Appelyard, Lesley White, Sarah Miller, Jenny Tabakoff, Rob Ryan, Christine Walker, Kate Flett, Peter Browne, Mal Peachey, Louise Chunn, Carl Hindmarch, Shane Watson, Nicola Jeal, Amy Raphael, Sally Brampton, Gill Morgan, Will Ellsworth-Jones, Charles Moore, John Connell, Michele Lavery, Ian Cranna, David Jenkins, Neil Spencer, Phil McNeil, Paul Rambali, Roger Alton, Shaun Philips, Philip Thomas, Veronica Lee, Steve Browne, Robert Posner, Lola Bubbosh and Auberon Waugh. I am more than lucky to have had them on my side – I am blessed. Special thanks to Tim Rostron – my best man, main man and mentor at *The Daily Telegraph*.

Previous plans to publish a collection of my journalism stumbled and fell because nobody could decide what such a book would look like. Should it be a music collection? Or a selection of pieces like 'The Tattooed Jungle', a bumper book of the kind of stuff that had the man on the Clapham Omnibus coughing blood? What about the travel stories? And the sexual polemic? Should the book be outrageously hilarious? Or merely hilariously outrageous? Nobody knew.

Mal Peachey came up with the perfect remedy over dim sum one lunchtime in Chinatown – chuck it all in, he suggested, expansively waving his chopsticks. Music, love, sex, travel and articles that eventually became documentaries on Channel 4's arts slot, *Without Walls* – wheel them all on! Let chaos reign! This book would not have existed without his enthusiasm and vision. Thanks, Mal.

The book attempts to be a comprehensive selection – some things have been left out on the grounds of space, the libel laws or common decency. But nothing has been left out because it was the immature ravings of someone who had a lot to learn. I have to live with the chortling, highly-strung ghost of my younger self and so must the reader. Sorry about that.

'A professional writer has only so many shots in his locker,' wrote Auberon Waugh in the introduction to his brilliant autobiography *Will This Do?* (the question, said Bron, that every journalist asks himself when submitting an article – and the question we will ask 'in trembling hope', when we finally face our Maker). I have been fortunate that the shots in my locker were all the things I love. It has been one hell of a day job.

When I was a very young boy I wrote to Keith Waterhouse asking him how to become a writer. Because Mr Waterhouse is a gracious man as well as a great writer, he took the trouble to write back. 'Get a good agent,' he advised. I have been lucky enough to have a great agent – Caradoc King of A. P. Watt, whose faith in me has never faltered. Keith Waterhouse was right.

Stories come in and out of a journalist's life like bus boys in a restaurant. It doesn't seem *so* long ago that I was floating down the Thames with The Sex Pistols or speeding around the Circle line with the Clash – but already those adventures are a quarter of a lifetime away.

And now I find that young journalists come to me asking for advice, just as I once shyly approached Keith Waterhouse. What am I supposed to tell them? As I tentatively turn through the eighteen years of journalism collected here, it seems to me that this is the sum total of what I have learned.

Stay close to the things you love. And take a baseball bat to the rest.

Tony Parsons
London 1994

Music

Blank Generation out on the Road

Sex Pistols; Damned; Heartbreakers; Clash: Leeds

New Musical Express, 11 December 1976

ENNETH ANGER CALLED James Dean 'a human ashtray'. Maybe he should have waited twenty years to see the self-inflicted fag burns on Rotten's arms. 'It's my body and I'll do what I like with it.'

The Pistols come onstage at Leeds Poly to a smattering of applause, lots of abuse and a few objects thrown at them. No way is this mob gonna be like their pogoing London supporters.

Glen Matlock & Steve Jones plug in and Paul Cook sits behind his kit as Rotten just hangs from the mike stand, rips opens a can of beer, and burns the crowd with his glassy, taunting, cynical eyes: Spiky dyed red hair, death white visage, metal hanging from lobes, skinny leg strides, red waistcoat, black tie and safety pins – he looks like an amphetamine corpse from a Sunday gutter press wet dream.

Something thrown from the audience hits him full in the face. Rotten glares at the person who did it, lips drawn back over decaying teeth. 'Don't give me your shit,' he snarls, 'because we don't mess . . . This first number's dedicated to 'a Leeds councillor, Bill Grundy and the Queen – fuck ya!'

And straight into a searing rendition of the Blank Generation anthem, 'Anarchy In The UK,' done even better than the single which just charted at 43. The rhythm section of Cook on drums and Matlock on bass are tighter than tomorrow, fully complimenting the pneumatic guitar work of Steve Jones and Rotten's deranged dementoid vocal.

It's a blistering start, but unfortunately for both the Pistols and the crowd it turns out to be the high point of the set. The crowd are way too restrained through 'Lazy Sod', 'No Future' and 'Pretty Vacant', failing even to see the humour in the really cocked-up intro of this song.

Rotten glares at them. 'You're not wrecking the place', he says, 'The *News of the World* will be *really* disappointed.'

This gets a laugh, but the crowd don't seem to realise that the two things Rotten hates most are apathy and complacency, both of which are rife tonight at Leeds Poly. 'I 'ope you 'ate it!' he screams. 'You don't like it then you know where the *exit* door is!'

Earlier he had been taking a sip from a can of beer and then handing the can to the crowd. Now he spits at them . . .

Even with numbers that the crowd know, like the Who's 'Substitute' or the Monkees' 'Stepping Stone', the punters never really get into it. Rotten's going crazy with angry frustration. A token object thrown from the audience hits him in the face. 'You just stand there, you don't know whether you like it or not!'

The band eventually returns for a few more numbers. The Small Faces' 'What'cha Gonna Do 'Bout It' has its lyrics changed to 'Want you to know that I hate you baby, want you know I don't care,' and then it's the last number, with the audience finally putting some effort into lifting the band. It's Iggy's 'No Fun', arguably the definitive Pistols live number – even more so than 'Anarchy'.

Then they were gone and I felt for them. A string of cancelled gigs, the press labelling them Public Enemies No. 1, and a frightened element of the rock press saying they can't play (obviously a lie) – and when they finally get a chance to play the kids *ain't* all right. What a choker.

The Clash opened up the evening with a great set. Hard committed, loud brash, violent rock music, I got the impression they expected nothing from the audience or anybody else so that they didn't have the same problems as the Pistols. Joe Strummer, wearing a green sweat shirt emblazoned with the legend 'Social Security £9.70', ignored the hecklers as he did the spoken intro to 'White Riot'. It's their best song, all about what it was like to be caught up in the Notting Hill Riot without being either a cop or a black. 'I wanna riot of my own'.

Mick, the lead axe, in a paint splattered Union Jack shirt, bounds about like Townshend, looks like Keith Richard's grandson, and a lot of the time handles vocals with Strummer. Other songs include 'Bored With The USA', 'London's Burning', 'Career Opportunity' ('dedicated to all you students') and '1977': *'Hope I go to heaven, been too long on the dole . . .'* If you don't know why I call it dole queue rock then you ain't seen The Clash.

I enjoyed the Heartbreakers because they remind me of the New York Dolls – the way they play, their songs and *sometimes* their visual. With ex-Dolls Jerry Nolan on drums and Johnny Thunders on leads (both of them with neatly shorn locks as a concession to the UK) you couldn't help but compare them to their days with Johansen, Sylvain and Kane.

Well, they're not as good as the Dolls *yet*, the other two members of the band being less manic than the Dolls of old, but if they live long enough they could develop into something very fine.

'I Wanna Be Loved By You' by 'Needles' Nolan, as Johnny Thunders calls him, has got hit single stamped all over it. And the Heartbreakers are certainly better than The Ramones.

I had eagerly awaited the appearance of the dole queue supremos The Damned, but they turned out to be the biggest disappointment of the night. The downer of cancelled gigs, a far too short set, and behind-the-scenes problems all contributed to the lacklustre performance.

And no one knew it better than Rat, Brian, Dave and the Cap. But I'd lay odds that next time out, anxious to prove themselves again, they'll be playing at the heights we expect from them and they expect from themselves.

Now listen good. If the pious hypocrites who rule our land ban this tour from appearing in your town then get off your lazy butt, go to the next town, or even the next town, until you get a chance to check it out.

Because if you miss it this time round, I doubt very much if you'll ever get a chance to see a tour like this again. And if you don't see it then all I can say is you are no fun.

Sten-guns in Knightsbridge??

The Clash

New Musical Express, 2 April 1977

'❙ T AIN'T punk, it ain't new wave, it's the next step and the logical progression for groups to move in. Call it what you want – all the terms stink. Just call it rock 'n' roll . . .'

You don't know what total commitment *is* until you've met Mick Jones of The Clash.

He's intense, emotional, manic-depressive and plays lead guitar with the kind of suicidal energy that some musicians lose and most musicians never have. His relationship with Joe Strummer and Paul Simenon is the love/hate intensity that you only get with family.

'My parents never . . . the people involved with The Clash *are my family* . . .'

The Clash and me are sitting around a British Rail table in one of those railway station cafes where the puce-coloured paint on the wall is peeling and lethargic non-white slave labour serves you tea that tastes like cat urine.

Joe Strummer is an ex-101er and the mutant offspring of Bruce Lee's legacy – a no-bullshit sense of tough that means he can talk about a thrashing he took a while back from some giant, psychotic Teddy Boy without the slightest pretension, self-pity or sense of martyrdom.

'I was too pissed to deal with it and he got me in the toilets for a while,' Joe says.

'I had a knife with me, and I shoulda stuck it in him, right? But when it came to it I remember vaguely thinking that it wasn't really worth it coz although he was battering me about the floor I was too drunk for it to hurt that much and if I stuck my knife in him I'd probably have to do a few years . . .'

When The Clash put paint-slashed slogans on their family-created urban battle fatigues such as 'Hate And War' it's *not* a cute turn-around of a flowery spiel from ten years ago – it's a brutally honest comment on the environment they're living in.

They've had aggravation with everyone from Teds to students to Anglo-rednecks, all of them frightened pigs attacking what they can't understand. But this ain't the summer of love and The Clash would rather be kicked into hospital than flash a peace sign and turn the other cheek.

'We ain't ashamed to fight,' Mick says.

'We should carry spray cans about with us,' Paul Simenon suggests.

He's the spike-haired bass-player with considerable pulling power. Even my kid sister fancies him. He's from a South London ex-skinhead background; white Sta-Prest Levi strides, highly polished DM boots, button-down Ben Sherman shirt, thin braces, eighth-of-an-inch cropped hair and over the football on a Saturday running with The Shed because for the first time in your life the society that produced you was terrified of you.

And it made you feel good . . .

Paul came out of that, getting into rock 'n' roll at the start of last year and one of the first bands he ever saw was The Sex Pistols. Pure late-Seventies rock, Paul Simenon. In Patti Smith's estimation he rates alongside Keef and Rimbaud. He knew exactly what he was doing when he named the band The Clash . . .

'The Hostilities,' Mick Jones calls the violent reactions they often provoke. 'Or maybe those Lemon Squeezers,' Paul says, seeking the perfect weapon for protection when trouble starts and you're outnumbered ten to one.

The rodent-like features of their shaven-headed ex-jailbird roadie known, among other things, as Rodent break into a cynical smirk.

'Don't get it on their drapes otherwise they get *really* mad,' he quips.

He went along to see The Clash soon after his release from prison. At the time he was carrying a copy of *Mein Kampf* around with him. Prison can mess up your head.

Strummer, in his usual manner of abusive honesty, straightened him out. Rodent's been with them ever since and sleeps on the floor of their studio.

The Clash demand total dedication from everyone involved with the band, a sense of responsibility that must never be betrayed no matter what internal feuds, ego-clashes or personality crisis may go down. Anyone who doesn't have that attitude will not remain with The Clash for very long and that's the reason for the band's biggest problem – they ain't got a drummer.

The emotive Mick explodes at the mention of this yawning gap in the line-up and launches into a stream-of-consciousness expletive-deleted soliloquy with talk of drummers who bottled out of broken glass confrontations, drummers whose egos outweighed their creative talent, drummers who are going to get their legs broken.

'Forget it, it's in the past now,' Joe tells him quietly, with just a few words cooling out Mick's anger and replacing it with something positive. 'If any drummer thinks he can make it then we wanna know.'

'We're going to the Pistols' gig tonight to find a new drummer!' Mick says excitedly. 'But they gotta prove themselves,' he adds passionately. 'They gotta believe in what's happening. *And they gotta tell the truth . . .*'

The Band and Rodent have their passport photos taken in a booth on the station. Four black and white shots for twenty pence.

They pool their change and after one of them has had the necessary two pictures taken the next one dives in quickly to replace him before the white flash explodes.

When you're on twenty-five quid a week the stories of one quarter of a million dollars for the cocaine bill of a tax exile Rock Establishment band seems like a sick joke . . .

The Human Freight of the London Underground rush hour regard The Clash with a culture-shock synthesis of hate, fear and suspicion.

The Human Freight have escaped the offices and are pouring out to the suburbs until tomorrow. Stacked haunch to paunch in an atmosphere of stale sweat, bad breath and city air the only thing that jolts them out of their usual mood of apathetic surrender is the presence of The Clash.

Because something's happening here but The Human Freight don't know what it is . . .

'Everybody's doing just what they're told to/Nobody wants to go to jail/White Riot/I Wanna Riot/White Riot/A Riot of me own!/Are you taking over or are you taking orders?/Are you going backwards or are you going forwards?'

'White Riot' and The Sound Of The Westway, the giant inner city flyover and the futuristic backdrop for this country's first major race riot since 1959.

Played with the speed of The Westway, a GBH treble that is as impossible to ignore as the police siren that opens the single or the alarm bell that closes it.

Rock 'n' roll for the late Nineteen Seventies updating their various influences (Jones – the New York Dolls, MCs, Stooges, vintage Stones; Simenon – Pistols, Ramones, Heartbreakers; and Strummer, *totally* eclectic) and then adding something of their very own. The sense of flash of beach-fighting Mods speeding through three weekend nights non-stop, coupled with an ability to write songs of contemporary urban imagery that are a perfect reflection of the life of any kid who came of age in the Seventies.

The former makes The Clash live raw-nerve electric, a level of excitement generated that can only be equalled by one other band – Johnny Thunders' Heartbreakers.

The latter makes The Clash, or maybe specifically Jones and Strummer (as Simenon has only recently started writing), the fulfilment of the original aim of the New Wave, Punk Rock, whatever; that is, to write songs about the late Seventies British youth culture with the accuracy, honesty, perception and genuine anger that Elvis, The Beatles or The Rolling Stones or any others in the Rock Establishment could never do, now that they're closer to members of the Royal Family or face-lift lard-arse movie stars than they are to you or me . . .

But so many bands coming through now are churning out clichéd platitudes and political nursery rhymes. The Blank Generation is the antithesis of what The Clash are about . . .

Strummer and Jones disagree on the best environment for a new band to develop and keep growing.

Joe thinks it's all too easy right now and having to fight every inch of the way when the band was formed a year ago is the healthiest situation – whereas Mick believes in giving every help and encouragement possible while being totally honest with bands who are just not delivering the goods.

'I'm as honest as I can be,' he shouts over the roar of the tube train. 'All the new groups sound like drones and I ain't seen a good new group for six months. Their sound just ain't exciting, they need two years . . .'

The sound of The Clash has evolved, with their experience this year in the recording studio first with Polydor when they were dangling a contract, and more recently recording their first album after CBS snapped them up at the eleventh hour.

The change in the sound first struck me as a regulation of energy, exerting a razor-sharp adrenalin control over their primal amphetamined rush. It created a new air of tension added to the ever-present manic drive that has always existed in their music, The Sound Of The Westway . . .

And, of course, the subtle-yet-definite shift in emphasis is perfect for the feeling that's in the air in the United Kingdom, one quarter of 1977 already gone:

'In 1977 you're on the never-never/You think it can't go on for-ever/But the papers say it's better/I don't care/Coz I'm not all there/No Elvis, Beatles or the Rolling Stones/In 1977.'

'1977', the other side of the single, ends with the three-pronged attack shouting in harmonies derived from football terraces: '1984!'

The pressure. That's what they call the heavy atmosphere in Jamaica, the feeling in the air that very soon, something has got to change . . .

The Jamaican culture is highly revered by The Clash. They hang out in black clubs, pick up reggae import singles in shops where it ain't really wise for them to tread and express their disgust at the undeniable fact that in the poor working-class areas of London where they grew up and still live the blacks are treated even worse than the whites.

But, ultimately, they know that White Youth needs its *own* sense of identity, culture and heritage if they're going to fight for change.

A riot of their own . . .

But can the masses take to the incisive reality of what The Clash are about the way they lap up the straight-ahead rock bands who push nothing more than having a good time?

'Maybe the reason those bands are so big is because they *don't* say anything,' Mick says. 'But we ain't gonna preach and sound like some evangelist.'

I mention to Joe what happened when he walked on stage at Leeds Poly for the first gig that actually happened on the Pistols' Anarchy tour.

He said a few words before the band went into the set that they'd been burning to play for weeks, about how the gutter press hysteria, local council butchery and Mary Whitehouse mentality of The Great British people was preventing certain young rock bands getting on stage and playing for the people who wanted to see them.

I remember him saying that 1984 seemed to have arrived early as the Leeds Poly students bawled abuse at him.

With the minds and manners of barnyard pigs the over-grown school-children conveyed the message that they didn't give a shit:

'I think they will take to us, but it'll take time,' Joe says. 'But I don't want to go *towards* them at all, I don't wanna start getting soft around the edges.'

'I don't want to compromise . . . I think they'll come round in time but if they *don't* it's too bad.'

'We ain't *never* gonna get commercial respectability,' Mick says, both anger and despair in his voice.

Paul Simenon takes it all in and then ponders the nearest station that has a bar on the platform.

That's the difference between their attitudes to, how you say, Making It.

Strummer is confident, determined, arrogant and sometimes violent in the face of ignorant opposition (a couple of months back in a club car park he faced an American redneck-rock band with just his blade for support).

Mick Jones is a rock equivalent to a Kamikaze pilot. All or nothing.

The Clash gives him both the chance to pour out his emotional turmoil and offer an escape route from the life the assembly-line education the country gave him had primed him for.

When a careers officer at school spends five minutes with you and tells you what you're gonna do with your life for the next fifty years. More fodder for the big corporations and the dole.

Mick is beating them at their own game by ignoring all the rules.

'*Someone locked me out so I kicked the way back in,*' he declares in 'Hate and War'.

His uncanny resemblance to a young Keef Richard allowed him to relieve an early identity problem by adopting the lookalike con-trick which fools no one but yourself. Then he met Strummer who told him he was wearing a Keith Richard identikit as though he had bought it in a shop.

'I got my self-respect in this group,' Mick says, 'I don't believe in guitar heroes. If I walk out to the front of the stage it's because I wanna reach the audience, I want to *communicate* with them, I don't want them to suck my guitar off. . .'

And Paul Simenon: total hedonist.

His fondest memories of the Anarchy tour are hotel room parties and broken chairs, things trod into the carpet and girls who got you worried because you thought they were gonna die like Jimi Hendrix if they didn't wake up. He's a member of The Clash because they're the best band in the country and it gets him laid a lot.

So what did they learn from the Anarchy tour, so effectively butchered by the self-righteous Tin Gods who pull the strings?

'I learned that there's no romance in being on the road,' Mick says.

'I learned that there's lots,' Joe smiles.

'I learned that if they don't want you to play they can stop you,' Joe says seriously. 'And no one's gonna raise any fuss . . .'

'For the first four days we were confined to our rooms because the *News of the World* was next door,' Mick continues.

'We thought – shall we go out there with syringes stuck in our arms just to get 'em going? Yeah, and furniture seemed to have labels saying, "Please smash me" or "Out The Window, Please".'

And when they finally got to play, the minds in the Institutes of Further Education were as narrow as those in Fleet Street. So Strummer gave them something – even though they were too blind to see it . . .

'This one's for all you *students*,' he sneered before The Clash tore into the song that they wrote about Joe being on the dole for so long that The Department of Employment (sic) wanted to send him to rehabilitation to give him back the confidence that they assumed the dole must have destroyed, together with Mick's experience working *for* the Social Security office in West London, and, as the most junior employee, being told to open all the mail during the time of the IRA letter-bombs.

The song is called 'Career Opportunities':

'Career Opportunities/The ones that never knock/Every job they offer you/Is to keep ya out the dock/Career Opportunities./They offered me the office/they offered me the shop/They said I'd better take Anything They Got./'Do you wanna make tea for the BBC?/ Do you wanna be, do you wanna be a cop?'/I hate the army and I hate the RAF/You won't get me fighting in the tropical heat/I hate the Civil Service rules/And I ain't gonna open letter bombs for you!'

'Most bands and writers who talk about the dole *Dunno what the dole is*!' Mick shouts.

'They've never been on the dole in their life. But the dole is only hard if you've been conditioned to think you've gotta have a job . . . then it's sheer degradation.

'The Social Security made me open the letters during the letter bomb time because I looked subversive. Most of the letters the Social Security get are from the people who live next door saying their neighbours don't need the money. The whole thing works on spite.

'One day an Irish guy that they had treated like shit and kept waiting for three hours picked up a wooden bench and put it through the window into Praed Street.'

Mick shakes his head in disgust at the memory of the way our great Welfare State treats its subjects.

'Every time I didn't have a job I was down there – waiting. And they degrade the black youth even more. They have to wait even longer. No-one can tell me there ain't any prejudice . . .

We make for 'Rehearsal Rehearsals', the North London studio of The Clash. An enormous building once used by the British Rail for a warehouse. Only part of it is in use at the moment, a large expanse of property ruled by no lighting, rats and water.

Upstairs Joe, Mick and Paul look glad to have guitars in their hands again. The walls are covered with posters of Bruce Lee, Patti Smith, The Pistols and The Clash themselves.

A large map of the United Kingdom faces the old TV set where Hughie Green is being sincere with the speech turned down. Biro graffiti stains the screen. The television is not treated like the Holy Grail in *this* place . . .

I watch Joe playing a battered old guitar with all but two of its strings missing and think about his comments when I wanted to know he would cope with financial success when/if it came . . .

'I ain't gonna fuck myself up like I seen all those other guys fuck themselves up,' he said. 'Keeping all their money for themselves and getting into their head and thinking they're the greatest.

'I've planned what I'm gonna do with my money *if* it happens. Secret plans . . .'

I could be wrong, but at a guess the development of Rehearsal Rehearsals into anything from a recording studio to a rock venue to a radio/TV station seem like possible Strummer visions for when The Clash get the mass acceptance they deserve.

As we talk about how The Clash have reacted to putting their music down on vinyl I tell them that the major criticism people not cognisant with their songs have expressed is that the unique Strummer vocal makes understanding their brilliant lyrics almost imposs-ible for the uninitiated.

'The first time we went into a studio with a famous producer he said, "You better pronounce the words, right?" ' Joe remembers with his amused sneer.

'So I did it and it sounded like Matt Monroe. So I thought I'm

never doing that again ... to me our music is like Jamaican stuff –
if they can't hear it, they're not supposed to hear it. It's not for them
if they can't understand it.'

The Clash say that being signed with CBS has had no interference
with the preservation of their integrity and, even with the band's
attitude of No Compromise, a termination of contract in the manner
of the Pistols seems most unlikely.

They believe the sound on the album to be infinitely superior to
that of the single because the latter was cut during one of their first
sessions in the studio after the decision to let their sound man Micky
Foote produce the band even though he had no previous experience
in production.

'We tried the famous ones,' Joe grins. 'They were all too pissed to
work.'

'Outside, there ain't no young producers in tune with what's going
on,' Mick says. 'The only way to do it is to learn how to do it yourself.'

'You do it yourself because nobody else *cares* that much,' Micky
Foote, Boy Wonder Producer tells me, his sentiments totally in
keeping with the clan spirit in The Clash camp.

The band talk of their respect for their manager Bernard Rhodes,
who has been a major influence on all of them, and who has made
enemies because of his obsessive commitment to The Clash. But Joe,
Mick and Paul are free spirits, unlike a lot of bands with heavy
personality management.

'He really pushes us,' Paul says.

'We do respect him,' Mick adds. 'He was always helping and
giving constructive criticism long before he was our manager.' Mick
then points at the other members of the band and himself. 'But the
heart is there.'

I ask them about their political leanings. Do they believe in left
and right or is there just up and down?

They reply by telling me about a leftist workshop they used to
frequent because they enjoyed the atmosphere – and also because it
gave them an opportunity to nick the paints they needed for their
artwork.

'It was really exhilarating there,' Mick says. 'They used to play
Chinese revolutionary records and then one day the National Front
threw bricks through the window.

'The place didn't shut, though. So one day they burned the whole
joint down and they had to close down ...'

'In 1977 there's knives in West Eleven/Ain't so lucky to be rich/ Sten-guns in Knightsbridge/Danger stranger/You better paint your face/No Elvis, Beatles or the Rolling Stones/In 1977/Sod the Jubilee!'

'I always thought in terms of survival,' Mick says.

'And these people are the opposition of free speech and personal liberty. And they're trying to manipulate the rock medium.'

Then he repeats something he said earlier, reiterating the importance of The Clash: 'And I ain't ashamed to fight . . .'

It has been over a year since Mick Jones, Paul Simenon and their friend Glen Matlock first met Joe Strummer down the Portobello Road and told him that he was great but his band was shit.

Later Joe talked to Bernard Rhodes and twenty-four hours after he showed up on the doorstep of the squat where Mick and Paul were living and told them he wanted in on the band that would be known as The Clash.

And from the top of the monolith tower block where they wrote their celebration of the Westway you can gaze through the window of – as Mick Jones puts it – one of the cages and see that London is still burning . . .

'All across the town/All across the night/Everybody's driving with four headlights/Black or white, turn it on, face the new religion/ Everybody's drowning in a sea of television./Up and down the West- way/In and out the lights/What a great traffic system/It's so bright/I can't think of a better way to spend the night/Than speeding around underneath the yellow lights./But now I'm in the subway looking for the flat/This one leads to this block and this one leads to that/The wind howls through the empty blocks looking for a home/But I run through the empty stone because I'm all alone/London's burning, baby . . .'

'Each of these high-rise estates has got those places where kids wear soldiers' uniforms and get army drill,' Mick says quietly.

'Indoctrination to keep them off the streets . . . and they got an *artist* to paint pictures of happy workers on the side of the Westway. Labour liberates and don't forget your place.'

He looks down at the fire hundreds of feet below.

'Can you understand how much I hate this place?' he asks me.

1977 is the year of The Clash.

Supergod Bestows Blessing on Punks

Robert Plant at The Roxy

New Musical Express, 29 January 1977

A LITTLE WHILE AGO *Thrills* would have said that the chances of finding a Heavy Sheet Metal Machine Music Demigod inside the New Wave's premiere hangout, the Roxy, in London's Covent Garden, were roughly the same as the chances of finding Johnny Rotten at a Folk Festival.

How wrong we were . . .

On the Monday night when The Damned played the Roxy, supported by the potentially great The Boys, suddenly there appeared a familiar face across the crowded room. I started pushing my way through the coolly dementoid crowds in the direction of those cascading golden curls, knowing, or rather believing, that they could only belong to but one person.

What a drag to discover that it was only Led Zep's Robert Plant.

'Hi, I'm Angie Errigo,' he lied.

What's a heavy metal SuperGod doing in a nice place like this, Robert? (A few feet away the Pistols' Johnny Rotten eyed the amiable Zep vocalist with much suspicion).

'I came down here last Thursday with Jimmy Page to check out The Damned,' he said. 'Yeah, I was impressed by them, thought they were really good, especially Rat Scabies the drummer. He's really got it . . .'

Get a chance to talk to them at all?

'Yeah, I was talking to Rat for a long time and having a few drinks, y'know. He's all right, I like him, he's not like his name.'

Who'd you come down here with tonight?

'John Bonham.'

(For those of you not of The Faith, Bonham, as Nick K. put it, 'takes care of the beef-and-potato drumming chores.' On this night down the Roxy, he was also trying to take care of a young lady while informing her of his fame and position in the rock establishment, to which she replied, 'I don't care who you are, getcha bleedin' 'ands offa me!')

What prompted you to come down and check out The Damned and the Roxy in the first place, Robert?

'Ah, I'd heard about them and I like to see new bands, see what they're doing, how good they are, keep in touch with what's happening,' he smiles.

If you're a member, fan or supporter of any of the young rock bands causing so much controversy on the scene in the UK '77 then the Roxy in Neal Street near Covent Garden is the most important venue in London.

The Clash, Damned, Boys, Johnny Thunders' Heartbreakers, Adverts, Slaughter and the Dogs and more have all played sets there, with varying degress of success, but the important aspect concerning the very existence of the Roxy, is that at long last, with the opening of the club at the tail end of last year, there is now a club suitable for live rock music where the manager is not terrified of youth, energy, short hair and scrap metal.

Entry is about a quid when a band's appearing, depending on how big they are, and the place is open every night except Friday until one in the morning. The club starts letting people in at eight in the evening but things don't start warming up until about an hour later.

On the ground floor there's a small bar near the toilets and also a large posing area avec seating facilities.

And hey daddy-o, down in the basement (as The Ramones warbled) there's a bigger bar, large area for going crazy and everybody do the pogo, plus a large enough perimeter to step back and watch the action without actually participating if you're feeling delicate.

Checking out the opposition? I smirk at the Zeppelin.

He grins good-naturedly. (Real friendly character, this Robert Plant. Completely without pretension, totally open, helpful, articulate and none of the old Superstar bullshit around *this* guy). He then explains to me his feelings about the New Wave Bands.

'You ask me if it reminds me of when we were starting out, but it doesn't. It reminds me of when we were rehearsing this afternoon! There's that same *feel* for the music . . . and all the talk about Old Farts and Young Farts is nonsense, age doesn't matter and anyway, Scabies is no chicken!'

You seen any of the other new bands around on the scene?

'No, only The Damned.'

Have you met and talked to any of the others?

'No, but that's The Sex Pistols just there,' he says, and eyes Rotten uncertainly, maybe just a shade nervous of Public Enemy Number

One (if you listen to the Shrill Majority) surrounded by his cohorts. 'I think that I'd, uh, like to meet him, but, uh, when it happens, just let it happen. . . .'

How're the injuries that you got in the car crash in Rhodes?

'Well, they're getting better but it's all taking time,' he says and lifts his left arm, which is apparently still giving him trouble, up and down to test it. 'Hopefully they'll be healed by the tour . . .'

What did Jimmy Page think of The Damned last Thursday?

'Jimmy loved it, thought they were fantastic . . . the spirit of what it's all about really . . .'

A lot of people are gonna be really surprised to see you hanging out down here . . .

He grins. 'Yeah, I know,' he says and over his shoulder I see a blitzed Merry Punkster staggering over to the Household Face of Robert Plant . . .

'Are you Led Zeppelin?' the kid demands.

Robert Plant shakes his head. 'Nah, I'm Angie Errigo, that's who I am . . .'

Whether you're into late Heavy Metal or New Wave you've gotta admire Plant's stance in ignoring the prejudice emanating from both media and punters alike, surrounding the new young bands currently being starved of gigs by the Mary Whitehouse mentality of town-hall bureaucrats.

Like Emerson said, '*A foolish consistency is the hobgoblin of little minds.*'

Clean Punks: The Menace to Our Kids

Generation X

New Musical Express, 29 January 1977

GENERATION X may well be the 'punk-rock' group that many people have been waiting for; songs with lyrics about change and revolution but with melodies cute enough for boy meets girl. And a lead singer in Billy Idol who, while coming out with the standard lines putting down age, stagnation and establishment, looks pretty enough for girls whose big sisters used to swoon over Marc Bolan.

Oh yeah, and they don't take drink or drugs . . .

'They make you want to sit around all day and not do anything about the situation,' Billy Idol says blandly as we sit in The Ship in Wardour Street, all of us drinking orange juice although only one glass contains the demon Smirnoff. 'All that crap, it ain't worth doing . . .

Not all drugs make you feel like sitting around flashing peace signs . . .

'The revolution can't happen if you're knackered tomorrow,' Billy Idol retorts.

'It ain't worth taking drugs,' says Tony James, the bass player. 'The important things in our life are the band, writing songs and playing . . . we get no time for anything else. If we drink too much we can't play.'

'Most of the people you admire, like the Dolls, Iggy, MC5 . . .

'We don't wanna be like them,' Tony says.

'They failed,' Idol asserts.

They didn't fail for *me*. They made some of the best music I ever heard.

'It didn't win ultimately,' Tony says, at pains to show me exactly what Billy meant by that last statement. 'It didn't *last*. I don't want to be like Keef or The Who . . .'

'He couldn't be like Keith Richard if he tried,' Patti O'Doors said when I played the tape back in the office.

'Iggy was great, but he was smashed out of his brain all the time,' Idol says. 'I'm about seeing things change *now*. He led up to what we're about, but he was a totally negative stance. We're gonna be positive . . .'

Three of the members of Generation X used to be in Chelsea with Gene October – who was the lead singer – with Idol on guitar, Tony on bass and John Towes on drums. But it wasn't going in the direction they wanted, with not enough emphasis being put on, uh, social comment so the three of them left Gene to carry on with Chelsea and formed Generation X with Bob Andrews on guitar.

I only saw Chelsea once, but on that night I was impressed by their enthusiasm, their energy, their commitment to their music and the fact that they didn't give a shit if the mostly arty-student audience liked them or not. They were rough, but they showed promise.

But, like Billy Idol and Tony James say, (they do nearly all the talking for the band, with John Towes making occasional remarks and Bob Andrews saying nowt) Chelsea and Generation X are two different bands . . .

One of the ironies around them is that, despite the great belief in the lyrical content of their songs, the words are almost entirely unintelligible when they play live, like down the Roxy on Saturday night.

Idol holds the mike like it was a python going for his throat and screams and spits out the words as his face contorts and turns purple. James makes his runs back and forth across the stage, Bob Andrews stands motionless and Towes whacks hell out of his shiny drum kit.

Titles include 'New Orders', '70's Problems,' 'London Life' and, their *pièce de résistance*, 'Your Generation.'

'Trying to forget your generation/Using any way I see/The end will justify the means/your generation don't mean a thing to me.'

That's just one example but pretty indicative of where they stand – singing of new orders although they're breaking no new ground with either their music nor their attitude, unlike the Sex Pistols who by the way they perform, the songs they write and the uncompromising way they've *always* faced the media have made it possible for bands like Generation X to break on through . . .

And Generation X sing of trying for kicks without wanting to pay the price of *getting* kicks and they talk of being positive and forward looking although their song 'Ready, Steady, Go,' is all about not being in love with the Stones or Dylan, just being in love with Cathy McGowan.

And they talk about social ills and 'gonna change things' and other naive spiels, while coming out with statements that make them look like a mindless New Faces act compared to, say, The Pistols or The Clash. Like this . . .

'I was in a band called London SS,' says Tony James. 'The name was initially chosen for shock value; the great thing about Nazism is that your parents hate it – it was shocking. We didn't give a shit, we weren't in the war, so it was great because it was shock value – if it shocks and it's frightening then it's great.'

What about concentration camps? By this time I was feeling slightly sick. And it wasn't the booze.

'Yeah, but we were never in the war, we didn't know nothing about that. It's just something that happened, right?' James asks me.

Wrong. What makes you think it can't happen today? You talk about caring and commitment, but if six million corpses don't cut through to you then nothing will.

'Obviously we don't agree with it,' he says hurriedly. 'SS also stood for, sort of, Street Soldiers . . .'

Street soldiers fuelled on orange juice? Revolutionaries who don't give a shit about Bergen-Belsen? The orders-nouveau sung to pleasant pop-rock melodies?

If Generation X didn't hype themselves as being such a big deal then I would probably not be as turned off by the band as I am now. If they just admitted that they're another young rock band and dropped the boring platitudes and thoughtless (because that's what it is) political raps then I wouldn't mind, I'd wish them all the luck in the world.

But I think it's about time that every goddamn 'New Wave' band in the land realised that, at the end of the day, they will stand or fall *on their own merits* and not because they have learned the right media spiel lines.

The Pistols are good enough to kick out and replace The Stones and The Clash are good enough to make you forget about The Who.

What about the rest of you New Wave bands? Who are you good enough to replace? On stage at the Roxy Billy Idol wipes the sweat from his face after finishing 'Youth, youth, youth.'

'Can someone get me a drink of water?' he asks.

One of The Pistols turns to me, and smiles. 'Clean boys,' he says.

The Jam at the Roxy

New Musical Express, 5 March 1977

THE CROWD AT THE Roxy on Thursday night just didn't deserve The Jam. I've seen that club packed out and pogoing for bands that ain't fit to lick The Jam's plectrums.

Three months ago it wasn't cool to say you liked The Damned, now the black sheep of the new wave are The Jam. It makes me puke, that kind of bullshit is just as vacuous as peace signs and half hour guitar solos.

The Jam's set of updated Who numbers, '60s soul classics and self-penned songs like their new Polydor single, 'In The City' (that four-year recording contract will take them nicely up to the age of twenty-one), is performed with the kind of genuine manic urgency that is sadly lacking in all those tenth rate support derivatives coming in from the suburbs with their glib platitudes and parent-purchased shiny equipment.

Paul Weller on vocals and lead, Rick Buckler on drums and sun-ray lamp cool maintenance and Bruce Foxton on bass wear dark mohair skinny leg/lapel suits and white shirts/black ties. Their band logo is very similar to that of the Shepherd's Bush Old Masters, and so a lot of retards assume they're some kind of revival band – which is just so far removed from the truth that it's incredible.

'For the next number we'll let our guitars go outa tune, and maybe you'll like it better,' Paul Weller said, naturally bitter. If you miss out on them because you can't see further than the safety pin in the end of your nose, you're a dumb cluck, ain'tcha now?

. . . Ex Pistol Plans a New Band

New Musical Express, 19 March 1977

THE SHOCK OF recognition. Spiky haired kids making a pilgrimage out to the wilds of Harlesden mingle with the regular Irish clientele of this old fashioned Baroque-style London boozer and occasionally one of them does a doubletake at the geezer leaning against the bar drinking a pint of light.

Yeah, the Bill Grundy debacle has left the boat race of Glen Matlock imprinted firmly on their memory banks even though he's no longer in The Pistols . . .

'That telegram Malcolm (McLaren, The Pistols' manager) sent to *Melody Maker* saying they kicked me out was wrong,' Glen claims, without a trace of bitterness. 'It was a mutual agreement. I wanted to leave and they wanted me out. In the beginning it was just mates playing rock 'n' roll and then later all the business side came in and spoiled it . . .'

What was it like at the time of your, uh, departure?

'Like playing in The Monkees,' he smiles pleasantly. 'It just seems like now Malcolm has got to give the impression he's in total control. That press conference, y'know – the Fleet Street lot could just use the articles they wrote years ago about The Move when they were smashing televisions . . . Just change the names.'

Last time I saw The Pistols was months back on the local-council-butchered Anarchy tour. Matlock looked the part as much as any of them, and also seemed like the best bass player the New Wave had produced. But even then he had sussed it wasn't gonna work out . . .

'Even before the tour, I'd make suggestions or offer ideas at rehearsals and nobody wanted to know. There was no communication between any of us . . .'

Some musicians who leave big-name bands can't come down, and choose the self-destruct button, but there's no way that Matlock will be going down that route. He's intelligent, creative and a superb musician. He's not bitter about his split from The Pistols.

'I had a good time there for a while,' he says. 'But I've been through all the front page articles and the national scandal and all the rest of it. I've done all that and don't need to do it again. I just wanna make my music, get a band together. Maybe we'll call it The Rich Kids – with my mate Jimmy Norton, who plays guitar and sings . . . and I want it to be *good*! There's so much dross coming through, ain't there?'

Sure is, Glen.

He looks at the clock on the pub wall and bolts down his drink. It's getting late and we ain't come all the way up to Harlesden just to talk. The last time I saw Glen Matlock he was dancing to The Clash. And smiling to himself.

Rich Stars Play London Charity Performance

Sex Pistols; The Slits: Screen on the Green

New Musical Express, 9 April 1977

USICAL CREDIBILITY has never been one of the stated ambitions of The Pistols. Maybe that's why they chose all teenage girl band The Slits as their support act. These four ladies make The Runaways look like Girl Guides. I mean, who cares about such trivialities as staying in tune, playing together or striking the right chords when one possesses such a sense of *theatrics*?

The singer, the lovely Arianna, takes out her frustrations caused by an audience of abusive proles by laying into the drum kit of Palmolive, The Slits' sturdy drummer, her feet and fists flying. However, Palmolive doesn't take kindly to being kicked in the high-hat and retaliates by hurling her drum sticks at Arianna and lashing out at her bass-drum.

A punch-up seems inevitable as the other two girls on lead and bass grind sourly to a halt, but after exchanging vehement, wet-eyed tirades Arianna and Palmolive call a truce and they all get back into their own brand of rock muzak – Rimbaud meets the Ramones speeding down an *autobahn* (*Huh? – Ed.*). The Slits look set to self-destruct, although Arianna herself could be making records as good as 'Radio Ethiopia' by the time she's old enough to vote.

The packed-tight capacity crowd give the band a big cheer as they leave the stage, and elbow their neighbour in the face to increase the size of their Personal Territory.

The only advertising for this gig has been done by word of mouth, and it's taking place in the early hours of Monday morning. But, as it is the first live date this year by The Sex Pistols (not including the USA NBC TV filmed debacle at Leicester Square's Notre Dame Hall a few weeks back, when the windy management would only allow *fifty* punters inside), everybody who is anybody, my angels, has made the pilgrimage. And admission is free. Good to see some of the £75,000 that A&M gave the band along with the boot going to such a worthy cause.

Malcolm McLaren sits at the mixing desk at the back of the hall as various films are run for the crowd's delight while we're waiting for The Pistols to come on around two in the morning.

There is Nuremberg rally-type mass excited identification as reels are shown of The Pistols live, hanging around Sex in the King's Road, little old ladies in the street denouncing 'punk-rock', intellectuals, show business personalities and assorted others ridiculing the same in the warmth of a TV studio *plus* – best-received of all – a re-run of the Bill Grundy fiasco, where it seemed strange to recall that the instigator of The Pistols' cussing was none other than the since departed Glen Matlock.

With a superb sense of dynamics, the films build a uniform feeling of tense anticipation amongst the braying crowd.

But the mood is evaporated amid a few half-hearted cheers when the band comes on and seem to have hassles with equipment before they can even play a note. Lights go off, and so do The Pistols. A false-start. The audience seem subdued after this premature ejaculation. The stage remains devoid of Pistols.

Then they come back on again, and after raven-haired John Rotten has bitched a little while about the fancy lights, The Pistols launch into the A&M single that never was, 'No Future'.

It's tragic that the twenty-five thousand copies of this single that A&M pressed are to be destroyed, because it's a great song, really very amusing (*Huh? – Ed.*) and music to beat up corgis to . . .

'*God save the queen/A fascist regime/She ain't no human being/ But God save the Queen/There is no future to England's dream.*'

Steve Jones has improved immensely both as a guitar player and a stage presence since the last time I saw him. He slashes chiv-artist chords as he leaps, struts and swaggers across the stage, his new axe rammed into his groin and aiming at the front row chicklets. His performance very often outdoes that of Rotten himself, the well-mannered boy Skank-dancing and looking like a week-old corpse still shaking with the shock of the red-hot piece of wire that a sadistic undertaker shoved up his anal passage on the very instant of death.

Paul Cook is as solid and relentless as ever as he attacks his drum kit – and Sid Vicious on bass can hold down a line better than I'd been led to expect. As a musician he's not in the same world as Matlock, but with his dyed spike-haired coiffure atop a pallid visage and his six feet plus frame encased in expensive Sex shop threads, Vicious certainly looks the part of A Pistol, which is obviously Malcolm McLaren's major consideration.

They're into chaos, not music.

But the reaction they're getting right now is a mixture of sporadic outbreaks of The Pogo from the hard-core fanatics down the front, listless fascination a bit further back and in the aisles, and at the back of the movie house a sense of mild disappointment as if all this gig was doing for you was making you nostalgic for 1976.

Rotten adjusts his velvet bow-tie and stares bug-eyed belligerent with curling upper-lip contemptuous sneer in the face of Demon Apathy. 'Don't be embarrassed to show you're enjoying yourself,' he taunts.

The Anarchy tour non-originals – 'Whatcha Gonna Do 'Bout It?' by The Small Faces, 'Substitute' by The Who and 'Stepping Stone' by The Monkees – have all been discarded for self-written material like 'No Feelings' (the B-side of the aborted 'No Future' single), 'Submission', 'Out On View' and the autobiographical 'EMI'.

These blank gems helped The Pistols and the crowd build the atmosphere along with Fave Raves that we used to hear down The 100 Club, such as 'Lazy Sod' and 'Pretty Vacant', where Rotten sniggered at Jones, 'They'll never know the difference' as the audience applauded the screwed up intro (why it is always *this* song that it happens on?).

And, of course, between each number Johnny boy dished out the obligatory verbal acid. 'Fuckin' old hippies all over again,' he snickered drily as sections of the crowd yelled at each other to sit down or stand up.

'What a waste of effort,' he spat, still not happy with the energy level being generated down in the stalls, just before going into the last number of the set and catching fire like they should have done from the very start.

'Anarchy In The UK' still sounds like the best single of last year, and here The Pistols did it with more bottle than I've ever heard it done before, proving they can still burn like they did back in the summer, although it was a drag that they took so long to confirm it.

As the mob call for more I reflect that The Sex Pistols miss Matlock's vocal back-up contribution even more than his bass line. Because El Sid don't sing (although now and again he threatens members of the audience between songs) and with only Jones bawling into the mike Rotten loses a few degrees of his obnoxious power.

Iggy's 'No Fun', the only non-original now included in the set, is performed with the blitzed malevolence of old, as is the final number, a patriotic reprise of 'No Future'.

Then they were gone, leaving me hungry for Sex Pistols vinyl, with the realisation that it is British institutions such as this band that make our country Great.

Eye Witness Pistols Whipping

Jubilee Day with The Pistols

New Musical Express, 18 June 1977

W HILE THE MEDIA whips itself and its customers ('They must be Russians' – a Sunday Mirror reader) into fresh paroxysms of p★nk rock hysteria, The Sex Pistols' Jubilee Tuesday boat ride gatecrashed by over-zealous cops went largely unrecorded in the columns of our national dailies.

Yet to those who saw it the incident remains a far uglier pimple on the face of British Democracy than any on the vilified visage of Johnny Rotten, and a damn sight more dangerous than any spike-haired dance band disrespecting the Queen could ever be.

The ride was planned as a private party; selected guests by invitation only. The Sex Pistols were scheduled to play a set on board as the boat – the Queen Elizabeth – sailed down the Thames.

It didn't go according to plan and *Tony Parsons*, who was there, reports why.

So we should all know by now that The Sex Pistols are Public Enemies Number One who neither want nor expect a thing from the multitudes who hate their guts. Nevertheless the scenes that occurred when invading cops broke up their Jubilee Day river party have left me with something that will remain long after the bruises have faded: it's unlikely that I will ever again be able to look at a member of Her Majesty's Metropolitan Police Force without feeling sick.

Despite the 'Discretion appreciated' message on the numbered and signed invitations, a lot of staunch Pistols followers turned up in the hope of blagging a ride when the boat set sail from Charing Cross Pier.

'We wanted to bring *all* our mates,' Paul Cook had told me the night before. 'But we only got a few tickets each.'

Undaunted, Slits' drummer Palmolive showed admirable bottle by repeatedly attempting to jump aboard the boat as it pulled away from the pier. A member of the crew hanging from Queen Elizabeth's railings kept pushing her back to *terra firma* every time she leapt for the vessel until it seemed certain that one or both of them would end up floating in the Thames.

On the river, the word in The Pistols' camp was that the owner of the boat had attempted to have their equipment removed just before we hoisted anchor, that he hadn't realised the identity of his cargo until those four familiar faces were below deck and frisking back the inevitable cans of lager.

A river police boat tailed us for a while as we headed down river. You could sense their chagrin when no dead babies were thrown over the side of the boat and the Tower of London passed by without a napalm attack.

Below deck the Pistols and their friends sat talking and drinking. As Johnny Rotten talked I understood why so many people hate him – in a business that is run on lies, deceit and doublethink, Rotten is one of the few who believe in *honesty*.

'The Clash came down to see me in the pub before the Ramones' gig,' he recalled dryly. 'They didn't like what I said about their *political* songs in the interview we did in the boring *Melody Maker*. Well, that's just too bad. And Caroline Coon complained about what I said about *her*. They don't understand that I say what I think and if anyone doesn't like it I couldn't care less . . .'

At a guess I put the number of people on board at about 120 – fifty per cent of them record company and media executives getting their jollies by slumming among vital young proles. As they glided past Rotten to gorge at the buffet table, they eyed the Pistol with tentative, capped-tooth smiles. He sniffed disdainfully and regarded them with cold boredom.

'Poxy, innit?' he said. 'Look at her, she's got gold trousers, gold top, gold face . . . looks like a bleedin' statue. I don't *know* these people.'

Not surprisingly his enthusiasm to play a set for an audience comprised of dozens of people who didn't give a damn about The Sex Pistols a year ago and will not give a damn about them in a year's time was not very high.

'Waste of energy,' he sneered. 'Why should we play for them? They don't fuckin' care about us. They shouldn't even be here . . .'

'Everybody's bored,' Paul Cook, usually the last Pistol to be brought down, sighed in resignation. 'Five hours of *this*! Ahhhhhhrgh! Lemme off!'

'Why isn't everybody drunk?' asked Rotten. 'What does it take to get people drunk these days?' He pulled off his red and white mohair jumper revealing the well-worn white shirt underneath. His friends made jibes at his sartorial elegance and he just smiled and ruffled the spiky red barnet. Then he got serious as he talked about a recent incident in the Kings Road.

'Everyone's always going on about the violent punks,' he sneered with disgust. 'About how violent *we* are. Yet nobody says a thing when a crew of Teddy Boys beat up a 16-year-old kid down the Kings Road. Tough bastards, ain't they? . . . But they'll get what's coming to them.'

Talk of Teds reminded someone to ask if he could get a pair of brothel creepers like the ones Rotten was wearing.

'Listen, all I got is those shoes and these,' Rotten replied, hiking his leg in the air to display the quasi-jackboots that his black strides are tucked into. 'Are you asking me if you can have a pair for *nothing*?' he demanded.

'Yeah.'

'No,' said Rotten, and the matter was dropped.

Young Mark of *Scum* fanzine wanted to know about the time Rotten halted the entry of Mick Jagger into Sex and so John patiently recounted the episode, snickering with amusement at the memory.

'He (Jagger) was standing outside for *hours* trying to work up the bottle to come in, and after about three hours he decided to risk it and chance a look around. All that time to work up his bottle and then I slammed the door in his face,' Rotten chuckled. 'Pathetic old bastard . . .'

After three hours on board, the band still haven't played. Rotten has checked out the poop-deck where the gig is supposed to be and doesn't like what he's seen.

'Look at the Martini set,' he complained bitterly. 'They don't deserve it.'

I looked around at the affluent section of the guests as they preened and posed for Rotten's benefit and I sympathised with the band's position. After all the work, all the shit . . . is this all there is?

Upstairs on the canvas-shrouded poop-deck The Sex Pistols and their equipment crammed into an area about the size of an average sized paddling pool.

As Sid and Steve tuned up and tested the PA, the crowd jostled for positions on chairs or on the deck within touching distance of the band for the Pistols' smallest gig of all time.

Rotten grinned malevolently and they tore into 'Anarchy In The UK' with the venom of a band who have been denied gigs by bigoted, frightened bureaucrats for too, too long and are burning for a chance to prove how good, how *great* they are live.

Rotten snarled bug-eyed dementoid blocko as he hung like a savage monkey-man from a bar in the roof of the poop-deck and spat out the lyrics to 'God Save The Queen'.

The true Pistols' supporters in the crowd gave them their energy and together they built the atmosphere to a pitch where only the band's third gig of 1977 was undoubtedly their best gig of 1977.

Every now and again Rotten bared his teeth and swayed sideways while Cook whaled several shades of excrement out of his kit and grinned with the sheer *kick* of it all. Steve Jones hadn't got the space to swagger and strut through the full catalogue of his stage movements, but he tried hard, often colliding with John Boy Rotten when they both went for dancing space that just wasn't there.

'I Wanna Be Me', as in anarchy as self-rule (open your eyes – they practice what they preach), had Sid's bass stretching across Rotten's chest and the over-excited photographers getting so ridiculously close to the band that a fight broke out between one of Rotten's friends and a French cameraman.

It was a minor incident over in seconds, the kind that can happen anywhere people gather for good times, but since this was The Sex Pistols the owner of the boat panicked and called in the river police.

The word on board was that the boat owner now wanted the party ejected from his 'licensed premises'. It's the same law that permits pub landlords to call in the Old Bill anytime they want to kick out undesirables.

So it was that cop launches started appearing alongside the Queen Elizabeth as the Pistols slashed out killers that will be on the forthcoming album like 'Pretty Vacant', 'No Feelings' (their best song amongst some classics) and 'Problems'.

'An' der problem is yew!'

Rotten laconically clocked the half-a-dozen or so river police boats as they got close enough to touch our barnacles.

'Any requests?' he asked as we were escorted off the Thames and into Charing Cross Pier. There were cop boats all around us now and police officers standing by to board as the stalwarts called out for The Sex Pistols' favourite non-original, Iggy's 'No Fun'.

It had been four hours since we had cast off from this same point, and as they started 'No Fun' The Pistols looked as though they wanted to play all night.

But the river police, about seven of them, were coming up the gangplank and then the power was abruptly terminated as someone pulled the plug and made an announcement telling us all to vacate the boat. No fun, ma babe, and no justice no sense, ma babe. At first I thought that Paul Cook was doing a drum solo but then sussed that he was continuing to play 'No Fun' even after they'd confiscated the electricity.

The river police repeated the demand to get off the Queen Elizabeth. Nobody moved.

Malcolm McLaren shook his head in incredulous amusement. 'What is all this shit? I mean, we're having a *party*. Everybody's having a *good time. We haven't done anything!*'

The cops weren't moved. 'The owner complained about the noise,' one of them announced.

'The owner complained about a fight,' said another.

'The owner wants you off the premises.'

Etcetera, etcetera, blah-blah-blah. But, of course, this is the UK. Democracy and all that. They can't do this to us, can they? You place your bets and watch those river police leave the Queen Elizabeth and please note the 30 or so Metropolitan Police officers on the quay-side who are now coming up the gangplank because from this moment on we won't be asked to do anything, we will be *told*.

Big geezers they were and they swarmed over the top-deck, and then one of them saw a familiar face and he said something that made me realise that '*A Fascist Regime*' ain't no hyperbole ...

'There's that *cunt* Johnny Rotten,' I heard him remark to a burly colleague. 'Let's get him ...' I heard him *and* I saw his number if anyone wants to know.

After that things got fast and things got violent. Anyone taking pictures was having their camera trashed. Three cameras were smashed and more were quickly stashed away, impotent and safe.

Jamie, Malcolm McLaren's assistant, questioned his rights and two cops told him he was under arrest. I saw him beaten in a vicious, unprovoked attack.

A cop smiled and punched me in the chest.

There was a sadistic glee in the way they went about their task.

More people were getting manhandled, punched and kicked than I could keep tabs on. I felt that if I farted I'd have got arrested for GBH.

Once on the pier things started getting drastically worse. A middle-aged Japanese lady, the wife of a record company executive who had been on the boat with her husband, was standing placidly on the dockside waiting for him when two cops started roughly pushing her around.

There were several people being arrested now. Driven up the tunnel towards the Embankment road, some people fell and were trod on by heavy-duty, highly-polished flatfooted boots.

Vivienne, McLaren's lady, was one of those on the ground, dragged along and trodden on.

McLaren, now incensed by what he had seen happening to Vivienne, had drawn the cops' attentions. I saw him given one of the most brutal, sadistic and gratuitous beatings that I've ever witnessed.

Two blue meat-wagons were quickly filled, mostly with people close to The Pistols camp. Passers-by decked out in Jubilee colours walked obliviously by – as though it was a movie. Cops threw punches when you didn't move, and they got away with it because they are the law and they can.

For the first time since the quayside, I had time to look around for the band. Steve and Paul were by my side and when they saw a group of police identify them as Sex Pistols they wisely took off.

Someone said that Sid was one of those loaded into the meat-wagons. Someone else said not, but they had taken Rotten's brother Jimmy, and McLaren had been rushed across the road and had his arms pinned horizontally away from his body.

As the meat-wagons drove off for Bow Street Police Station with eleven people on board, I was left reflecting that the whole stinking episode smacked of Pistols-bashing and little else.

I went along to Bow Street to see if there was anything I could do. The cop behind the counter would not tell us a thing, only this; 'There were a few more people we would have liked to have arrested if we had known their identity . . .'

The eleven arrested will be in court in September. Anyone with a brain could see that the police tactics on Charing Cross Pier at ten o'clock on Jubilee Tuesday were senselessly violent because of the mindless prejudice of authority towards The Sex Pistols.

Whatcha gonna do?

Dial-A-Ramone: Gabba Explained

New Musical Express, 6 August 1977

'TEENAGE LOBOTOMY' 'Get Well' and 'The Cretin Hop' ... they're our latest songs.

' "The Cretin Hop" is a brand new dance, we gonna show der kids in der UK how t'do it when we come back at der end of der year.'

Dial-A-Ramone services has enabled Mrs Ramones' shortest son to elucidate the brothers' future directions as they prepare to slink back to the studio to record their third album.

'We wanna put der kids in anudder dimenshun ...'

But, Tommy, The Ramones are so *slow* on vinyl ...

'Yeah, well, we ain't so fast on der records coz we like to make it, like, two different bands: one fer doing it live and one fer doing it on record. Yeah, we getting faster all the time. The fourth album'll be a live one, should be able to get about 30 songs on two sides.'

Those of you who witnessed The Ramones on their recent UK jaunt will not be amazed by valuations of the band as The Seventies Beatles, The Perfect Pop Group, Trash Aesthetic Incarnate and all the rest. Forget all that obscurantist artistic minimalism crapola. Did you need an Oxford Dictionary to read *Spider Man*? A BA to enjoy The Ronnettes? An NUS card to chew on a cheeseburger? The musical brain-surgery of The Ramones is there to be *enjoyed*; my goodness, they're fun, coming over like their total experience on the planet has been restricted to watching technicolour USA TV and listening to high school juke boxes.

And hasn't The First Tycoon Of Teen himself expressed a longing to join forces with the brothers and try to recapture the glory of his Golden Age?

'Yeah, we visited Spector at his mansion,' Tommy recalls. 'He was real friendly until he pulled his gun and held us prisoner. But after Dee Dee told him that he wuz noo rotic Spector was okay again.'

And will The Man's vision of a Ramones/Spector liaison ever happen?

'Awwww . . . ummuummmm . . . ah dunno . . . maybe he'll call us up in der future . . . ah dunno.'

This red hot quote reminds me that all artists of true genius articulate chiefly through their work and often face accusations of being mumbling morons when limited to mere conversation. Believe me, kid, we don't have it easy . . .

'Dey say we're *stoopid*.' Tommy bellows over 6,000 miles of telephone wire. 'Whadda dey *want*? Fer us to use *flugel horns* 'n' *strings*, or sumting?' Tommy chuckles at their detractors' ignorance.

'Der Gabba – gabba – hey – we – accept – you – one – of us ting on "Pinhead" is our, uh, *statement* to all der people who call us *dumb* an' give us exaggerrated Noo Yawk accents when dey write about us.'

Where's it come from, Tommy? Like, wherefore the source of information, pinhead?

'We sorta picked up on it from this silent '30s movie called *Freaks* by this guy Tod Browning,' Tommy reveals. 'And when der freaks admitted someone noo into their ranks dey carried signs saying, "Gabba, gabba, we accept you". An' "Pinhead" is a parody of that.'

Last time I spoke to The Ramones they were all skint. Tommy says that their financial situation has improved somewhat of late.

'At dat time I didn't have a dollar,' he says glumly. 'Now I got a dollar,' he quips. '*Haw-haw-haw!*'

And the uniform of leather jacket, tee-shirt, cheesy sneakers and ancient Levis with knee ventilation? Are they the only clothes the brothers have got?

'Yeah, dat's all the clothes we've had for tree years now,' Tommy sighs.

How long?

'*Tree years!*' he repeats impatiently.

Ain't it getting a little . . . *samey*?

'Well, it kinda smells,' he chortles. 'Especially in the hot weather. But we jest hang it out the window fer a while an' den it ain't so bad.'

Despite their casual attitude to personal hygiene, The Ramones were considerably pissed off with the vast quantities of bubbling gob spat in their direction on their tour of these isles.

'It's funny, all dat spitting you got over dere,' Tommy reflects philosophically. 'We got some spitting in Manchester, but most of it happened at the two London gigs . . . see, we're entertainers, an' we wanna put der kids in annudder *world*, annudder *dimenshun* when we're on stage, an' when you're playing an' ya suddenly get a stream of gob in your face ... boy, dat's real *distracting*!'

Tommy's thoughts on the British Youth Apocalypse are diplomatic, although he concedes that him and his brothers find politics nowhere near as inviting as showbiz.

'Yeah, we seen dem bands,' he says. 'Dey're real good. Met Sid and Johnny of The Sex Pistols and dey were real nice guys. Said, "How's everything?" an' stuff.' All in all though, Tommy Ramone reckons that the '70s are musically not in the same league as the '60s, and says that The Ramones' favourite bands are still the likes of The Beatles, Stones, Kinks and other dinosaurs, their influence tempered with primal Heavy Metal and classic pop pulp.

'Most of the bands in the '70s are fifth generation Led Zeppelins,' he concludes. 'The Ramones is a reaction against *dat*.'

Bowie: Two Hours and Ten Minutes of Excellence

David Bowie at Newcastle City Hall

New Musical Express, 24 June 1978

FIVE YEARS (cough) and one month (count it) have elapsed since the opening date of David Bowie's last UK tour.

Back then, MainMan were flogging studied decadence as if it was a trademark, the 'Ziggy Stardust' blue-print for ultimate pop-deity had long subsumed its architect into his own platinum artefact and – with that year's mutant 'Aladdin Sane' a new product in the market square – it seemed *so* inviting, *so* enticing to play the part . . .

Bowie's attempt to perform the first ever rock show in the Earls Court abyss confirmed that inside every Leper Messiah there's an Ideal Home Exhibition trying to get out. Bouncers fought running battles with large numbers of the 18,000 stage-props who refused to confine themselves to allotted seats where we were denied the gift of sound and vision.

The Nazz repeatedly left the stage while his security tried to restore a semblance of law and order among his ego-receptacles. Studied decadence came face to face with social disease and discovered that the forelock-tugging disciples had now become an incensed lynch-mob out to do more damage than crush somebody's sweet hands. The Pistols epoch began *here*: Bowie – always the movement's major influence and agitator.

Not sticking around for the fulfilment of his assassination prophecy, Bowie backed off fast. Within two months of the Earls Court debacle he announced his retirement (a polite euphemism for emigration to America).

Over the next five years, Bowie annually continued to recharter course rather than reinforce the commercially viable direction of his career by producing for the converted. Utilised and eventually discarded (along with the USA itself) were theatrical Never-Mind-The-Ballads SF excess, WASPlastic-soul, inverted festering *discomotorik* psychosis, before Bowie's eventual arrival at synthetic Stax and in-

dustrialised folk-muzak for the factories, inevitably created by someone who doesn't have to work for a living.

In the half-decade since his last UK tour, Bowie's live appearances
in this country have been restricted to the 1976 Empire Pool dates
(the austere death throes of the Cracked Actor's Fractured Follies)
and his low-profile session musician role playing keyboards on Iggy's
Idiot tour in the spring of 1977.

At that time, the controversy surrounding 'Low' was at its apex,
and Bowie's contrived flat-cap lumberjack-chic seemed to satirise the
critical theory that he had taken the optical illusion device to its
logical conclusion and submerged his ego in the infinite void (then
how come I'm still making albums, sucker?).

Tonight, some of the Geordie kids crammed into the City Hall
(the size of a large club!!!) appear to have missed out on the post-
punk awareness that being 'natural' is the biggest pose of all, and
have dressed down for the occasion in a plethora of ethnic wood-
chopper togs. Elsewhere in the compact auditorium the more sentimental *kinderclones* reverently commemorate the myriad Ghosts of
David's Past.

You will (not) be like your dreams tonight ... Not surprisingly,
Bowie's latest stage persona bears absolutely no relation to the atro-
phied *alter-hyperegos* (now leg warmers), nor to anything else you
could have anticipated.

House-lights dimmed but not out, a smiling David Bowie strolls
on stage with his seven-piece band. Sandy barnet shorn to Just A
Gigolo length, dapper in open-necked green and yellow satin jockey-
jerkin, baggie beige canvas strides and azure training shoes, Bowie
positions himself stage-right behind a Mini-Moog as the rest of the
band ready their instruments – except for Carlos Alomar, stage-
centre, who holds a conductor's baton instead of his customary
guitar.

The musicians, not least Bowie, intently follow the magic waving
wand of Carlos the conductor as he guides them through 'Warszawa'
and the audience sink back into their seats, somewhat subdued.

It is, of course, a deftly calculated effect. The song's (?) emotive,
quasi-religious soundscape of doom and desolation, with its experi-
mental phoneticism the nearest it gets to lyrics, opened side two of
'Low' – unprecedented musical departure for David Bowie.

Performing it as the opening of a gig which some of these kids
have waited five years to see may result in Newtonic alienation for
parts of the audience, but Bowie is only giving them an accurate

representation of his current work and it's the punter's prerogative to walk away and let the artist commit commercial hari-kari if he so desires.

With 'Warszawa' over, Bowie abandons keyboards, grabs hand-mike and dances to the front of the stage as the band pump out the riff to 'Heroes': the audience finally has the chance to erupt. The running-order is arranged so that whenever Bowie's band perform one of the more inaccessible instrumentals, they'll reward the audience before or after the reading with one of Bowie's golden 45s. It works brilliantly.

Despite the much touted coldness that Bowie is meant to exude from every pore, his rendition of 'Heroes' makes the vinylised version seem positively tame by comparison.

The band he's got behind him is the tightest outfit he's ever worked with, and that includes the Spiders . . . The awesomely relentless black rhythm section of Dennis Davis on drums and bass lines by George Murray at the heart, with the guitars of Alomar and Adrian Belew, Simon House's violin, Sean Mayes on piano and the multi-synthesisers of Roger Powell – disparate elements operating at their own pace in the rich, abstract blocks of open-tuned synthetic noise that act as backdrop to the most powerful instrument on stage, Bowie's voice.

'*And the shame was on the other side . . .*'

Love under fire but holding out, the wall could just as easily be Lewisham as Berlin. The most moving spectacle I've ever witnessed at a rock gig.

Four songs from side one of 'Low'; 'Be My Wife', 'What In The World', 'Speed Of Life', and 'Breaking Glass', anti-narrative, random cryptic cut-up imagery and fatalistic futurist-funk, Bowie practising intricate soul-shoes steps as he moves across the boards, the most compelling stage presence since Sinatra.

'Jean Genie' is the solitary pre-'Low' song in the first half of the show. It provokes the most enthusiastic crowd response so far, but the Stones riff is given a false-ending so that you're left clapping with one hand. This happens with a few songs in the set, and after the first time it gets boring.

'Blackout', 'Beauty And The Beast' and 'Sense Of Doubt' from 'Heroes' bring the first hour of the show to an end. After the intermission, Bowie returns dressed in white T-shirt and white tent-dimension shitstoppers to crank up the pace to fever pitch and indulge in some nostalgic funtime, seeing as we sat and appreciated David's new, left-field subject matter so well in the first segment.

Half a dozen Ziggy vignettes – 'Five Years', 'Soul Love', 'Star', 'Hang On To Yourself', 'Suffragette City' and 'Ziggy Stardust' – are sufficiently overhauled to prevent them sounding anachronistic with some inventive vocals by Bowie, the theatricals kept down to his sporadic use of mime.

Bowie's rapport with the audience is astounding, light-years away from the contemptuous, contemptible Thin White Duke of two years back. During his mini-moog stint in the extra-terrestrial 'I Can't Stand The Rain' called 'Art Decade', he grins at the kids like a good-natured shark modelling Ambre Solaire. He looks glad to be back.

Next up is the night's only non-original, a cover of the Bertolt Brecht/Kurt Weill number 'Alabama Song (Whiskey Bar)', which The Doors brought to the public eye on their first album. The members of Bowie's band wail a harrowing banshee chorus while Bowie swaggers across the boards, and it hits me that he'd do a fine version of Bertolt Brecht's 'Mac The Knife' with them railings.

'Station To Station' closes the two-hour set with Powell's synthesisers and Adrian Belew's guitar combining to produce some panoramic-paranoia sound effects that have got to be heard to be believed.

'It's not the side-effects of the cocaine!'

The expressionist banks of white neon strip-lighting explode into dazzling brilliance and your mucous membranes are still burning after the encores of 'Stay', 'TVC15', and 'Rebel, Rebel', and Bowie has exited smiling broadly with a red velvet dressing gown draped around his shoulders like a triumphant heavyweight.

Bowie played for two hours, ten minutes and it was the best gig I've ever seen since mid-'76 down the 100 Club.

David Bowie is alive and well and no longer living only in theory.

Bruce: The Myth Just Keeps On Coming

Springsteen in New York

New Musical Express, 14 October 1978

REETINGS FROM THE New Jersey shoreline's omnipresent leisure industry of endless beaches, broadwalks, amusement parks, souvenir arcades, piers, clubs, pubs, bars and sideshow booths ... greetings from small town life in Asbury Park, NJ.

Our story begins circa the early '60s. At a strict Catholic school, a strange, solitary boy of eleven has been caught skipping lessons. His punishment is being placed in a class of six year olds.

His arms and legs feel too long for his body as he sits at the dinky table and chair built for a mere mite. Stared at by the room full of curious Catholic ankle-biters – immobile Lilliputians to his awkward, embarrassed Gulliver – he grins self-consciously, his face burning.

The Sister of Mercy's voice breaks the silence.

'Let's show this young man,' she intones, her eyes never leaving the boy, 'what we do to children who smile in this class.'

One of the six year olds stands up and walks over to where the big kid is sitting. Their eyes are level. Then the small child pulls back his fist and, with all the force he can muster from the spirit of the Holy Mother Mary, rams it home into the older boy's face.

'Very good,' smiles the Sister.

Stunned with shock, shame and pain, the boy clutches his face, fighting back the tears.

'There's a dark cloud rising from the desert floor/I packed my bags and I'm heading straight into the storm//Gonna be a twister to blow everything down/That ain't got the faith to stand its ground/ Blow away the dreams that tear you apart. Blow away the dreams that break your heart//Blow away the lies that leave you nothing but lost and brokenhearted/The dogs on mainstreet howl 'cause they understand/If I could take one moment into my hands/Mister, I ain't a boy/No, I'm a man/And I believe in a Promised Land.'

* * *

Some seventeen years later he's slumped in the dressing room at New York City's Palladium. After his usual three hour sound check that afternoon, where he personally covered every last inch of the 3,400 seater theatre to make sure that the sound was absolutely perfect for every kid in the house, he performed the greatest rock 'n' roll show that I will ever experience. It lasted for nearly four hours. It will be almost dawn before he finally leaves the Palladium.

Out back there's several hundred kids waiting for autographs, a chance to talk to him, an opportunity to thank him. None of them will go home disappointed. He's got time for all of them and he doesn't make a big deal about it. If you press him on the subject, he'll just get thoughtful and reply, 'My music gave me everything that I got, I was *nobody*, I had *nothing* . . . I will never put anyone in the position of being humiliated. It happened to me for too long.'

And if any other musician in the world said that to me – as you've no doubt noticed – I'd wait until I stopped laughing and then it would be news-sheet mince-meat time. But this geezer is unique; when Bruce Springsteen comes out with emotive statements like that I don't sneer, I *believe*.

When Springsteen played New Orleans on his last American tour a middle-aged woman reached up from the stalls and handed him a ring, saying that it had been her grandmother's engagement ring. There was a plethora of precious stones encrusted on the ring and it was obviously worth thousands of dollars. Springsteen thanked her for the thought, but said he couldn't take it. The woman refused to take it back, told him that she wanted him to keep it and disappeared back into the darkness of the auditorium. Shaken, Springsteen handed the ring to the hall's management after the show and told them to keep it safe in case the woman ever came back to claim it.

She never did.

'It gives you a feeling of responsibility, a real heavy feeling of responsibility,' Springsteen reflects. 'I had all these kids coming up to me all the time we were making the album and they'd say, '*We know it's gonna be great, we know you're gonna do it, it's gonna be great!*' . . . I don't wanna let the people that have supported me down. And it ain't good enough just *getting by*, I wanna take it all the way, every night . . .'

There ain't nothing else that he can do.

All duded up for Sunday night, the last of three Springsteen dates at the Palladium (all ten thousand-plus seats sold in under two hours) this is a partisan crowd, hard-core Springsteen followers since the early days. They're mostly in their late teens or early twenties; wild and loud but without the glass-chucking violence so beloved by the mob-handed morons with a mile-wide yellow streak down their backs who contaminate gigs back in the good ol' Yew Kay.

'These kids that come to my shows, they ain't here for trouble, they're here to have a good time,' Springsteen tells me. 'They get kinda noisy and excited but the last thing on their mind is busting somebody's skull.'

Before every show he plays Springsteen talks to the Security and tells them that he doesn't want any rough stuff. He tells them that if there *is* any heavy-handed bouncer antics he'll do everything in his power to make sure the individuals responsible are looking for a new job in the morning.

What he doesn't tell them is that if they start beating up on the kids then they better be prepared to go through him, too; he personally dives into the audience to sort out Security-provoked aggravation. It happened time and time again on his last tour.

'You guys work here?' he demands. 'These guys you're roughing up are my *friends*!' And his fans love him for it . . .

'But the Security at the Palladium are okay,' he grins. 'Never any trouble here. They know me.'

About half of the crowd are from New Jersey and a lot of them remember Springsteen jamming in the Upstage club, which he remembers as 'some of the happiest nights of my life'.

'If there was ever a chance of any of us making a living through music, we figured it would be through Bruce,' says his guitarist Miami Steve Van Zandt of the E Street Band.

Springsteen had first picked up a guitar (for mirror-posing purposes) at nine, the day after gawping at Elvis on the Ed Sullivan show, but he didn't start playing until he was a friendless thirteen year old, two years after the nun's rough justice in the Catholic class-room. His distaste for organised religion ('The smell of the convent made me literally throw up'), his lack of self-respect ('I definitely did not dig myself') and his loneliness ('It was a very solitary existence, I didn't have the flair to be the class clown, it was like I just didn't exist') left a life of such awesome nothingness that he was soon practising eight hours a day to fill it . . .

'My sister, my youngest sister, she's sixteen and she's very pretty and very popular. There's no way that she's gonna sit in her room for every waking hour.' He grins ruefully. 'I didn't have that problem.'

By the time he was fourteen he was in his first band, by sixteen he was so good that when he practised in a garage kids would stand on milk crates with their noses pressed against the window panes to watch him.

At first none of the countless bars and clubs in New Jersey would allow him on their stage because he refused to play Top Forty golden greats. Then he was given a chance to strut his stuff at the Upstage and struck while his plectrum was hot. From then on he packed out the club for four nights a week until he finally met his first manager, Mike Appel. They decided to be Elvis and Colonel Tom but it really didn't happen that way at all.

After the CBS contract in the early '70s came 'Greetings From Asbury Park, NJ' and 'The Wild, The Innocent and The E Street Shuffle', both in 1973, with only a handful of songs – 'Lost In The Flood', 'Spirit In The Night', 'Incidents On 57th Street', 'Sandy', 'Rosalita' – giving a clue to the quality to come, the rest of the records too verbose for comfort, Springsteen subsequently getting lumbered with one of the New Dylan albatrosses that in those days they were giving away instead of Green Shield stamps.

Springsteen went into his studio for a year or so to record his third album, co-producing it with Appel and *Rolling Stone* scribe Jon Landau, and when he came out again the shit was already poised to splatter against the proverbial fan, man. 'Born To Run' was grandiose, heroic, magical, worthy of some unholy alliance between Phil Spector and Leonard Bernstein, a romantic fantasy of sleazy street-life, enormously accessible.

As the hysterical hyperbole of the CBS publicity machine went into overdrive, Springsteen played ten sold-out dates at New York's Bottom Line to consistently ecstatic audiences, 'Born To Run' became a platinum album and the single of the same name broke into the American Top Twenty: Top of the world, Ma! Then everything began to fall to pieces . . .

Jon Landau had written an incisive, sensitive, trenchantly subjective article on Springsteen for *Rolling Stone* in which he succeeded in expressing the unique brilliance of the man in intensely personal terms; Landau spoke of his love for his girlfriend asleep upstairs as he worked at his typewriter, of what the music he had grown up with had meant to his life and how witnessing Springsteen that night had been the purest exposition of the rock 'n' roll spirit that he had seen in many years. Landau's piece remains one of the best articles on Springsteen.

But CBS instigated all-out critical backlash by latching on to one quote from the article – 'I have seen the future of rock 'n' roll and its name is Bruce Springsteen' – taking it completely out of context and using it as the masthead for the hard-sell marketing technique overkill that rebounded on the record company and Bruce himself with a vengeance. 'At last London Is Ready For Bruce Springsteen!' was another one, and I remember sneering at it as I walked down City Road, N1, on my way to work one night late in 1975.

In fairness to Springsteen, no-one was innocent when it came to the extravagant claims being made on his behalf except for Bruce Springsteen himself. As soon as he saw the *future of* quote screaming from a 'Born To Run' advertising billboard he was on the blower to the Fat Cats telling them to cut the crap. And when he discovered gratis *'I Have Seen The Future etc'* badges being handed out at one of his gigs, well . . .

Meanwhile; back in the boardroom, Appel and Bruce were having the initial argument over the distribution of the newly acquired wealth that would eventually degenerate into a permanent rift twixt manager and musician, both parties filing million-dollar law-suits against the other alleging breach of contract.

Jon Landau became Springsteen's new manager and Appel filed an injunction preventing Landau from entering a studio with Springsteen and preventing Springsteen entering a studio at all. There followed nearly three years of lay-off and litigation. When Bruce should have been out on the road consolidating the 'Born To Run' victory (he loves touring, says he's always fascinated by what his hotel room will look like, how big the bed will be, what colour the carpet and wallpaper will be, if there'll be any weird pictures on the wall. Isn't he a lovely bloke?) he was in front of the legal bar.

The basis of the disagreement between Appel and Springsteen is rooted in Bruce's naivety when it comes to contracts. Appel had always told Springsteen that he paid the E Street Band far too much money but it wasn't until the royalty cheques for their first hit album began getting delivered by the truckload that Bruce realised how little say he had over the fruits of success he and the boys had been working towards for the best part of a decade . . .

'We'd suddenly made all this money and contracts we'd signed three years before became important. It wasn't so much the money . . . I wanted *my songs*. Mike had the publishing rights to all my songs . . . when I signed those contracts I didn't even know what publishing *was*! That whole period was just a time in my life that seemed completely out of my hands. Business is something that I'm pretty easily intimidated by . . .'

Remarkably, Springsteen holds no grudges against Appel.

'Even when we were in court . . . he was still a guy that I kinda liked and knew that he kinda liked me.'

The final proof that Springsteen survived all the hype, the two years in court and the *looooong* time in the wilderness of enforced retirement is 'Darkness On The Edge Of Town'. He has returned with infinitely more maturity, power, soul and fire on his fingertips than he ever had in his life.

'That album . . . it's about people refusing to let go of their humanity. No matter what they go through, no matter what life does to them, they never let go of their humanity.'

'Brooooooooose!!!' from three and a half thousand throats and the lights go on as the E Streeters hit the opening chords of 'Badlands': the same epic, awesome waves of invigorating beautiful noise as before; but Springsteen, striding the planks grinning, his Fender hanging loose on his back, gripping the hand mike tight in both hands, dapper in black jacket and strides . . . once he starts spitting out the lyrics, makes it plain where he's been all this time, how he's not the same anymore . . .

'*Lights out tonight/Trouble in the heartland/Got a head-on collision/Smashin' in my guts, man/I'm caught up in a cross-fire that I don't understand!/But there's one thing I know for sure, girl!!*'

'I was disappointed that the reviews of the album said it sounded depressed,' Bruce told me later. 'I spelled it out for 'em on the first track . . .'

'*I don't give a damn for the same old played out scenes/Honey, I don't give a damn for just the inbetweens, Honey, I – want – the – heart – I – want – the – soul – I – want – control right now.*'

Raw, exhilarating, inspirational . . . the superlative dictionary is right down the dumper, John. Springsteen – be it in conversation, on record and *especially* on stage often appears too good to be true. You look for the catch, the flaw, the giveaway. And you look and you *look* and you keep looking until you finally concede that there isn't a catch. He's the one.

After two years of showbiz decadence, all the free albums and concert tickets, Springsteen is the only one I'd actually pay money to go and see. He's the only person who makes me feel like a fan again.

'*I believe in the Love You Gave Me/I believe in the faith that can save me!/I believe in the faith and I pray that someday it may raise me ... above these ... badlands!!!'*

This is joyous, optimistic rock music. It's what rock 'n' roll should have been about and rarely was. He's not, unfortunately, the future of rock 'n' roll, but he's so good, so vital, so honest that he shows the majority of the rest of 'em up for the squalid cretins they are. The day he quits is the day the music really dies ... this guy, this rocker, has actually got some backbone to his work, some *moral fibre*.

'Yeah, there's a lotta morality in the show, and it's a very *strict* morality. Anybody that works for me has gotta understand that. I know how *I'd* feel if I paid money to see a show and what I wanted wasn't delivered. It comes back to the responsibility thing ...'

I've seen great gigs before; The Clash at Harlesden in '77, The Who at the Rainbow in '71, Bowie in Newcastle earlier this year, the Pistols on the Jubilee boat trip or at the two Screen on the Green dates, but what Bruce Springsteen does transcends all of those without a photo-finish. This ain't just the best gig I've ever seen in my life, it's much more than that. It's like watching you're entire life flashing by and instead of dying, you're dancing.

Springsteen sings a love song and he doesn't make you smirk the way you would at some fat-zero axe-hero mucho macho man; he makes you ache for the girl you love, he makes you remember her and wish she were here tonight so you wouldn't have to go home alone and without her. I didn't know music could do that to you.

And Springsteen documents the conflict between father and son better than anyone since Steinbeck in *East of Eden*. There's the raging 'Adam Raised A Cain' but the real killer is the unrecorded 'Independence Day', possibly the most poignant, moving ballad he's ever written. I was close to tears. At first I thought it was because either I'm too sensitive or else I'm getting soft but then I realised that rock 'n' roll rarely gets this *real*.

'*Well, Papa, I don't know what it was with the two of us/We chose the words and, yeah, we drew the lines/This house, no how could it hold the two of us/I guess that we were just too much of the same kind/So say goodbye, it's Independence Day/All boys must run away ... come Independence Day/Oh say goodbye, it's Independence Day/All men must make their way/Come Independence Day ...*'

You want it, you take it you pay the price ... Springsteen, apart from everything else, is also a born performer, frequently jumping off stage and running into the heart of the auditorium, one hand on the mike and another wrapped around a kid in a display of genuine affection.

The E Street Band is a revelation; Danny Federici on organ and Roy Bittan on piano, Steve Van Zandt on guitar, the golden sax of The Big Man Clarence Clemons as always the most important instrument after Springsteen's impassioned, howling voice and with it all nailed down solid by the relentlessly strident rhythm section of Garry Tallent on bass and Max Weinberg on drums. The sound is as full and vibrant as on vinyl but Springsteen's meticulously perfectionist attitude to sound checks and the electric urgency applied to performing live by everyone on stage takes Springsteen's music to awesome, unprecedented extremes of excellence.

'Something In The Night' and 'Streets of Fire' were both recorded for 'Darkness' in just one take. The latter is yet another gem on stage, Springsteen alone at the front of the darkened stage, haunted, tortured, agonising like some tormented Prince of Denmark yet totally believable.

'*When the night's quiet, and you don't care anymore/And your eyes are tired/And someone's at your door/And you realise . . . you wanna let go/And the weak lies and the cold walls you embrace . . .*' The vocal building, the bitter bile of undiluted fury rising in his throat. '*Eat at your insides and – leave – you – face – to – face with streeeets of fiii-rrre!!!*'

And 'Factory', possibly the most accurate recording of the drab, dull, soul-destroying boredom of working class existence ever put on black plastic. Kraftwerk, Devo and all those other industrial-togged turds . . . do you *really* believe that their product is 'industrial factory folk-muzak of mass-man in the machine-age' *undsoweiter*. You *do*? You poor, deluded git. I bet you never done a day's work in your miserable life.

'*Early in the morning factory whistle blows/Man rises from bed and puts on his clothes/Man takes his lunch, walks out into the morning light/It's the work, the working, just the working life/Through the mansions of fear, through the mansions of pain, I see my daddy walking through those factory gates in the rain/Factory takes his hearing, factory gives him life/It's the work, the working, just the working life/End of the day, factory whistle cries/Men walk through these gates with death in their eyes/And you just better believe boy/Somebody's gonna get hurt tonight/It's the work, the working, just the working life . . .*'

I love that song. But then I'm still a bit mutt 'n' jeff from Distiller's so then I'm biased.

Springsteen performs *all* of 'Darkness On The Edge Of Town', *all* of 'Born To Run', early songs like 'Spirit In The Night' and 'Incident On 57th Street'.

He performs great songs that he gave to other people – 'Faith' (Robert Gordon), 'Fever' (Southside Johnny), 'Because The Night' (Patti Smith) – all of them cutting the cover versions to shreds, smouldering lust paeans, love bites back . . .

That's Bruce's one fault to my mind – he's too *generous*; nobody else in the history of rock 'n' roll has given songs of that quality away. Still, I guess he can afford it, he is a genius, after all.

And when he's played for nearly four hours and it's way past midnight and the houselights have been on for over half an hour but we just won't go away, we refuse to leave the auditorium, we just stand on our seats and scream *Brooooooose!!! Moooooore!!! Brooooose!!!* he comes back and plays on, all old Juke Box giants, Buddy Holly songs, 'Quarter To Three', 'Devil With The Blue Dress On' and many, many more (no, I didn't take notes). And then your heart sinks because it's all over.

What can I tell you? God, I wish you could have been there.

'Bruce has collapsed,' his manager Jon Landau tells me thirty minutes after the end of the show. 'We'll have to cancel the interview. He's in a state of exhaustion. He can't talk to anyone now.'

Usually, I'd know that I was getting served bullshit and the rock star I was ready to interrogate had pissed off, back to a gram of coke in the Ritz and was at this moment writhing around in the back of his limo with leather strides around his ankles and a big, fat groupie sitting on him.

With Springsteen it's different: all I can think is . . . Christ, I hope he's gonna be all right.

But I stick around inside the Palladium, just thinking about the gig. Shit, I got a plane to catch early in the morning so I might as well stay up all night. I couldn't sleep after a show like that anyhow.

'You can come backstage and meet Bruce if you want to,' Landau tells me and my heart starts a-pounding. Kid, I've met 'em all . . . Led Zeppelin, The Rolling Stones, the Pistols, Mike Batt, you name it. Never in my life have I felt awe at the thought of meeting a musician before . . . Well, I was afraid I'd be let down. Of course, I wasn't; he's exactly what he seems to be – open, honest, warm, personable, friendly, funny, probably the most likeable geezer I've met in my life.

Five feet nine inches with a muscular, tanned, athletic build, an easy smile and a hoarse, rasping laugh, he's relaxed and talkative, ready to listen and you feel like you've known him all your life.

As you've no doubt sussed, I was meant just to say hi and split but me and Bruce got talking and we just couldn't stop. He talks about the album for a while and when he asks me what I think of it and I tell him it's nowhere near as accessible as 'Born To Run' but after repeated playing it stands up as by far the best thing he's ever done, he actually breathes a sigh of relief.

'Phew, *that's* good . . . that's what we want people to react like when they hear it.' But, Bruce, surely you ain't *worried* about it . . . you must know how good it is . . .

'Ah, people tell ya so many different things . . . I just want the people who *care* about me to know what I'm trying to do. See, it couldn't be an innocent album like "Born To Run" because things ain't like that for me anymore. The characters on the new album ain't kids, they're older – you been beat, you been hurt – but there's still hope, there's always *hope*. They throw dirt on you all your life and some people get buried so deep in the dirt that they never get out. The album's about the people who'll never admit they're buried too deep to get out.'

Bruce talks about the three nights he sold-out Madison Square Garden in the summer. 'I don't usually like playing places that big but that was for all the long-time supporters, so they could all get in and see us . . .'

On the first night he brought his sixteen year old sister Pam on stage after dedicating 'Sweet Little Sixteen' to her.

And before the final encore on the last Garden date he was dragged back on stage by his Italian mother Adele (his father, Douglas, is Irish, once a factory worker in New Jersey and now a bus-driver in Northern California). Bruce was screaming in protest as Adele dragged him to the mike, 'Aw, Mom! I can't do anymore! I just played four hours! I can't do no more!'

The Garden dates were typical Springsteen gigs; intimate and cha-otic both, more like a great party than a rock 'n' roll show, yet paradoxically the greatest rock 'n' roll show in the world.

I informed him that I was at Madison Square Garden a few days ago, standing out front and trying to sell two ELO tickets that CBS had given me. After getting hassled by the local spivs and unable to unload the tickets I decided to take a look inside and use the tickets myself. After seeing that the Garden was just another Wembley and reluctant to watch an ELO show, I decided to leave. But though, the Garden was geared to take thousands upon thousands of people *into* the auditorium, there was no provision for letting people *out*. All stairs, all halls, all escalators were strictly one way. Travelling in the opposite direction just wasn't allowed. Eventually, I got out. I had to get thrown out by the cops, Bruce.

But this fat cop called 'Heavy' was very nice about it, he only bounced me on the pavement once and waved his nightstick at me but never hit me with it.

Bruce cracks up with laughter. 'Hey, I never thought what would happen if somebody wanted to get *out* of one of my shows!!'

And the dogs on Main Street howl, 'cause they understand.

George Michael

Is it true you're an arrogant bastard, George?

The Face, August 1985

T'S REALLY BAD. He has just moved into this flat but he can't furnish it. Because every time he goes into a store he gets chased out. He really is shockingly famous! He stops traffic. Even when we're sitting at a back table in a very discreet oyster bar – and he has his back to the window, for God's sake – out in the street cars are slowing to take a look. If you had never listened to the records you would think he was a real bimbo. If you had never listened to the records you would never guess that he really is exceptionally talented. At his best – 'Careless Whisper', 'Everything She Wants' – it could be Cole Porter crying in the Wag. At his worst, great lines like '*We've got plans to make, we've got things to buy, and you're wasting time on some creepy guy,*' are drowned by screaming. In America, where Wham! are about to play a sell-out stadium tour, 'Make It Big' has yielded three number one hits – the first LP to do that since 'Saturday Night Fever'. He is the biggest thing since John Travolta (and he has yet to make a movie). To listen to his detractors you would think that under his tennis shorts was a 666 birthmark. To listen to his detractors you would think his politics make General Pinochet seem like Shirley Williams. It could be the classic pop life story except . . . he pulls his own strings. In every facet of his career, he calls the shots. He thinks the fan newsprint ('With his Moon in the sign of Leo, George loves to make every little thing about the home special – he probably likes a bubble bath, a teddy bear and loves to play little tricks on people') is just as phoney as the stuff the grown-ups get from Fleet Street ('Wham! Man In Hara-Kiri Terror!'). To listen to the gossip about him in the powder rooms of the music business you would think he was a belligerent glutton on the verge of a mental breakdown. Lies, all lies. He is intelligent, touchingly loyal, ferociously ambitious, very down to earth. He is real. And – I'm sorry, but you are going to have to come to terms with this – he really is exceptionally talented. By the time you read this he will be celebrating his birthday. He will be 22. Are you ready to raise your glass to George Michael?

TONY PARSONS: Are Wham! the cause of famine in the Third World?

GEORGE MICHAEL: I think so. I think most of the people who bought the last Wham! album would have given their money to charity had they not bought it.

TP: Were you upset about the way the miners' strike ended?

GM: I must admit that when we did the strike benefit I was at a turning point. Not as to what I thought about the issue, because the issue was clear enough. But when I met Arthur Scargill I got a terrible impression of him. He really did annoy me. He just seemed to be enjoying it all far too much. When I met him I got the impression that the only place he was leading the miners was further and further up their own asses. It was good that they were fighting, because nobody had been fighting for years, but I started to feel that by carrying it on all they were doing was damaging their own industry and they were not going to make any ground. I was hoping that Scargill was going to become a realist and see that the Government wanted to make an example of the miners. He didn't. I thought it was really sad when it came to an end because they really hadn't got anything out of it. When we did the benefit, I really thought there was some kind of hope.

TP: You got a lot of stick for doing that benefit from people who supported the strike. They didn't like your hair, the clothes you wear. Do you get hurt by what people say about you?

GM: They can knock shit out of you. But in the end it doesn't really matter unless they call you a child molester.

TP: Did you react to *Saturday Night Fever* the same way that a previous generation reacted to The Pistols?

GM: Definitely. Andrew and I became fully fledged suburban soul boys at 15. We wore dungarees and bright colours and got sent home from school. All this shitty minor rebellion. I loved all that '77–'78 disco stuff but then it started getting into jazz-funk and I thought, fucking hell, all these 17-year-old kids haven't got a clue about jazz music, they just think it's the trendy thing to do. We just got out of it, stopped going to those clubs. We got into 2-Tone because that was the next thing that happened that was young and energetic, then when that faded we were flailing around for about a year in terms of what we liked and what we wanted to write. Then there was this resurgence of soul-pop, stuff like 'Burn Rubber', and we decided that was what we wanted to do. 'Wham Rap' was meant to be a piss take of rap records, it was meant to be a parody record – *I am the most beautiful*. Rap was quite funny at first but it got really boring. Punk-disco they called us. The ridiculous things they called us!

TP: A lot of people thought you were black.

GM: Especially in America. In America they were doing the old job where they send out your record to the R&B stations without your picture on. It's disgusting, it's so disgusting. Getting you through the back door.

TP: You haven't got any kind of rock heritage at all, have you?

GM: None whatsoever. I have so little respect for the type of glamour that people see in rock and roll.

TP: What's that? And how is it different to your glamour?

GM: Rock 'n' roll glamour is MTV. Fast women, fast cars, larger than life.

TP: While *you're* still down on the street . . . (*sings*) 'Easy girls and late nights, cigarettes and love bites'?

GM: Rock 'n' roll believes that music can elevate you into something you're not. If you play aggressive guitar music then automatically your cock is three inches bigger. It's brainless.

TP: How was China?

GM: The people in themselves seem blissfully ignorant. Any sympathies that I've ever had with extreme Socialist views, when you actually see it in practice it's just a load of bullshit. The leaders there are just the same as leaders anywhere else. They were screwing us for money left, right and centre. Anything you want to do, anything at all, if you're Western they screw you for a bit of money before you do it. That whole filming trip ended up costing us about a hundred million more because everything we did, they said we had to pay. Most of the people at the top are more Capitalistic than even the people in the American government – they have this basic greed about them.

TP: So why did you go? Surely it was all down to ego?

GM: You're absolutely right. The basic reason for going to China was not to introduce our wonderful culture. It was to *do* something. How many things does a band do that are of any significance whatsoever? Just for once it was nice that you were the first and quite possibly the last. There is a certain privilege attached to that. But once we got there I just thought the whole thing was a shambles. What was basically going on was that the Chinese government was trying to encourage the Western world to accept Chinese product.

They were saying – look, we have our arms open, we are going to accept Western music. That was total bollocks! They used us. We were a propaganda item. There are factions in China who do want to open up but the people who are still in power were so fucking scared as to what might happen. At that first gig they disallowed dancing! The Minister of Culture made an announcement on radio two days before saying – go and see Wham!, enjoy the concert but do not learn from it. How can you say anything more ridiculous than that? Yet over there it works. The most incredible thing about China is that the people seem almost totally drained of any kind of initiative. There's no point in using any initiative there because you can never get anywhere. It's a denial of what all those people are capable of. Saying that everyone is equal is a denial of where we've got to. For all the awful things that one can say about America or England or the Western world, it is at least ... *honest*. People follow their instincts. And in that country there doesn't seem to be any.

TP: What does it look like?

GM: It is *so* barren – the drive between Peking and the airport is absolutely and totally barren. To me this is not an intelligent government. Twenty years ago they decided to kill all the birds because the birds were eating the crops. Now it doesn't take much working out that if you kill all the birds then the birds are not eating anything else. So ten years ago when all the insects had eaten all the crops because the birds were not eating all the insects, they just fucking pulled up all the grass! Can you believe it? There is no grass in China because if you have grass you have insects and if you have insects they eat the crops. What kind of government makes decisions like that? The latest one is they are encouraging the people to eat rats – because there are four hundred million rats in China so they are asking the people to eat them. In some ways it is so primitive it's frightening. People were saying to us – if you had been here 18 months ago you wouldn't recognise the place. They are supposed to have come so far in 18 months! It is *unbelievable*. I'd never go there again.

TP: Does this mean you won't be touring Russia?

GM: I think Russia is something totally different. I think it's probably a lot more depressing.

TP: Do you believe in trying to be faithful?

GM: My honest view is that if you can actually find someone who you can be faithful with then you're a lucky bastard. Because there are some people who are totally satisfied with one partner. I don't believe that fidelity is all it's cracked up to be. I think if your girl-friend or husband or wife or whatever is screwing other people on the odd occasion throughout a marriage or a relationship they can get into a situation where somebody's throwing themselves at them. If they're sleeping with that person because they're not getting what they want from you then you've got problems. If they're just sleeping with that person because they're curious sexually and they can't con-trol it – or not that they can't control it but they don't want to control it – then I don't think there's any big problem. As long as people still have affection and don't think any less of you than they did when they first met you, then I don't think your relationship is in any jeopardy. I don't think it's that much of a trauma. I think a lot of people believe that without saying it.

TP: Mrs Thatcher must love you – a self-made millionnaire at 21. Born in Finchley!

GM: We have capitalised on what we do well at the worst possible time. There's a difference between getting rich and being right wing. A lot of people don't see that difference. The music press is just so far removed from what is going on in the mind of the kid on the street where five or six years ago it wasn't.

TP: Did you grow up feeling like any kind of an outsider because you come from a Greek family?

GM: My dad's Greek but my mum's English. My mum's very Eng-lish. My dad was working so hard up to the age when I was about four that I got no Greek language. I didn't like Greek music when I was a baby, when I was a kid. I've really got very little association with the Greeks at all other than the fact that I'm hairy.

TP: Hirsute.

GM: Hirsute. Good word. I don't feel any affinity for the Greek way of life and I never did. The only way that I did feel an outsider was the fact that from the age of six or seven I had no interests other than music. Everything else bored me. I would sit in lessons thinking about music, thinking about the record I was saving up for, I was so totally preoccupied with it that in that way I was an outsider. It made me stronger.

TP: Did you have a happy adolescence?

GM: I don't look like the same person I was when I was 13. Andrew is one of those people whose faces never change, he looks exactly the same as he did then. I had all the things not going for me that 13-year-old kids don't have going for them. Apart from the spots. The only thing I didn't have was the spots. But I was well overweight, taller than everyone else, I had really frizzy, curly hair, very thick glasses – nobody looked at me, absolutely no girl ever looked at me. Then suddenly when I was about 15 I cut my hair and I got contact lenses. The optician was saying I was too young but I wanted them so badly. It's not vanity not to want to have specs, is it? And it suddenly became fashionable to have curly hair – *the perms, the perms* . . .

TP: Kevin Keegan!

GM: The Kevin Keegan look! All of a sudden people started inviting me to their parties. I was still on very dodgy ground because I had no idea how to throw my weight around or how to pull. Andrew and I just used to get absolutely pissed, every single place we went to we got paralytic. Then there was this one night when I was well over the top and just this one night, Andrew stayed totally sober. That's the night that got around about me wandering home saying, oh, I must be so ugly, no girl will ever look at me. I burst a blood vessel in my eye that night, I was so pissed. I had a red eye for three weeks.

TP: That's how Genghis Khan died. On his wedding night, old Genghis drank so much he burst a blood vessel in his brain.

GM: I missed it by a couple of inches. But everyone throws one real whopper when they first start drinking, don't they? I still throw a few now.

TP: I know I've got too drunk when I lose a contact lens . . .

GM: The worst thing about contact lenses is when you decide to go home with somebody and then, when you've done whatever you're going to do with this person, you suddenly realise you haven't got your contact lens case, right? And you lay there with nowhere to put your contact lenses. What kind are yours?

TP: Gas permeable.

GM: Mine are soft. If you put them in water they're *agony* when you put them in the next morning. I've done it two or three times. I have had to keep them in and actually had to lay there in bed all night and in the morning pretend I've been asleep. But I've just been laying there all night with my eyes glued open – it doesn't look totally superstud when you say in the morning, I'm very sorry but I've been awake all night because I didn't take my contact lenses out.

TP: When did you lose your virginity?

GM: I was 12, almost 13. There was a long, long gap between that one and the next one.

TP: It's supposed to be best to lose your virginity with either a virgin or a prostitute.

GM: I certainly didn't lose mine with a virgin! She was a right old dog. Basically, it was one of those jobs where I was so young and I was so absolutely inexperienced that – you know how it is, when people have their first screw they go back to school and they tell everybody – it was so embarrassingly bad that I went to school and didn't tell anybody. Because I couldn't lie straight-faced to them and tell them I'd had a good time. Sex is a great leveller – for those years between that time and the next I really thought that I'd been conned. I thought it wasn't just me but that sex really wasn't that much fun. I don't think that many people do have much fun that first time. It's a leveller. The great leveller.

TP: Did you ever fall out with Andrew over a girl?

GM: It's strange . . . your sexual role is reversed when you become some kind of teenage idol. You become chased. Not *chaste* as in chastity but *chased* as in – down the street. You become the one who is sought after as opposed to the one who has to do the chasing. It makes you – you see it in our photographs time and time again – we suddenly adopted this *feminine* attitude to the camera. It's very subconscious . . .

TP: You're coming on to the camera?

GM: You're coming on to the camera in the same way as a woman would do to a man. I try not to do it anymore. What I'm saying is – there's a similarity between Andrew and I now which there wasn't before. Because Andrew was always the feminine looking one and I was much more masculine. Girls who liked me didn't like Andrew and girls who liked Andrew didn't like me. There was a definite barrier. But now they'll take either of us. It's the honest truth. And it's something that I never saw before. If we both fell for the same girl *now*, that's the girl we'd fall out over.

TP: How do you feel about marriage and children and all that jazz?

GM: I always looked at it and I always hated it. Except when I see a young bloke and he's got a little boy with him I think, fuck, I would love that. I would love a little boy. I don't want a little girl. I love little boys. And to still be young, that's the thing. I know that by the time I get a kid I am not going to be very young. Because I know the way I think about my career I'm going to be easily 28, 29 before I get married. But I love the idea of still being a young man and having a little boy. The way I work now I can't see it stopping for quite a while. I just would not be happy to leave the kid and go flying around the world.

TP: 'Everything She Wants' is such a great song – it's not a song you would expect from a 21-year-old.

GM: Actually I've been married and divorced three times. No, I'm very proud of that one. It's the most hard-hitting lyric I've written, though I've got a lot more that I've started on that are a lot harder than that. To most people 'Everything She Wants' is the same as 'Wake Me Up Before You Go' because it's just a pop record. To me it's something totally different. That's where being a scream band has held us back in terms of recognition of that we have actually been trying totally different styles over the past two years. There's an audience out there that I desperately want to win back because I think the music we make merits it. But if you make uplifting, euphoric, optimistic records and you also happen to be 21 and not ugly – even if you're just reasonable looking – you automatically get screamed at. You can't say, fuck this, I don't want it.

TP: There's an interesting quote from Springsteen where he says that for years his albums sold a million copies and he could still walk down the street, then when he made a record that sold three million copies, suddenly walking down the street was a very difficult thing to do.

GM: There's a difference between people who are pop stars and people who are Fleet Street pop stars. Right up until the last four or five months, right up until the Christmas single when they decided that George Michael and Andrew Ridgeley would be on the front page when Princess Di wasn't having her hair done – it's hard to get across to people that you're not trivia just because you're treated like it – right up until then I could go on a train, in a store. I'd get a little hassle but I could do it. Now the honest truth is that I can't go into a shop, I can't go into a department store, I can't get on a train. Because it is literally a joke! But up until a little while ago I refused to stop doing things like that because it worried me a lot, having to skirt round things, just as someone who *writes*, and as someone who has a career to live out. You have to have some kind of relationship with what's going on. I still go to all the London clubs even though they're fucking awful. I get stick. Before we were successful I was going to vaguely underground clubs for a couple of years and then when we became successful I felt the resentment from those people so I moved out of those clubs and started going to real shit-holes where the place would be full of real wallies but they still played decent music. Because I always like dancing to late-Seventies music. I like some of the stuff that's come out over the last couple of years but that's what I love – a nostalgia trip for when I was 15, 16 years old. These clubs were full of wallies but at least they were wallies

who wouldn't bother me. But then it got to the stage where they *would* bother me. So I had to go back to the vaguely underground clubs. By that time the people in them were so far removed from us – inasmuch as they *thought* they were so far removed from us – and those people are so self-important that they wouldn't actually come up to you and hassle you. When I go *now* I tend to have a couple of arguments. Because if you've had a few drinks and some wanker comes up to you and says, 'They shouldn't let you in here because what you play is shit,' I can wipe the floor with them. So I tend to do that a lot – and then I dance till three.

TP: But the girls outside your management offices are very relaxed with you.

GM: Because they see me every day! They see me every single fucking day that I go in that place! They say things to you like, 'Oh please please can I have another autograph because I've only got 42 of your autographs and Debbie's got 46?' I'm not a board game! But what can you do? They think they love you or whatever. I don't know what they're using us for. It's a shame because some of them are real bastards and some of them are really sweet. A lot of them are unemployed.

TP: Although your marketing has always been very aggressive, a lot of your early stuff had a real sense of humour about it. I mean, when Duran Duran did that video for 'Rio' they really looked like rich rock stars being filmed in exotic locations but your 'Club Tropicana' promo looked like you were on a package tour to Benidorm.

GM: At the beginning there was a real sense of humour. There's no way that I'm going to deny that's gone. You go from being two kids who have got this chance they weren't expecting to being . . . professionals. My absolute all-time low career wise is the video to 'Bad Boys' – because by the time we got round to making the video I had forgotten that it was meant to be a joke. That video is the worse thing in our entire career. We look such a pair of wankers in it. How can anybody look at those two people on screen doing what we were doing in that video – with all those fucking camp dancers prancing around in the background – and think it's *good*? We lost a lot of ground with that video.

TP: I had heard you're an arrogant bastard, George.

GM: I'm definitely very self-confident but people have different conceptions about arrogance. Some people who have got nothing have an arrogance. As far as I'm concerned it's a ridiculous business and I happen to be very, very confident in the one thing that's made all the success – ie, the fact that I write songs. I'm confident as a writer, as a performer – but, all round, I am not an arrogant person. The way we act on stage, the way we act on video is definitely – I love me. The people who are best at that are nearly always totally, totally different off stage. I came into this thing as a songwriter. On stage I come on like I think the world of myself. It does two things – it makes people buy the records, because people like to buy confidence, and it puts a lot of people's backs up.

TP: Do you feel like saying to your partner, 'Who writes the bleeding songs anyway?'

GM: In terms of songwriting, Andrew Ridgeley is probably my greatest fan. I think he's almost as proud of me as I am. He had no qualms about standing back. At a certain point we decided that our ambition was to be the biggest band in the world. When we realised that was our ambition – and we certainly haven't achieved that yet – the quickest way to do that, and the most likely way to do that was for me just to let my own writing take its natural course. So he stood back, very graciously, and in terms of the relationship in the band since then we have the type of relationship where we tend not to argue about things and then we get to a certain point – it's usually me – where we have to come clean with each other. Because otherwise we are really going to fall out. A real clear-the-air job. And that's probably happened about three or four times in the last three years. But because of it, and because it always gets to that stage and we let it go, there's definitely no kind of jealousy there.

TP: I think on your gravestone should be inscribed – Honour Thy Mate. Do you love him?

GM: Yes I do.

TP: Have you kept your other old friends?

GM: Sometimes some of my old friends will say something and I will think, oh, don't say that, don't be that impressed – because you know me better than that. And then you think to a degree you've got to allow them that because you've never been in that situation, you've never had a friend of yours go from just being a friend to having all this crap written about them and all this kind of elevated stuff. But you have to allow for human nature. You can't expect people to see it the way you do. You can't expect people to see the truth. But I've got a couple that really do and I hang on to them desperately. Because I need them more than they need me ... you see, I started off this interview answering in very interview-like answers and now because I've had a couple of glasses of wine I'm getting very conversational.

TP: Yeah, a sniff of the barmaid's apron and you're anybody's.

GM: It's true, it's true.

Rave From the Grave . . .

Jim Morrison

The Sunday Times, 7 July 1990

T IS NOT DIFFICULT to find the grave of the only man who ever looked good in leather trousers. Jim Morrison – poet, drunk, lead singer of The Doors – is one of more than a million souls laid to rest in the Cimetière du Père-Lachaise in Paris, but to get to his grave you need only follow the signs.

Half a mile from where he lies, the directions of long-gone hippies stain ancient tombstones, their felt-tip runes pointing pilgrims on the right path. 'Jim Morrison', it says, next to the rough arrows. Graffiti start to appear, a curious collection of weird European pet names – 'Titti' and the like – rubbing up against snatches of Doors songs, love letters to Jim and assorted pop culture refuse. On a nearby sepulchre, someone has carefully inscribed the names of the members of Australian heavy rockers AC/DC.

At the grave itself, the atmosphere is as reverential as a belch. In the mid-Seventies, a few years after Jim's untimely death in a Parisian bath tub, this grave was a shrine for freaks and heads of every description. The mourners all had long hair, called everybody 'man' – even girls – and would offer a hit on a weak joint. Somewhere between then and now, the hippies have gone off to cut their hair and run multinational corporations while Jim's touchingly simple grave has been overrun by 16-year-old Italian kids who are into Madonna. They pour through the scarred tombstones, chewing gum, jabbering excitedly and wearing their brightly-coloured 'Jolly' knapsacks. They stare dumbfounded at one dead pink rose resting on a slab of stone with an inscription almost obliterated by nearly two decades of graffiti. You can just make it out – 'Jim Morrison 1943–1971' – because someone has traced around the engraved words with a particularly virulent purple.

There's not much to look at. Beer cans, wine corks and cigarette butts are everywhere, reinforcing the aura of pimply squalor. Once a mawkish bust of Jim – all faraway eyes and doomed pout – stood by the grave, but that was stolen. Thieves also tried to make off with the headstone, but they managed only to drag it around so that it now rests across the grave, pressing down on Jim from what would have been the top of his luxuriant, black hair to the bottom of his silver belt.

Most of the visitors to his grave on this rainy day were nowhere near being born when 'Riders On The Storm', the last Doors single, was posthumously released. Occasionally you see some cool dude in mournful leather standing silent vigil, a Doors fan from way back, shedding a quiet tear behind impenetrable Ray-Bans, but for most of the young necro-teens – I counted more than 50 before I gave up – this is a Mecca for gauche Euro cool, a kind of Hard Rock Café of the afterlife.

Possibly Jim's early death gives them their first sense of tragedy. Perhaps they will get into The Doors a little later. Maybe they will just buy a T-shirt. But they are here, paying a sort of brash, unthinking homage.

Jim Morrison was the last in the line of twentieth-century American expatriates who came to Paris with dreams of a life that would be limitless and free, totally creative, a line that stretches back to Hemingway, Fitzgerald and Gertrude Stein. He was in Paris for only a few months before he died, but he did more than enough in his life to deserve to be buried among the heroes of Père-Lachaise. The cemetery is the fourth largest tourist attraction in Paris, though you certainly don't see the kind of crowds that Jim draws around the graves of Chopin, Bizet, Seurat or Oscar Wilde. Despite such competition, it's Jim that pulls them in. He is bigger box office than ever. A young Italian finished writing 'Emiliano' on a neighbouring tombstone. 'Jeem eez not dayd,' he told me.

In fact, he is a growth industry. The day before I left for Paris, the window of the Virgin Megastore on Oxford Street groaned under the weight of his painfully oblique poetry. Slim volumes originally published in private editions of a few hundred are now on sale in the Sainsbury's of the record industry. *The Lords, The New Creatures* and *Wilderness – The Lost Writings of Jim Morrison* are available at all good book shops now.

There are videos galore, a major biography (*Dark Star* by Dylan Jones, published by Bloomsbury) and WEA have 14 Doors LPs out there, though the band recorded only six studio albums. The numbers are made up with a collection of live recordings, various compilations, Jim reading his poems etcetera, etcetera. And they are currently shifting over a million units every year. At this rate James Douglas Morrison is going to leave every other pop icon, every other secular saint – Monroe, James Dean, Hendrix – trailing in his wake. Jim Morrison is on course to become the Elvis of the millennium. And we are still a year away from 3 July 1991, the 20th anniversary of his death.

By that time Oliver Stone's film, *The Doors*, now in post production, will be out on release, just in time for a global wake. Rock bio pics are notoriously hard to pull off, and it says a lot for Morrison's enduring appeal that a film maker of Oliver Stone's quality – *Platoon, Wall Street, Born on the Fourth of July* – is willing to risk a major pratfall by attempting to translate Jim's dark magic to the big screen. Tom Cruise was first cast as Jim Morrison but Stone has since settled on Val Kilmer, a brooding ex-Cher toy boy who had a meaty role in *Top Gun*. Billy Idol, Bridget Fonda and Meg Ryan are also cast.

Jim Morrison fulfilled all the criteria of pop culture martyrdom – he had youth, fame and beauty, and he casually squandered the lot – but what he produced in his lifetime remains more important than the manner of his death. Someone described The Doors as three great musicians and a genius, and that's about right.

'Their music insists that love is sex and sex is death and therein lies salvation,' Joan Didion wrote in *The White Album*. 'The Doors are the Norman Mailers of the Top 40, missionaries of apocalyptic sex.' In the late Sixties, an age of strict cultural apartheid, The Doors brought the underground to the teens and they took the hit parade to the avant-garde. 'The Doors begin where the Beatles and the Stones leave off,' said one critic. They were a truly great singles band, knocking out a string of classic 45s like 'Love Her Madly', 'Touch Me' and 'Hello, I Love You'. Then, delving into their albums, your mind was bent into a thousand different shapes by hard-core acid noir, 12-minute songs – not remixes or extended plays but real songs – grandiose epics like 'When The Music's Over', 'L.A. Woman' and 'The End', full of tortured, twisted visions that left you feeling like you had dipped your school plimsoll into Dante's inferno. 'After The Doors' people used to say, 'dinner with your parents was never the same again.'

Back in the Sixties, whether your tipple was Thai sticks or Tizer, The Doors spoke to you. Morrison was a cultural totem to the heads, an American dreamboat to the little girls. His voice embraced the two great genres of modern American song – the blues man and the

torch singer. He could sing like Howling Wolf and he could sing like
Sinatra and he often did both in one song. 'Come back, baby, back
into my arms,' he croons – really croons – in *When The Music's
Over*, just a few seconds before he screams, 'We want the world and
we want it . . . *nowwwwww.*'

Jim Morrison started out as a beautiful man, a man who looked
as if he was born for heroism. The definitive portrait is the Joel
Brodsky photograph that appears on the cover of *The Best Of The
Doors* and the poetry album *An American Prayer*. It also appears on
the cover of the seminal Doors biography *No One Here Gets Out
Alive* by Danny Sugerman and Jerry Hopkins. It appears, in fact,
almost everywhere because it perfectly expresses the most popular
and long-lasting image of Morrison. The photograph is Adonis Cru-
cified, a phallus in leather trousers, the picture of a sullen, cheek-
boned beauty with a bare lean torso and every unkempt curl in place.
'Isn't he handsome?' said old Ed Sullivan when The Doors appeared
on his show, and the little ones understood.

Jim Morrison was a military brat. His father became a rear ad-
miral and commanded a fleet of aircraft carriers in the Pacific while
his disowned son protested the Vietnam war in a song called 'The
Unknown Soldier', a song about the senseless waste of young lives.
Hearing Jim Morrison sing it now, it seems painfully ironic.

'The child of a military family, I rebelled against church after
phases of fervour,' Jim wrote in *As I Look Back*, a memoir included
in his book *Wilderness*. 'I curried favour in school and attacked the
teachers, I was given a desk in the corner. I was a fool and the
smartest kid in class. History of rock coinciding with my adolescence. Came to LA to film school. Venice Summer – Drug Visions –
Rooftop songs – early struggles and humiliations. Thanks to the girls
who fed me.'

While at UCLA film school, Jim Morrison met Ray Manzarek, a
classically trained pianist who played keyboards in a blues band with
his two brothers. Jim sang 'Moonlight Drive' to Manzarek – later
described as looking like a hip undertaker – while they sat on Venice
beach.

'Let's swim to the moon,' Jim crooned, eyes closed. 'Uh-huh, let's
climb through the tide. Penetrate the evening that the city seeks to
hide . . .'

Manzarek was impressed.

'Those are the greatest f★★★★★★ song lyrics I ever heard,' he
said. 'Let's start a rock 'n' roll band and make a million.'

'That's what I had in mind,' said Jim.

For their drummer, Manzarek recruited the pock-marked John Densmore. Drummers are traditionally the pinheads of any group but Densmore was a physics and psychology major that Manzarek knew from his meditation class. There were no pinheads in The Doors – not even the drummer. The efficient Manzarek brought in the dazed-looking Robbie Krieger, a guitarist who was also trained in the classics and was steeped in the blues. William Blake had written, 'When the doors of perception are cleansed, man will see things as they truly are, infinite.' Aldous Huxley had shortened the quote for his drug travelogue, *The Doors of Perception*. Jim Morrison shortened it further for the name of his band. The Doors began to rehearse and Jim Morrison had never been happier.

Right from the start, The Doors had more intellectual and musical muscle than any band that ever appeared on the Billboard Hot 100, before or since. They had their roots in the blues and Blake and high-faluting theories of confrontational theatre – Artaud was as big an influence as Elvis and Sinatra, Jim's favourite singers. It could have been awful and sometimes it was, but mostly it was glorious, the three musicians weaving a dense spell, the sound of a fairground in hell, behind Morrison, sex symbol and sage, a doomed poet in black vinyl pants.

The Doors' eponymous debut album was released in January 1967, and by the time the summer of love blossomed, they had their first million seller. And while everybody else – even the Beatles and the Stones – wore flowers in their hair, Jim Morrison sought a crown of thorns. 'Some are born to sweet delight,' he sang on that first album, a direct quote from Blake's *Auguries of Innocence*. 'Some are born to the endless night.'

The Doors were always a real band, never just Jim Morrison and some exceptional backing musicians. Still, he was always a man apart and nowhere is this clearer than in Granada TV's 1968 documentary *The Doors Are Open*.

Filmed in the days when you could play rock over footage of Vietnam and everyone would get it, *The Doors Are Open* features a scene where each member of the band comes through Customs to be met by the director. He asks all of them the same three questions – 'Name? Date of birth? Occupation?' Manzarek, Densmore and Krieger answer the questions with the same formality. 'Raymond Daniel Manzarek . . . February 12th 1939 . . . musician . . .' And then Morrison appears.

'Hi,' he says.

'Name?'

'Uh ... Jim,' he says, sounding doubtful.

'Occupation?'

'Uh ...' he says, and, lost for words, he gives the camera one of his rare smiles, a smile of impossible sweetness, the smile of a stoned seraphim. It is clear from the film that Morrison was a man of enormous personal charm. It is also clear that he was permanently blitzed.

'Jim,' a reporter asked in 1967, 'were you stoned up there on stage tonight?'

'Man,' said Jim, 'I'm always stoned.'

It was no idle boast. As the Sixties wound down Morrison became buried alive in his own myth-making. The Doors never made a bad album – Jim's voice merely became a little coarser, he had lost some of that smoochy crooner quality – but his behaviour became increasingly erratic. Once at the Château Marmont on Sunset Strip he fell two storeys, bounced on his head and walked away. In an age when rock stars were starting to drop like flies, it was suggested that Jim would be next. 'No,' said a record executive. 'Not Morrison. Too obvious.'

The Doors live became more and more confrontational, Jim habitually baiting his audience and abusing the police. 'Morrison has an authoritarian personality,' Albert Goldman wrote. 'I think he's more like his father than he realises.'

Jim was tear gassed by a cop for refusing to stop heavy petting with a random chick backstage at a gig in New Haven. Then in Miami in March 1969 he asked an audience, 'Do you want to see my cock?' A warrant was issued for his arrest.

'Morrison, a white male, age 25, reportedly pulled all the stops in an effort to provide [sic] chaos among a huge crowd,' said the FBI report. 'Morrison's programme lasted one hour, during which time he sang one song and for the remainder he grunted, gyrated and gestured ... He screamed obscenities and exposed himself, which resulted in a number of people onstage being slugged and thrown to the floor.'

Jim was found guilty of vulgar and indecent exposure but not guilty of the more serious charge of gross lewdness and lascivious behaviour. None the less the Miami débâcle and the subsequent trial marked the start of Morrison's final decline and the extent of his desperation. 'I drink so that I can talk to assholes,' he said. 'This includes me.'

Alcohol was Jim's poison. The good looks became podgy as he drowned himself in booze. He covered his podginess with a beard. 'What kind of sex symbol can a group have,' asked *Creem* magazine, 'once the lead singer has grown a full beard and a beer belly?' Jim Nash of the *Village Voice* saw him at a party in New York in 1970. 'Looking at him,' Nash wrote, 'I could smell death.'

The final Doors studio album, *L.A. Woman*, fulfilled the band's recording contract with Elektra and Morrison left for Paris with his long-term old lady, Pamela Morrison, a red-haired hippy beauty.

'After four years,' he wrote, 'I am left with a mind like a fuzzy hammer. I pissed it all away. American Music.'

Jim Morrison arrived in Paris on 10 March 1971 and moved into a small apartment in the Marais with Pamela. He was happier than he had been since the early days of acid and the ocean and rehearsing with The Doors in Venice. 'They threw away the blueprint when they made this city,' he said. Less than four months later, on 3 July, he died of a heart attack in a bath tub on a Saturday night. He was 27.

The Sixties feel like they ended with Jim Morrison. But his death was ripe for that great Seventies phenomenon, the conspiracy theory. When a representative of his record company arrived in Paris to identify the body he discovered only Pamela and a sealed coffin. There was no autopsy, no doctor present and, although there was a signature on the death certificate, Pamela couldn't remember who it belonged to. By the time the world knew about Jim Morrison's sudden demise, his coffin was in Père-Lachaise.

Rumours persist that the grave that Emiliano and his fellow young Italians mob is empty. Pamela isn't talking – within three years she was dead of a heroin overdose. But it is said that there are people in Paris who still insist that Jim Morrison was seen boarding a plane the night he is supposed to have died. And it has long been pointed out that the very last Doors single, 'Riders On The Storm', seems to suggest that Jim was going to split this crazy scene for a while and check back with us later. 'Take a long holiday,' he croons. 'Let your children play . . .'

Who knows? Maybe Jim Morrison will turn up for the premiere of the Oliver Stone movie, dressed in a snakeskin tuxedo. Now wouldn't that be a trip?

What Kylie Did Next

Kylie Minogue at Wembley

The Daily Telegraph, 31 October 1991

A FTER watching Kylie Minogue at Wembley Arena I feel that I am finally ready to take that GCSE in Sexual Molestation. Strutting around the stage like a waterfront strumpet, Kylie was pawed by leering dancers, had her frock torn off, and her buttocks were given a thorough medical examination by one of her chorus boys. But it has to be said that the show also had its bad points.

These are difficult days for Kylie. The Aussie *ingénue* has decided to ditch pop stardom and become a serious artist. It should be noted that Kylie's idea of a serious artist is not Henry Moore or Arthur Miller but Madonna – a woman who wears her underwear on top of her clothes and bras so pointy that they could take your eye out.

At Wembley Kylie defiantly showed that long gone are the days when she would coo inane tosh like, 'I should be so lucky, lucky, lucky'. These days her songs reveal a sophistication that was unknown when she was the sheila next door. 'I guess I like it, I guess I like it, I guess I like it like that,' goes one of her new numbers.

A sold-out Wembley lapped up the little madam. It was a strange crowd – a large turnout of five-year-olds in high heels accompanied by their parents in shell suits, but also lots of acne-clogged youths bellowing out of a lager haze. It was like wandering into a crèche at a football ground.

Minogue gave them a heady mix of material from the new album – slushy ballads, sweaty exhortations to pump it up, get it down and take it off – plus all the Kylie classics. The old stuff was updated to suit Kylie's new image with much miming of fornication. 'I should be so lucky, lucky' snarled the new Kylie, and gave her tiny breasts a good squeeze. I'm not making this up.

Kylie also showed us this new dance move where, wearing a pair of black tights and not much else, she turns her back to the crowd and pretends to give birth to a baby calf. She demonstrated her

mastery of crack dealer argot by calling for her chief dancer –
'Where's my main man? Yo, Darryl!' and then proceeded to come
within an inch of sitting on Darryl's face.

She can loll about in a leather fig-leaf and sing about pumping it
up all night long – but Kylie is half a pint of semi-skimmed milk and
she always will be.

Bitter Triumph of a Pop Catalyst

Brian Eno

The Daily Telegraph, 18 September 1992

Bᴙɪᴀɴ ᴇɴᴏ's ᴛɪᴍᴇ has come at last. For years Eno lived in the urbane shadow of Bryan Ferry, his former colleague in Roxy Music. But now Ferry is nowhere to be seen and the *New Musical Express* is hailing Eno as nothing less than 'the most important man in pop'.

They could just be right. Eno is probably the most distinctive record producer since Phil Spector. His collaborations with David Bowie on records like *Low* and *Heroes* have resulted in some of the most interesting and original records ever made, while Eno's production work with U2 on *The Joshua Tree* and *Achtung Baby* have helped transform a second-rate rock band into artists of a rare and special magic.

Even more than his considerable achievements as a producer and musical catalyst, Eno is being hailed as a musical heavyweight because he is the man who invented ambient music.

Legend has it that Eno was in bed recovering from being knocked down by a taxi when he discovered that his stereo was defective, rendering the harp music he was listening to almost inaudible. Eureka! Eno realised that he *liked* the way it sounded. And so ambient was born – gentle and profound, beyond music, beyond songs, into the twilight zone of ideas. Imagine *Tubular Bells* with the tunes taken out and you are halfway there.

Right now nothing has more credibility than ambient, largely thanks to *U.F. Orb*, the dreamy, chart-topping CD by The Orb, ex-ravers who make Eno music for the dance crowd. The Orb freely admit that they would never have existed without the musical experiments conducted by Brian Eno, the crazy professor who quit the hottest band of the '70s so he could invent music for the millennium.

And so it came to pass that an *NME* writer recently went to share tea and biscuits with Brian Eno. Munching an Ostler, the *NME* writer reflected on Eno's new position in music. Eno invented

Nineties pop, declared the man from *NME*. He is a freelance theorist, a random ideas generator, an egg-headed visionary, the founding father of ambient.

But incredibly Eno – almost choking on an Ostler – did not accept these compliments with a very good grace. 'Yes, and I'd like you to put that in your paper,' he raved. 'For four years, the *NME* was so obscenely rude about it [ambient music]. Just because it wasn't some ballsy, flesh-and-blood testosterone rocker thing. Eno-esque was a term of abuse ... There were five of them [journalists], and I will never forget them. Two of them I'm delighted to say, are dead, and I look forward to the day when I read the obituaries of the other three.'

Even by the hyperbolic, hysterical standards of the music business, this was an extraordinary outburst. It's a chilling thought that an intelligent, sensitive man like Brian Eno could seriously be scouring the obituary columns looking for the names of the jeering music journalists who thumbed their noses at records like *Music For Airports, Another Green World, Ambient Four: On Land* and *Thursday Afternoon.*

My first reaction was one of amazement. Who does Eno think he is? Van Gogh? It's not as though he's an impoverished, tortured genius languishing unloved on his death-bed. At least people came round to his way of thinking eventually. The depth of his bitterness is truly shocking.

And I fear I may be one of the names he is waiting to discover in the obituary columns. As I get older I find I like his stuff much more than I once did. But I was certainly never a fan of ambient music and, though I cannot remember sneering at Eno during the years that I worked for the *NME*, it is quite possible that once or twice I let slip some casual jibe while leaning up against the bar with assorted testosterone-enriched rockers. I remember we often used to stand around in our leather jackets swapping Eno jokes.

I regret that now. And the fact that this man I have never met might hate me is profoundly depressing.

It's not *quite* as depressing as listening to Eno's new record, *Nerve Net* – his usual collection of electronic squeaks, beeps and burps – but it comes very close.

But there's something in the writing; I felt that he understood very deeply the ambiguity of sexuality.

TP: He said, 'I see myself as a bisexual man who has never had a homosexual experience. That's the way I approach my songwriting. If you are asking am I insincere to pose as a sodomite when I've never had someone's cock up my arse, then no, I'm not. The sexuality you express is not limited to the things you've experienced. I mean, if you're a virgin, does that make you asexual?' He's been accused of hijacking gay imagery. Blurring the borders to make things more interesting for everybody.

DB: It amuses me that gays are often so protective about being gay. It has got to be black or white. There is often a limited response amongst gays to people who have ambiguities about their own sexuality. You have to come out and be one thing or the other.

TP: The Brett quote came in a debate about sex in music. Funnily enough, your name came up quite a bit. Boy George was there and he said that in the early '70s you gave him something to hope for, you showed him that there were other people like him in the world. But George also said that he always thought you were more gay than you actually were. And then later, when it became clear how much you liked women, he was disappointed in you. You were not the gay Elvis after all.

DB: Yeah, with gays it is very much us and them. That's unfortunate. In the States, towards the end of the '70s, I think the gay body was pretty hostile towards me because I didn't seem to be supporting the gay movement in any kind of way. And I was sad about that. Because I had come to the realisation that I was pretty much heterosexual. Now I even have a problem relating to my life and my sexuality in the early '70s.

But it annoys me when people say, oh, but you were gay, like it was something bad to have been. And I say – well, what's wrong with that? Although I no longer consider myself gay or even bisexual it shouldn't be assumed that therefore I have decided that heterosexual is correct and gay is wrong. That is the furthest thing from my mind. It is just that psychologically it was a decision that was made for me, in my head somewhere. There was never the thought, oh well, I'll be straight now. Because life isn't like that. And gays will tell you that. They didn't wake up one day and make a decision to be gay. They are gay. It just happens to be the reverse for me.

I was exploratory and there was so much that fascinated me. I guess it came from my own ambivalence about what my sexuality was when I was young. And then I remember reading – sometime in the late '60s – *City of Night* by John Rechy. A gay novel. A stunning piece of writing. I found out later that it was a bible among gay America but I didn't know it at the time.

There was something in the book akin to my feelings of loneliness. I thought – this is a lifestyle I really have to explore because I recognise things in this book that are really how I feel. And that led me a merry dance in the early '70s, when gay clubs really became my lifestyle and all my friends were gay.

I really opted to drown in the euphoria of this new experience which was a real taboo with society. And I must admit I *loved* that aspect of it. But as the years went on it became a thing where, sexually, I was pretty much with women the majority of the time. But I still had a lot of the trappings of gay society about me. In terms of the way I would parade or costume myself or my attitudes in some of the interviews I did. I remember doing the Russell Harty show – and I was definitely doing my gay bit on that show.

TP: I remember that, you were really camping it up.

DB: Yeah, in a really decisive way, to make a point. It seemed to be the one taboo that everyone was too afraid to break. I thought – well, if there's one thing that's going to put me on the edge, this is it. Long hair didn't mean much any more. So I thought – right. Let's really go into the gay lifestyle and see what that's about and see how people relate to me. If they can.

TP: What excited you as a child?

DB: The most exciting thing was the remnants of the Teddy Boys. It was exciting seeing them still on the streets. And I remember seeing two of them having a fight. I was on the other side of the road and it was really exciting. And I felt quite scared because I was near them. I was only about ten or 11 and couldn't take my eyes off them. And they had chains. Bicycle chains. I didn't run away, I wanted to watch them beating the shit out of each other.

TP: Has your accent changed since you were a kid?

DB: No, not at all.

TP: Your eyes are different colours because of a famous teenage fight that damaged the sphincter muscles of your left eye so that the pupil remains permanently open. Did getting your eye mashed up affect your vision?

DB: Dramatically. I was very worried about it. It was very bad in the early days. It's got a little better but not much. The further away I get everything's just brown. Everything's blurry with the left eye.

That was quite a shock for both George [George Underwood, Bowie's lifelong friend, who punched him in the eye] and I.

I was shocked that anyone could be that angry. It was over this girl that we were both going out with. George is the kind of guy who would probably remember her name. It was my fault. I knew he was going out with her. And I decided that I wanted to go out with her as well. Then he came at me! One lunch hour! And whacked me so hard in the eye . . .

I thought I had learned my lesson. I had a black eye. And then a couple of days later the eye just exploded. My dad rushed me to the London Eye Hospital and I had an emergency operation on it. The only other person I've ever seen with eyes like this is Little Richard.

TP: The new album, *Black Tie White Noise*, sounds like *Heroes* in love. Or a black Kraftwerk.

DB: With this album I feel that it's going to get a really good reaction among my hard-core fans. But how much of an audience something gets is really down to the singles these days and I really don't know what they would release as a single.

TP: Your great gift is to slip in and out of the mainstream. *Low* was a retreat from the mainstream. *Let's Dance* was slipping back into it.

DB: God, was that slipping into the mainstream! The success of *Let's Dance* was very disconcerting. It was terribly rewarding financially and it was rewarding seeing so many people going back to my old albums. To see relatively young kids come up with things that I'd done maybe ten years previously. But I'd become used to being a cult artist. And that's where I had grown to be comfortable. So suddenly being on television all the time and a stadium act – it was very odd. It was very strange for me and it really put me off balance.

I was not in great shape to accept success at any level. So it could not have come at a worse time for me. I was still fighting desperately to stop the drug thing, which was intermittent by then, but kept coming back. I told everyone that I was no longer an addict – including myself – because it was only occasional. But of course those occasions got closer and closer together. I would have a great spree for a few weeks, then stop and turn back to alcohol. It's an absurd situation because you say, oh, I've kicked everything – but you're a virtual alcoholic.

Drink is the most depressing of all addictions because it takes you so far up and throws you back down. And so as a writer and an artist I really didn't have much to hang on to any more. And it has been a very, very slow process of coming back again. And I dare say it isn't over. I dare say that none of our searches are really over.

TP: Your work often seems to hold up a mirror to itself.

DB: I think I have a certain vocabulary that, however much I change stylistically, there is a a real core of imagery. I don't see any abrupt changes in what I've done. To a symbolist, which is what I am, characters and situations are manifestations of things that he can't explain.

But what often amuses me is the reaction to a song like 'Loving The Alien' – where so many reviewers said, oh, Bowie out in space again. And the alien in this case was Muslim, which is prophetic because here I am married to one. I was talking about people being aliens to each other.

TP: I get the feeling that you didn't think you would get married again. Do you find it difficult to combine sex and romance?

DB: All sex and no romance was the problem. Or there were a number of platonic friendships, which I still have. The human bond was rarely there – another drugs spin-off. Sex becomes a release of energy. All that energy just ends up as sex.

When I was trying to straighten everything out in my life I met Melissa [the young dancer Bowie was engaged to in the late Eighties], who is such a wonderful, lovely, vibrant girl. I was immediately drawn to her exuberance and natural curiosity about life. And I guess it became one of those older man-younger girl situations where I had the joy of taking her around the world and showing her things. But it became quite obvious to me that it just wasn't going to work out as a relationship – and for that she would thank me one of these days. So I broke off the engagement.

That was three years – a big part of my life. I was depressed. It was like starting out all over. And I really wasn't looking for another relationship. But then over dinner I met Iman.

We were brought together by a mutual friend who thought we would get on very well. We were wary of each other but the attraction was mutual right from the beginning. She had also gone through a broken marriage and wasn't looking for a permanent relationship.

But so much of what we shared was similar. We had both achieved success. We knew the same people throughout the world. We both had children. A year and a half later we got married.

TP: Have you become more capable of loving someone? Or is she the right woman at the right time?

DB: I hope I have become more capable of loving someone without being possessive of them. And wanting to control them. It's knowing how to let go of the other person and let them be who they are. A major character fault of mine is that I do try to control people.

But my wife has a very strong sense of who she is. She comes from a strong clan system in Somalia. Her family go back many generations. And that's probably what I need in my life – someone who doesn't have a fractured personality, very down to earth, not flippant.

Life has become more precious to me. For a long time I felt that I was treading water. I kept looking at my watch – well, life should be over pretty soon, I'll soon be out of here. I was totally nihilistic. It wouldn't have bothered me if I had died tomorrow. But I have retrieved my passion for life. But death won't come as a shock when it happens. I have been too near to it.

TP: What do we tell our sons about sex and drugs?

DB: Not all experiments end up in a discovery. Some of the drugs we were playing around with were a cul-de-sac. So many of us have been casualties and some of us have been fortunate enough to come back. But we shouldn't be afraid to experiment.

Experimentation is about pushing the parameters of our knowledge. It is the spirit of Dionysus – the energy that makes us what we are.

What scares me at the moment is that we are becoming narrower and shallower. There's a loutish consensus that seems to be sweeping the Western world and reducing us to Philistines – which is quite hard on the Philistines. We are becoming cultural thugs.

AIDS is being used as a manipulative device to keep people in their place. That's the one thing that really scares me. Even when it began to dawn on me that my orientation was heterosexual, I was still experimenting and playing around in gay and bisexual areas. I needed to feel comfortable within my own sexuality. What really worries me about young people today is that they are going to be screwed up by their own orientation.

We are aware that for the first time in our history that the sexual act can bring about death. But we must not let AIDS become a banner that can be waved by right-wing elements to herald some new morality. AIDS is being used as a reason why nobody must experiment. But we have to be aware that everybody *must* feel comfortable in their sexuality.

I feel that a lot of what happened in the early '70s was good – it brought sexuality into the open and people didn't have to feel like a prisoner or a victim or outsider. But whatever was discovered then has been receding over the last few years. We can't allow society to make us sexually impotent, which is what it is trying to do. We shouldn't shun that curious investigative spirit. It's the greatest gift we have.

Mick Ronson: Spider From Mars

'It's not easy being David. I don't think it's easy for anyone being that successful. You have to keep on top of it, don't you? The more successful you are, the harder it is. There's your whole past to live up to.

'We met in 1969. I was in Hull. I met David through a drummer called John Cambridge who was in a group called Junior's Eyes. John was a right prankster. Still is. We backed David on a radio show – a John Peel session or something. John was on drums, a friend of his on bass and me on guitar.

'He definitely had a way about him. He wasn't your regular kid on the street. He was a great singer and they were great songs. A bit classier, a bit different from everybody else.

'I was brought up on classical music so I was very conscious of melodies. The rock thing didn't happen until I was in my teens. I was still into classical music when I was 16. I played the violin. But I always had one eye on the Everly Brothers and The Shadows. I thought it looked better than playing the violin. Then when the Stones came out it was all over. I wanted to be one of them.

'Not long after I met David, I moved to Haddon Hall, the big house he had in Beckenham. David said, "Why don't you move down? Play regularly." I was working as a gardener at the time for Hull Council. And it was a job I liked a lot. I was getting paid. So I had to think about it. But I didn't think about it too long.

'Haddon Hall was a huge, strange house with musicians sleeping on mattresses and everyone dreaming of glory. The main part of the house was a huge hallway when you walked in, with a balcony all the way around at the top and three rooms coming off it. These rooms were *huge*.

'Haddon Hall was great. The world was wide open. It was a particularly good time around then. There was some great music coming out – T Rex, Roxy Music – they were exciting times. There was hope everywhere.

'I was there pretty much from the start. We played a gig at the Roundhouse as Hype but I don't remember much about it. I got so stoned. I don't really smoke dope. And all the hip crowd were in the dressing room, the Warhol lot, and I was wandering around not knowing where I was or what I was doing. All my lips were stuck together. I was totally confused. God knows what the gig was like. It was fun. But afterwards. Not at the time.

'Ziggy Stardust happened before you realised it. It was hard to grasp exactly what had happened until it was all over. It was a lot of fun. More fun than work. We weren't constantly on the road.

'What we did on stage, the playing off each other, that was all instinctive. When I play, I play. It's not planned. You can't think about it too much. You get messed up if you think too much.

'The make-up and all that wasn't a brand new idea. It wasn't as though it had never been done before. Elvis used to slap on a bit of make-up. The Kinks used to wear frilly shirts. But it had gone. Everybody was into looking authentic.

'Ziggy definitely affected him. To do anything and to do it well you have to become completely involved. He had to become what Ziggy was, he had to believe in him. Yes, Ziggy affected his personality. But he affected Ziggy's personality. They lived off each other.

'The association ended around the time when he was moving into soul music. David wanted to have a lot of time off, he wanted to write a Broadway show. So there really wasn't a lot going on. Making my own album seemed like a good idea – because what else was I going to do? David was searching, his career was moving off into other areas.

'The Spiders From Mars didn't really last that long. It fulfilled me creatively because I didn't really have a chance to fall out of love with it. Two or three years go by in a flash. But David and I always stayed friends. There was never any real reason to fall out.

'I was a bit awkward when I was younger. I think David used to get frustrated with me. I was very stubborn. Very opinionated. There was still a lot of growing up being done. And he had to deal with all that. You look back on your life and say – why was I like that? But David doesn't like arguments. He walks away. Best way.

'It was an incredible experience to go through. One minute you're dreaming about the world listening to your music and the next they *are* listening. It makes you feel great. Your dreams literally come true. But it happens so fast you don't realise it's happening. And I'm proud that it's one of the most memorable periods of his career.

'I remember the first time I did some string arrangements. We were producing some tracks for Dana Gillespie. And she said, "Well, I want strings, I want a string quartet." And David said, "Oh, Mick does that." I had never done it in my life. But I started writing arrangements for strings. The great thing about David is that he pushes people to do things. Most people just try to keep you in your place. He brings out the best in you. What a wonderful quality to have.'

Morrissey: England Made Me

The Daily Telegraph, 8 May 1993

'THERE'S THIS LONG STANDING IMAGE of me sitting in the library – next to the radiators – which bores me stiff,' says Morrissey. 'I always liked – for want of a more tragic expression – quite *laddish* groups. I loathe the wimp image and the fact that I'm supposed to be some cross-legged, flowery *Carry On* extra. Most of the concerts I have performed have been pretty dangerous and, if I really were such a flowery, cross-legged character, I can't imagine that I would survive situations like that. I don't ever remember being particularly pacifist. I wouldn't back off from any confrontation.'

In the pale, hairy flesh Morrissey is something of a shock to the system. Can this really be that wan youth who swanned to fame as the sickly lead singer of The Smiths? The Oscar Wilde fan with lyrics full of laconic self-pity and back pockets full of gladioli? He seems so *beefy*. You expect someone who is going to banter *bons mots*; and who should appear but a stocky 33-year-old Mancunian who talks football and drinks his lager from the can.

Yet, though he looks like an unshaven fairground greaser, Morrissey still talks like a particularly waspish member of the Algonquin set.

'The slimy, unstoppable urges,' he says, speaking of love, trying to reconcile his famous celibacy with the unabashed romanticism that sometimes rears its lovely head in his songs. 'Because I am not involved with the slimy, unstoppable urges, that makes me see them in a more serious way. I think I was meant to have other things.'

Have you given up on love or has love given up on you? 'I think we came to a mutual agreement,' says Morrissey, reaching down to stroke my cat.

I am talking to Morrissey in my living room. Murray Chalmers of EMI had told me that Morrissey would grant me an interview if we could think of an 'interesting' location. I suggested Père Lachaise,

Paris, where Wilde is buried, or perhaps Fairmount, Indiana, the final resting place of James Dean – another of Morrissey's guardian angels.

'Morrissey says what about somewhere in Hounslow?' said Murray.

In the end, we settled for my home – Morrissey's idea. He turns out to be hugely entertaining company; yet, although our knees are almost touching, I feel a distance between us.

Does he find it easy to make friends? 'No, I don't. It takes me years with people. If I am having a conversation with someone and somebody new walks into the room I can't speak.'

Why is that?

'It's basic mistrust,' he says. 'I don't want to impart any information to anyone who will misuse it or not be listening. They say – how are you? And you say – well, I'm quite depressed. And then they say something *completely away from the subject*. That infuriates me. I can't stand shallow people.'

I tell Morrissey that I decided to be a Smiths' fan when he took his shirt off on Top of the Pops to reveal the words 'marry me' written in blue biro on his chest.

'Hmmm,' he says, unimpressed. 'Yes. Lest we forget.'

Morrissey is one of the few people in the country not nostalgic about the passing of The Smiths, who broke up six years ago and are now widely considered to be the last great British pop group.

'The death of a group brings on lots of rosy cheeks,' says Morrissey. Then he laughs: 'Well, perhaps not so rosy *cheeks*.'

Perhaps rose-tinted glasses?

'Oh yes, but I didn't really want to say *that!* I never wanted to be a solo artist or record under the name of Morrissey, so when The Smiths ended I was pushed out to sea and it was up to me to sink or swim. And there was a strong sense that I couldn't function without Johnny.'

Johnny Marr – the other half of the greatest songwriting team since Jagger and Richards – was the man whose jangling guitars made such a beautiful backdrop for Morrissey's arch meditations.

'Even very close friends said it's all over now,' says Morrissey. 'And I would say – well, I'm actually about to go into the studio. And they would pick up the Evening Standard and turn to Patrick Walker. But I don't miss being in The Smiths. Things are better for me now, I even get occasional twinges of happiness.'

Morrissey has now been a solo act for longer than he was a Smith.

Though life without Marr looked as though it would be difficult for him, he has created a canon of songs – 'Everyday Is Like Sunday', 'Suedehead', 'Disappointed', 'Hairdresser On Fire' and an album, *Your Arsenal* – that is the equal of anything he did with The Smiths. He has done enough now to be hailed as the most interesting British musician since David Bowie, who covered a Morrissey song on his *Black Tie, White Noise*. Yet he never gets the praise he deserves.

'*Everybody's* more celebrated than me,' he moans.

Over the past couple of years, Morrissey has enjoyed enormous success in America. Prince wants to record with him. He sold out the Hollywood Bowl faster than The Beatles, packed Madison Square Garden and appeared twice on Johnny Carson's *Tonight* show. And yet his work remains peculiarly English, its concerns ranging from the grimy back-streets of provincial cities to the over-excited hair-dressers of Sloane Square. So what does being English mean to Morrissey?

'I think it's the village atmosphere, the small-mindedness, which is still very much a part of me. I can't shake it off. I can't become internationalised and I don't think of the world as a place that is mine. I don't feel that I can go anywhere I choose to go. But I think I've pounded my Englishness into the ground. It's just me. I don't claim to have copyright on the English stamp.'

But you would be a different man if you were a Belgian. 'Well, I'd probably have a moustache,' he quips. 'Being English does inspire me in a very poetic way. I walk to Wapping for absolutely no reason. I walk to Bethnal Green for absolutely no reason. Nobody, I believe, would actually choose to go to those places.

What did you like about Bethnal Green and Wapping?

'Absolutely nothing! But I find that the working-class areas of London are more English than any of the more affluent areas.'

Really? My mother comes from Poplar and she doesn't recognise the East End she grew up in. You live in London now – do you still find the East End quintessentially English?

'Certain images catch the eye,' he reflects, 'but, yes, on an overall point, I suppose that there has been a complete invasion.'

Doesn't that enrich our culture?

'No, not at all. But it's a subject that can't really be discussed. Because if you try to open it out and have the broad discussion it's almost like admitting that there is a case for racism.'

Morrissey enjoys being an Englishman. He likes the flag. Sometimes he even enjoys waving it. He did so last year at a concert supporting Madness at Finsbury Park. As he pranced with his Union Jack in front of the backdrop featuring a couple of suedeheads (a slightly furrier version of skinheads), he was struck by a couple of missiles from the crowd and had the music press howling that he was a racist.

'I think that whole Finsbury Park thing and that which followed was just simply latching on to absolutely anything. There is a hate campaign against me. There have been *many* other groups with Union Jacks and nobody has commented on them. But of course I do it and I'm Hitler.'

Morrissey is no racist, he says. But he does have an abiding passion for what he sees as a disappearing culture. And he also has a platonic love for the world of ordinary boys – young, male, working-class lives that are lived without intellect, without thought, without agony.

Your Arsenal included a poster of Charles Richardson, a contemporary of Ronnie and Reggie Kray. Does he envy people like that?

'Yes, I do, because their existence is purely physical. I don't mean sexual – purely physical. Because obviously my life has never been that way it's fascinating to me. But I think if you are not like that then you never can be. You can't suddenly decide to forget, unlearn, obliterate everything. But yes, I am quite fascinated by people who – quite happily – steam through life with an astonishing lack of thought. But I know it's just me prodding with a stick again and saying, "How fascinating." '

Though he is worshipped by his fans – the collection of 'high-IQ misfits and fervent introverts' that *Rolling Stone* described as his constituency – Morrissey remains unforgiven by his detractors. Does he ever feel like leaving England?

'Yes, I do now,' he concedes, 'because it's particularly insulting, year after year. The slightest untidy moment, shall we say, is magnified beyond all reasonable human proportion. If I did something really offensive – can you imagine? If I put my hand around the Pope they would assume I was trying to pick his pocket.'

Brett Anderson

Vox, March 1994

'**P**EOPLE MIGHT THINK that we are a bunch of fainting woofters who are going to release one album and then disappear,' says Brett Anderson. 'I desperately want to prove them wrong.'

He walks into my house, tears off his jacket and goes straight over to the record collection. Soon he is fondling an old vinyl copy of the *Clockwork Orange* soundtrack. Brett Anderson is not what you are expecting.

In his photographs he can make Oscar Wilde look like Mike Tyson. In the pale, translucent flesh he is completely different. The wanton fop you see pouting and teasing in all the pictures is replaced by a young man who is very tall, very thin and very rumpled – like a high school basketball player who sold his soul to amphetamine sulphate. Anderson is made of sterner stuff than you think.

All week I had been seeing predictions of Suede's imminent demise. Justine Frischmann – Suede's former rhythm guitarist and leader of the latest Great Indie Hope, Elastica – was predicting that the media feeding frenzy made it impossible for Suede to produce a strong second album (after seeing Elastica perform 'Line Up' on *The Word*, I hereby predict it will be impossible for them to produce one good single). Meanwhile everyone from *Q* to the inkies was saying that America had proved immune to Suede's sultry charms while support act, The Cranberries, were whipping up scenes that recalled Beatlemania. For the first time since they were being booed by two people in a toilet, genuine doubts are being expressed about Anderson's outfit. Can this really be the end for Suede? Are you kidding?

Suede came into my life when they sent me a copy of 'Metal Mickey' autographed by Bernard Butler and Anderson. It was the first time in my life I had ever received a record autographed by people *I had never heard of*. It transpired that Suede had the lot –

the youth, the looks, the haircuts, the arrogance, the attitude. But before you got to any of that, there was the music.

Suede swept the country with songs of squalor in the suburbs and glamour in the gutter, a canon of love and loneliness that couldn't fail to set your heart racing no matter if you were old enough to have seen The Sex Pistols at the Screen on the Green or young enough to believe that the good old days were when the Stone Roses were around. Suede went thermonuclear the way they did because they were everybody's idea of a great band.

There is never a shortage of mindless cockiness in the music business but sending an autographed record to someone who didn't know you were alive revealed something else – a supreme self-assurance that turned out to be completely justified. And despite the gathering of the sceptics, Anderson is contemplating the future with exactly that same confidence, though he knows that Suede could soon be on the receiving end of the mother of all backlashes.

'The music press don't build you up and knock you down,' he says, sipping instant coffee (milk, no sugar). 'They can't. They don't have that power. You fuck yourself up and then it becomes fashionable to knock you. I think nothing can go wrong as long as we keep making good music.'

Anderson is wearing a dark, two-piece suit that is either second hand or in need of dry cleaning. A dark V-neck sweater that fits him like a second skin (no vest – in this weather!). And an assortment of beads and bracelets, those vaguely ethnic accessories that you see Jim Morrison sporting in his classic photographs. When his fringe – Bryan Ferry on steroids – falls forward, it covers his face. He sweeps it back with long, pale fingers. This is a happy man.

Anderson's dreams have come true and have yet to turn sour. Where he is now makes me think of a story by F. Scott Fitzgerald called 'Early Success', in which the writer recalled that blissful moment when he woke up and realised that he was famous. 'The fulfilled future and the wistful past were mingled in a single gorgeous moment,' wrote Fitzgerald, 'when life was literally a dream.'

'The excitement of every day is quite daunting,' says Anderson. 'There are moments when I feel like I'm Oliver Twist – have you seen that scene in *Oliver!* where he wakes up in the rich house? He has just been saved from Bill Sikes and he looks out of the window and there are all these people singing and selling cakes in the square. I feel exactly like that. Because I really did go through a lot of shit before we started to get anywhere and that was a depressing time, something which I wouldn't wish anyone to go through. And then to be saved by music in this romantic fashion . . .'

Anderson's social circle is divided between friends his own age who are unemployed or working at low-paid Mcjobs – his best friend, someone he knows from the old neighbourhood in Haywards Heath, works in a chip shop in Oxted – and the high and mighty. Unlike most growing young rock stars, he does not pretend to be disgusted by the celebrity whirl.

'I've met quite a few people that I really like,' he says. 'It sounds really crappy, but lots of people that are quite famous have become friends of mine. Not because I want to join some crappy celebrity club, but a wonderful thing about getting well-known is that you get the opportunity to meet some amazing people. Bowie is ridiculously charming. People say how cool and icy he is but I don't think so. He's like someone's dad or something. He's so down to earth. He phoned me up the other day – he wants us to do a cover version of one of his songs – and he left this really funny message on my answer machine. I've got this bit from *Performance* on my answer machine and he said, "Ah, *Performance*, Nicolas Roeg, 1971." Like some kind of Geography teacher or something. He's very approachable and very nice. But I wonder what he was like back in the Seventies. I think the cocaine would have destroyed some of the humour.'

Last year Anderson had a public falling out with Morrissey, his other spiritual guide. Harsh words were spoken on both sides and it seemed unlikely that Moz would ever sing 'My Insatiable One' again. But at the Q Awards, the pair patched it up and restored their mutual admiration society.

'I think Morrissey has decided that he is going to enjoy life rather than suffer for it,' says Anderson. 'He was there with his beer, you know what I mean? Come along to party. He was nice. We talked a bit about America, a bit about drugs. I told him to come round and have an E. I tugged on his quiff and he felt my furry collar.'

If you talk to Brett Anderson about the music he grew up with, he is fond of saying that he missed everything – punk, Bowie, the lot. All of his favourite things had to be excavated from his older sister's record collection. Or almost all – because of course he didn't miss The Smiths, who he cites as the supreme consolation of his suburban adolescence.

'I did feel that The Smiths were a piece of armour to help me fight my way through life. They had power and a presence that couldn't just be put down to some effeminate poncing around with flowers coming out of his back. It was much more sinister, much more sexual and much more real than that. The thugs of the world hated them and tried to attack their weak points. But to me they had no weak points.'

Like Morrissey in the Eighties and Bowie in the Seventies, Anderson currently wears rock music's twin crowns. He is both golden boy and whipping boy, and with Suede was the recipient of a wide range of awards in the current round of music paper polls. So how does it feel to be both man of the year and twat of the year?

'I can see why we would wind some people up,' he concedes. 'It's to do with my personality. I can imagine millions of long-haired students everywhere having voodoo dolls of me – because I don't *rock*, in the traditional sense of the word. I think we are truly quite threatening.'

After two years of relentless attention, Anderson says that England sometimes feels as claustrophobic as Haywards Heath, where the houses smelled of cat's piss and there was always baked beans for tea.

'I do get quite sick of the cynicism here,' he sighs. 'We won the Mercury prize and there were about *two* people clapping in the room. Other bands get away with murder. I think we have quite high standards, compared to some trash gets released in the name of music.'

There are two ways of regarding Suede's first album. One is that it is the Nineties equivalent of *The Smiths*, only the first kiss of what is destined to be a beautiful relationship. The other is that it is another *Never Mind The Bollocks*, the flamboyant final curtain on two years of headlines. Certainly there are no shortage of people predicting the decline and fall of Brett Anderson.

Justine Frischmann told *NME* that Suede have been, 'Overexposed ... it's been incredibly damaging to Suede personally – it's going to be difficult for them to produce a second album on the back of it. Very difficult.'

Anderson disagrees.

'I feel incredibly confident about the second album. I have written probably over three quarters of it by now and I think the standard of songs is on a different level from the last one. Lots of songs on the first album like "Animal Lover" and "Moving" were left over from years and years ago. Good live songs but I wouldn't write songs like that any more.'

But I like those rabble rousers.

'Yeah, but they don't form part of a coherent album for me. When you start your only forums are practising rooms and playing live with some shitty PA so all the songs have to be incredibly bombastic – just to express yourself. In the studio you can be a lot more subtle. I have always loved albums that pull you around – almost like a play. You have to go through the trauma and be dragged through the hedges and laid in honey.'

We talk a bit about 'Stay Together', the memory of an Eighties nightmare that is Suede's Valentine's Day single, and its B side, 'The Living Dead', a love song with track marks. But Brett is almost dismissive of Suede's first new product since last April's album.

'Those songs are old songs for me now. We recorded them so long ago I've practically forgotten them. I'm really excited about the new album. It's going to be *really brilliant*.'

Because he comes from a drab dormitory town five stops from Brighton, Anderson has often been portrayed as an average working class lad. In fact his background is much more complex than that. This was a childhood of Bohemia on the breadline. His father was an unemployed ice cream man who was obsessed with classical music and both Brett's mother (who died in 1989) and his sister were artists. They were certainly poor but there was far more culture *chez* Anderson than in the average working class home, even if it wasn't the kind he liked.

'It was like some kind of Victorian house,' Brett says. 'My dad had Hector Berlioz blasting down the stairs. Aubrey Beardsley was on the wall. There was a very classical tradition in my upbringing and I revolted against that. I wanted to do something in the gutter. And I quite cherish that because it stops me from being pompous – which could happen.'

Anderson's lyrics are peculiarly rootless. In 'The Next Life', Worthing briefly holds out the promise of a Mcjob selling ice cream, but apart from that, they could come from anywhere in the post-industrial world. Anderson puts it down to coming from the sprawl, the Cockney diaspora that stretches out one hundred miles in all directions from the capital.

'I don't feel any kind of affinity to the place that I come from. I think that's generally true of people that are born in the south of England. People born in the north are much more territorial. Coming from Darlington – it's almost like a football mentality, a fierce pride. And the further north you go, the worse it gets, until you're in Scotland where everyone is champing at the bit to defend their city. The south is such a wasteland that you don't have that community spirit. The only place you could feel that is London, which is almost like a bucket for restless souls. London is just a waiting room for stray waifs who have wandered in from all over the world. And I guess I'm one of them.'

He is a good talker and, when you hear some of his more striking soundbites, you are reminded that this is the man who brought you the famous line, 'I see myself as a bisexual man who has never had a homosexual experience.' It is a statement surely destined to live forever in quote heaven alongside John Lennon's 'The Beatles are bigger than Jesus,' and Johnny Rotten's 'Sex is two minutes of squelching.' Does he regret saying it?

'I wouldn't entertain regret,' he says. 'I do get pissed off with the misinterpretation of it. But I wasn't really talking about sex. I was trying to express a universality. It sounds as though I am trying to dig myself out of my own trap, but it's perfectly true. I was trying to say that by being unmanly it doesn't necessarily mean you're womanly. People say – oh you're not much of a man? But does that mean that someone's a woman? It can't necessarily be confined to something as vulgar as sexuality.'

Anderson – or rather Anderson's stage persona – is very much in the tradition of Jagger, Bowie and Morrissey, those very English rock stars who perceived sexuality as something as malleable as a haircut.

'A nation of fags, aren't we?' says Brett. 'A nation of fags! That's what they think in America. But I love all those people – Mick Jagger, especially. I've been thinking a lot about him recently. I try to tap into his spirit on stage. I think Jagger was the greatest performer who ever existed. He was like some sort of dog on heat. He has that knife-edge quality, that duality, almost like a fool and a superstar at the same time. He's almost like some stupid monkey at times – a millimetre away from being laughable. But the key to being a true star is to be almost laughable – and then just flip it, and turn it into something serious. I think that Jagger did that incredibly well – he's like an ape but at the same time he's this sexual superman.' Anderson was genuinely hurt when he received flak from the gay community for the alleged crime of posing as a sodomite.

'There was a time when the gay community decided that we were a load of fakes and that we were messing with their imagery and their lives. And that made me quite unhappy because it was *never* intended to be like that. I've never tried to be patronising towards the gay community – fifty per cent of my friends are gay – and I talk about their lives as much as I do mine. I was trying to be compassionate. I think a lot of gay men must take our songs to their heart because they are love songs that involve them in quite a real sense. Gay people weren't being represented so I wrote love songs for gay people, like "My Insatiable One" and "Animal Nitrate". What's always bothered me about gay entertainers is that they are incredibly vocal when it comes to political causes but where it counts – in their art – they don't really say anything worth saying. They just do silly cover versions.'

Recently Suede have been jeered for their failure to shag the USA. Statistics are wheeled out to prove that Radiohead did better than Suede on their first American tour and The Cranberries did better on their second – statistics that ignore the fact that there was a time when Gerry and the Pacemakers were outselling The Beatles.

'The number of times I've heard this about The Cranberries outselling us. Yeah, they did – they had a hit in America, it was a really good song and they *deserved* it. And maybe we *won't* dig into the American heartland the way people predict we won't. But in places like San Francisco, LA and New York, it's quite insane. We did two gigs in LA and we were getting chased down the street after the gig. It was like when we started becoming successful in this country, when people were going insane and tearing my shirt off.'

It is always liberating for English boys to wake up in America and find themselves in a land uncluttered by tradition and the class system. But there's always the paradox of anally retentive old England with its seemingly limitless supply of wonderful, idiosyncratic talents and liberated America churning out one conservative act after another. Perhaps Suede are not corny enough for America.

'I've always had a horror of that American corniness,' says Brett. 'And maybe we are not manly enough in that traditional sense. But there are different ways of cracking America. There are lots of bands that do it over a number of albums and I think that if we do get success in America it will be that way. The whole scene over there is much less cyclical and based around fashion. Grunge is still fashionable and probably will be for another five years. If you look at any of the bands that are big over there, they are *so straight* it is ridiculous. There is no leeway for anything a little bit off kilter, and that's not in our favour. Grunge is a worldwide trend. Suede aren't a worldwide trend.'

Anderson has great hopes for the Suede comeback.

'We'll be fashionable again soon,' he predicts. 'It's getting much more into a musical realm now, which is the way to survive. Music should, after all, be about music. Ultimately music isn't about image and ideas. To be a great band you've got to be musically good. You can't look at The Sex Pistols and say it was just a load of furore and hype – *Never Mind The Bollocks* was a brilliant album. And the same with The Rolling Stones – they had another dimension, an ability to play with people's perceptions and aggravate and intimidate – but behind it all was music that was inspired and magical. And I would like to think that the same is true with us. I don't think you can stay on top if there is nothing behind the hype. We have been on top for eighteen months now. You look at these fleeting little fancies like Riot Grrrl and nobody even remembers it any more.'

Brett recently came out as a Billy Joel fan – a brave and noble gesture that will surely be an encouragement to secret Billy Joel fans everywhere.

'I hope so – I thought "River Of Dreams" was brilliant. "*In the middle of the night!*",' he sings. 'I'm a big fan of the mainstream. I liked the Terence Trent D'Arby album. I am not going to have some kind of misguided loyalty to alternative music because I think it should be championed. I don't. I think there's a lot of amateurism in there. We happen to be on an independent label because it gives us control. I wouldn't want people to think of us as an indie band.'

But surely Suede are considered the standard bearers of the entire indie nation?

'I don't have any real affinity with the indie scene,' he insists. 'As music gets more in bed with finance I think it's the only stamping ground where people get any space for experimentation and being a bit maverick. But as an idea to be championed and upheld, I haven't got one second for it. Because I think it's populated by middle class, inverted snobs, who have taken refuge in the fact that their parents have a load of money so they can become some grubby little indie band. I think there are a lot of fakes in the indie business. Great music has always been made by people who have *had* to make a living out of it. I haven't come from a rich family. I want to sell records. Not just any records or I'd be in Take That – *great* records. Even at Motown they went into the studio thinking what was going to be a hit.'

Just before Brett leaves my house he meets my wife and son – who have both met their share of the rich and famous – and he completely charms the pair of them. He is friendly, self-deprecating and down to earth. And yet, unmistakably, he is also every inch a star. Anyone waiting for Suede to fall flat on their fringes is advised not to hold their breath.

'I feel the desire to stick in people's flesh for quite a long time,' Brett Anderson tells me, just before he wanders off into the rainy Islington night in search of a cab. 'I remain a big fan of Suede.'

You and me both.

Diana Stands Alone

The Daily Telegraph, 23 June 1994

THE SECRET OF HER SUCCESS is that she has never been afraid to move on. The Supremes, Tamla Motown, her first husband, her mentor Berry Gordy – she has always known when it was time to leave.

'I have learnt not to settle for unhappiness,' says Diana Ross.

In photographs she is striking. In the flesh, close up, she is more than that. Her head is not big but everything about it is huge. When she laughs, which she does often, the mouth is as wide as her face. The hair, which is real, tumbles halfway down her back. The eyes would not be out of place on a baby seal. It is a shockingly familiar face. But the woman herself remains out of reach.

We can only learn so much about Diana Ross from her records. In thirty years of hits she has often been cast as a sighing, star-crossed lover brought low by *amour fou*. But the reality is very different. You do not make it from the Brewster Projects of Detroit to a fortune estimated at $75 million unless your spirit has a thread of steel.

'My work is my love made visible,' says Diana Ross. Yet this artist is also an astute businesswoman. She was moulded at the Tamla Motown charm school, where through the Sixties she played Trilby to Berry Gordy's Svengali. But for many years she has managed herself through Diana Ross Enterprises Inc.

'The direction comes from me rather than from someone else,' she says. 'I'm my own manager. I sign my own cheques. I make my own choices. And that way you can take the credit when things go right and can't blame somebody else when things go wrong.'

Ross was nominated for an Oscar for her portrayal of Billie Holiday in *Lady Sings the Blues*. But Lady Day was vulnerable, self-destructive and dominated by men. Miss Ross – as everyone around her calls her – is nobody's victim.

She left The Supremes in 1970, when the jealousy of the other members became too much to bear. 'The girls had treated me very badly,' she writes in her memoirs. 'They had gone against me with a vengeance.' Then in 1981 she left Tamla Motown for a $10 million deal with RCA.

'Leaving The Supremes, leaving Motown ... yes, I was very scared. Change is frightening. But I have learnt that change isn't bad.'

We met up in Stockholm, where she was giving a private performance prior to her British tour, which starts tomorrow. At fifty, she is infinitely sexier than she ever was as a skinny Supreme, the original superwaif. She is still slim, but five children and thirty years have made her voluptuous. She is dressed completely in black, the colour she dons for travelling and rehearsing.

'I don't wear my gowns *all* the time,' she says.

Apart from Michael Jackson, Diana Ross is probably the only artist ever to transcend her status as an ex-Motown act. To understand why she has flourished when so many others have slipped into obscurity or the oldies circuit, you need to see her live show. In concert, Ross is mesmerising – a genuinely charismatic performer who spends a large amount of time wandering among her spellbound audience.

'It's not stage technique,' she says. 'One of the things that I learnt a long time ago is that to really get comfortable on a stage, I need to see the audience's eyes. Something about it relaxes me. I feel like they're not strangers to me any more.'

She is unsentimental about The Supremes. Even before her spangly stage sisters turned against her – not long after The Supremes became Diana Ross and the Supremes, funnily enough – she recalls that beyond the stewardess grins was nothing but hard grind.

'I remember the hard work. Rehearsing all the time. The stress of it all. Never having the time for a private life.'

On the very first Supremes tour, Ross's mother Ernestine acted as chaperone, insisting that Diana and the other Supremes left every hotel room exactly as they found it, which included making their beds.

'I hate it when people say I have gone from rags to riches,' says Ross. 'My family were never raggedy. My mother was a seamstress. She would make us pretty dresses and put bows in our hair. We didn't have a lot of money. My dad worked two jobs. My mother did domestic work. But I always had what I needed. We didn't think of our neighbourhood as a ghetto. My childhood was wonderful.'

Scrawny little Diana was a physically tough child – killing rats with bows and arrows and defending her five siblings from bullies.

'I was a tough kid. My sister says, "Diane used to fight to kill." I used to get bullies down and get my knees on their throat.' She jumps up to demonstrate, crunching her knees down on an imaginary throat. 'I was unsinkable,' she says proudly.

By her teens she was singing with The Primettes, the group that would become The Supremes. Her mother, who died ten years ago and whom she misses desperately, was always her best friend. But her father Joe was far less supportive, insisting she got home 'before the street lights came on'.

'I started to understand him more when I became a parent. His daughter was sixteen years old and going out of the house with her hair piled up and lots of eye make-up on. My dad used to say, "Why do you have to put that *black* stuff around your eyes all the time?"'

When Diana Ross met Berry Gordy, the man who built Motown, she was 16 and he was 31. Always the jewel in Motown's crown, Ross went solo in 1970 and a year later became pregnant with Gordy's child. They never married.

Instead Ross married a Los Angeles press agent called Robert Silberstein. She gave birth to a girl, Rhonda, and only six years later, after she had divorced Silberstein – and given birth to two more daughters, Tracee and Chudney – did she admit that the father of her first child was Berry Gordy. Despite some bad patches, especially when she left Motown, their relationship has endured for a lifetime. She now says that Berry Gordy 'means more than a romantic link'.

After splitting with Silberstein, she moved to New York and spent nine years as a single parent. She demurs when I suggest that she enjoyed having complete control.

'You make the decisions alone but the truth is that you really want the support of the other half. I do think a woman or a man can raise their children by themselves. I was able to do it. But I didn't love it.'

In May 1985 Ross met a Norwegian millionaire called Arne Naess in the Bahamas when their children were playing together. She married him five months later. Naess, a shipping broker, had just climbed Mount Everest when he met Diana. I saw him in Stockholm – a short, fit fiftysomething, wondering aloud if he should run in the Stockholm marathon.

Diana and Naess have two small sons, Evan and Ross, the youngest born when she was 45, giving her a total of five children, ranging in ages from 23 to five. They live apart. Naess is based in London while Ross stays in a rambling house in Connecticut with their sons.

lives. As Lydon's book reminds us, punk was liberating because, 'it made people realise the creative potential within themselves'.

Rotten: No Irish, No Blacks, No Dogs is a great story weighed down with arthritic prose, too much padding and petty spite. Lydon is an egocentric, mean-spirited old git and *Rotten* is often exactly that – yet for all its flaws, I would recommend it to anyone who has any interest in punk rock. These are, after all, the memoirs of the man who was king for a day. John Lydon's golden years ended with The Sex Pistols but, impressively, he is not nostalgic:

> If you stormed into my room and looked through my closets you wouldn't find any of the old Pistols clothes. I don't even have photos. It's all somewhere in the jungle I call a brain. I couldn't be a sentimental Sex Pistol, now could I?

Love and Sex

The Wham, Bam Baby

Arena, September/October 1992

H OW DOES The Rock Chick turn off the light after sex? She closes the car door!

The first time I ever saw a Rock Chick was the first time I ever went on the road with a band. The band were Thin Lizzy, and the late Phil Lynott, being the kindest of men, had decided he would take care of me. I spent a lot of time in his company and I soon realised that, like a sailor, Phil Lynott had a different girl waiting for him in every town. And they all looked the same. The look was lots of leather (trousers or skirts – worn tight and short), black stockings, lots of make-up (white face, red mouth) and high-heeled shoes. Their favourite colour was black. Hair was dyed black or blonde. They were all Rock Chicks. They were for sex.

This was 1976 and the Rock Chick was in her golden years. But the Rock Chick still exists in large numbers. And they still look exactly the same, a cosmic amalgam of tight clothes, dyed hair and high heels.

You can see the Rock Chick on the street of every major city in the Western world, click-clicking in her Fuck Me heels to some office. The Rock Chick has her own personal income. Money is never a problem (though she prefers using yours).

Favoured Rock Chick jobs are working for a record company (press office), journalist (music press) and advertising (receptionist). The Rock Chick tends to work in mildly creative fields where no creativity is required on her part.

It is not that the Rock Chick is dumb. But her hedonism takes precedent over higher interests. She believes in having a good time, all the time. The Rock Chick tends to be a hardened drinker and, although she sometimes gets drunk, she is never a bore. Drunkenness is an excuse for raucous laughter and sexual innuendo. She likes drugs but never buys them. She will take whatever is around but she can live happily without artificial stimulants.

In bed the Rock Chick always does it twice. And she insists you do it twice too. She seems to find it impolite to just do it once. The way the Rock Chick encourages you to do it twice is by manipulating you with her mouth prior to your second coming. *Every Rock Chick does this* – they must learn it at Rock Chick School. You will be nodding off when the Rock Chick's head will disappear below the sheets, her mouth slurping away. But the message about safer sex has got through and Rock Chicks all carry condoms.

Rock Chicks are not groupies. However, they are not so difficult to get into bed. Sleeping with a Rock Chick is about as difficult as taking off your socks. And every Rock Chick has slept with at least one famous man. One day you will be looking at your Rock Chick's photograph album when suddenly a famous face will be leering back at you. God, you will say, what is *he* doing here? But you know exactly what he is doing here. And of course Rock Chick heroes are women like Jerry Hall and Yasmin LeBon, women who model until they marry rock stars. This is why so many Rock Chicks look like one of Rod Stewart's wives.

The Rock Chick is somewhat retro in her taste in music. The dance craze has passed her by (she enjoys dancing – but to things like 'All Right Now' and 'Satisfaction'), she is essentially a fan of rock music. U2 (she still has a crush on Bono), the Stones ('Still the best rock 'n' roll band in the world') and Springsteen (she bought the new records without hearing them first). She would have been happier in the Seventies. Safer sex and dance music are not really her thing. The Rock Chick is out of time.

And where do all the Rock Chicks go? To the suburbs, to raise children. They are sentimental about animals and old boyfriends (unless the relationship ended in abortion or violence – infidelity she expects) and babies.

As she staggers home from a night of expense-account sex and drugs and rock 'n' roll – her make-up a mess, her tights torn – the Rock Chick still gets a pang in her throat when she sees a young mother pushing her baby.

And it is said the Rock Chick makes a good wife. When she hangs up her leather trousers and moves to the suburbs, the Rock Chick still plays the music too loud, slaps on too much make-up, wears her heels too high. But she is always a devoted lover, and though she is sometimes messy around the house, the Rock Chick can become surprisingly domesticated. That's where the Rock Chick goes. She becomes a good wife. And two weeks after the wedding she runs off with your best friend.

Say It With Fishes

Anatomy of Love – A Natural History of Adultery, Monogamy and Divorce, by Helen Fisher (Simon & Schuster)

The Literary Review, January 1993

W HAT IS LOVE? Why do we marry? Why doesn't it last? Will your secretary sleep with you if you give her some beads and a piece of fish?

Helen Fisher, a Desmond Morris for the boudoir, attempts to answer these and many other burning questions in *Anatomy of Love*. I know it sounds like a Mills & Boon book about a randy doctor but it's not. This is where the naked ape gets laid. To write her exhaustive investigation into the mating game through the ages, this American anthropologist has researched divorce in 58 societies and adultery in 42 cultures. And she has brought back some pretty amazing conclusions.

'Nowhere in the world do people regularly have coitus in public,' she exclusively reveals. 'Human beings almost never have to be cajoled into pairing. We flirt. We feel infatuation. We fall in love. We marry. And the majority of us marry only one person at a time.'

Powerful stuff. From the blind dates of Cro-Magnon man to the business trips of the modern American business executive, this is the human animal's secret sexual history. We preen, we display our genitals, we buy another round of drinks. Fisher finds many echoes of our mores among our furry friends in the animal kingdom. The monogamy of birds; gang bangs among pygmy chimps; the glint in the eye of a bitch in heat – all animal life is here.

A wild female chimpanzee in estrus will stroll up to a male, tip her buttocks towards his nose, and pull him to his feet to copulate. When he has finished, she copulates with almost every other male in the community.

I'm sure we have all been on dates like that. Ultimately, the author argues, the differences between man and other species are mimimal. Boy marmoset meets girl marmoset, boy marmoset loses girl marmoset. If we could talk to the animals, Fisher suggests, they would probably ask if they can come in for coffee.

Most mammals caress when courting, she observes. Blue whales rub each other with their flippers. Male butterflies stroke and rub their mates abdomens as they couple. Dolphins nibble. Moles rub noses. Dogs lick.

Fisher has delved deeply into the dating *dos* and *don'ts* of the !Kung people of the Kalahari (though she never explains their bizarre exclamation mark), she has examined the exchanging of bodily fluids in ancient China and she has spent a lot of time hanging around in singles bars in Manhattan. Folks, she concludes, are pretty much the same all over.

There is no more widespread courtship ploy than offering food in hope of gaining sexual favours in exchange. Around the world men give women presents prior to lovemaking. A fish, a piece of meat, sweets, beer, are among the countless delicacies men have invented as offerings.

Fisher has cast her net wide. Her subject is nothing less than love, marriage and what men get up to when their wives are out of town since the dawn of time. All the more disappointing, then, that all she has come up with is the spectacularly obvious.

We search for true love, find him or her, and settle in. Then when the spell begins to fade, the mind begins to wander.

For this she peered into the primordial mists? Another problem is that Fisher can't write for toffee. She favours sentences of two words or less – such as, 'Cannibals?', and 'Fire!' – and she has all the descriptive powers of a children's author in a coma.

'Thwack, thwack, thwack,' she writes, attempting to conjure up a vision of 5000 BC. 'A giant willow cracked, swayed, then thundered down beside the lake.'

Thwack, thwack, thwack? But Fisher does know her way around a *homo erectus* and her years of research into the Darwinian dating game have produced a few interesting facts.

For example, did you know that the disconcerted stirring in our M&S underpants that we think of as the seven-year itch is, in biological terms, actually a four-year itch? Or that married couples are more likely to divorce in their 20s than later in life? Or that the problem of sexual harassment at the office will only get worse because for millennia men and women had separate workplaces? Not a lot of people know that.

But considering the woman has investigated 57 varieties of horsing around, these modest nuggets are very few and far between. For the most part this is the painfully self-evident tarted up as major revelation.

> We may plausibly propose that, as the twenty-first century begins, our ancient human reproductive script will remain basically unaltered: young couples fall in love and form pair-bonds; many will then leave each other and find new mates. The older people get, the more children they produce, and the longer they remain together, the more likely spouses will be to mate for life.'

Is that it? Fisher takes three hundred pages to tell us what we already know. We meet, we fall in love, we reproduce, we get drunk and drag a workmate into the stationery cupboard at the Christmas party. Birds do it. Bees do it. We may plausibly propose that, ethnologically speaking, even educated fleas do it.

Commitment

Elle, May 1994

WOMAN WILL FORGIVE a man she loves almost anything. She will forgive infidelity, drunkenness and premature ejaculation – although probably not all on the same evening. She will forgive him if he falls asleep immediately after sex. She will forgive him if he falls asleep immediately *before* sex. But the one thing a woman will never forgive in a man is a lack of commitment.

I recently had one of those lunches where your friend is nursing a badly bruised heart and a stiff drink and all you can do is commiserate and try to make some sense of the whole sorry mess.

'Listen,' I told him, as he reflected on the woman he had loved and lost, 'women are only after one thing – romance.'

I was trying to be a good friend and help him to understand why it hadn't worked out. But I was giving him bad advice. What I *should* have told him was – women are only after one thing. Commitment.

You would think that after nearly 30 years of feminism men and women would want the same things. But our different interpretations of what we mean by commitment continue to provide us with our most bitter source of conflict.

The end of my friend's affair had been painful and messy. He had loved – truly loved – this woman and, as far as I could tell, she felt the same way.

But there were other people involved – aren't there always? – and it became clear that sooner or later they would have to decide if they were going to build a life together or go their separate ways. And after agonising about it for months, my friend decided he could not bring himself to leave his wife and three young daughters.

So they split – his lover's choice. They did not part because they did not love each other. Or because passion had died. Or because someone had been unfaithful. They split simply because he was not prepared to make that final, ultimate commitment.

They never show up in the statistics, but more relationships are killed by conflicting notions of commitment than any other cause. To women, it seems, men who have difficulty with commitment are feckless bastards who want their cake and a slice of choice gateau on the side. But from the male point of view, women often want more commitment than a man is prepared to give.

The way we see it, women are commitment junkies. Commit yourself to one night and a woman wants a relationship. Commit yourself to a relationship and she wants a marriage. Commit yourself to a marriage, she wants to stop you going out with your friends, to cut back on travelling and to go to Sainsbury's instead of Arsenal on Saturday afternoon.

One late, unlamented lover of mine was so keen to increase my commitment quotient that she cut up my passport. Little wonder that so many men associate commitment with claustrophobia. Of course not *all* women start looking around for a mortgage, kids and a dishwasher as soon as they hit puberty. But even powerful, high-stepping career women who have carved out lives that can quite happily sustain themselves without a man – in fact *especially* these powerful, high-earning career women – complain about the male aversion to commitment. Many of my female friends seem to long for that unqualified commitment from a man more than anything else. It seems that real commitment has replaced true romance as the ultimate goal of the modern woman.

And what is commitment? A pledge that love and affection will be translated into something more concrete. That is not an unreasonable expectation. What *is* unreasonable is that men who are reluctant to commit themselves are invariably demonised in the female imagination.

Women always tell men about their previous affairs and there is always one man (usually the most recent one) who gets a particularly harsh press. He hates women, you are told. He fears women. He is a 24-carat scumbag.

And what did the scumbag do? Was he violent? Was he cruel? Did he try to sleep with one of her friends? It often transpires that the worst thing this scumbag ever did was to get cold feet. Often it sounds as though his only crime was that he wasn't ready to commit himself – at least not to her.

It would be ridiculous to paint all women as paragons of loyalty and all men as totally incapable of commitment. But it is undeniable that our biological programming means that men and women have different notions of commitment. You see it most graphically in our different attitudes to a one-night stand.

A one-night stand is always a mistake for both parties – the experience is either worth repeating or it was not worth doing in the first place. But most men are quite capable of walking away from a one-night engagement while most women are not. And it is not because the earth moved and angels sang that a woman is reluctant to walk away from this hasty exchange of bodily fluids. It is because women are deeply and profoundly offended by such an obvious lack of commitment as demonstrated by these briefest of encounters.

That's why so many one-night stands produce such a horrible morning after, that's why *Fatal Attraction* rang a bell with so many men. You get stupid drunk when your partner is looking in the other direction and the next thing you know you are being harassed by vindictive phone calls and someone is boiling your pet bunny rabbit. Hell hath no fury like a woman who has a man's lack of commitment shoved in her face.

And who can blame her? Sometimes a man's lack of commitment looks suspiciously like a lack of common human decency. A man's reluctance to commit, a determination to maintain the free and easy lifestyle of a big swinging dick about town, is sometimes just an excuse to treat women badly. That's undeniable.

But it is equally true that nothing is a greater turn-off than a woman who is desperate for commitment. Nothing is more repellent to a man than a woman who – after one heavy date – is ready to pick out curtains.

The male fear of commitment is often a fear of domesticity. Commitment, that unspoken vow to another human being, is the bridge a man crosses on his way from being a dog-like creature – free, wide-ranging, sniffing at any passing stray – to being cat-like – domesticated, docile, grateful for a saucer of semi-skimmed milk.

And what if you choose the wrong person? The male nesting instinct, his desire for a home, hearth and children, is no less than that of the female. But men seem more aware of how incredibly easy it is to commit yourself to the wrong person.

There are many men who have no problem making a commitment to a woman. They will do their best to be supportive partners, faithful lovers, good friends. But, crucially, to a man there are gradations of commitment.

There is the commitment you feel for someone you have spent years with and gone through all manner of highs and lows. And then there is the commitment you feel for someone who makes your heart pump faster every time you hear her name. That is why the male conscience is untroubled by the thought of having both a wife and a lover. But all women seem to care about is the size of your commitment. If it's not big enough, they are not interested.

If you can't promise eternal devotion, if you can't give her the kind of commitment she wants – if all you can offer is friendship – then she will spit in your eye as she walks down the aisle with another guy.

Men feel incredibly bitter about this all-or-nothing attitude. Time and again women promise everlasting friendship at the start of a relationship and then when it is all over, they are not interested in wiping their shoes on your friendship. How about that for a lack of commitment?

Commitment – real commitment, commitment everlasting, commitment without end – could well turn out to be a thing of the past. My father was with my mother from the time he was 17 until his death, aged 63. Now that's commitment. But they don't build relationships like that any more. It is time to revise our notions on what we mean by commitment. Otherwise we will end up constantly disappointing each other.

Our lives are being shaped by a new breed of commitment. In our time serial monogamy is the new orthodoxy. You have a partner for six or seven years and then you move on. There will of course be happy exceptions to this rule but that is the fact behind the divorce statistics and the reality we see all around us. There can still be commitment in this world – but not the kind that lasts for forty years. If we could accept the commitment that people are prepared to give, it would be better for all of us.

But I fear that our different definitions of commitment will always be a source of conflict between men and women. This is because women seem to believe in The One – the love of their life, the man of their dreams, Mr Right. Men, for the most part, do not believe in The One. Most of us think that Ms Right is not out there. Instead men believe that there are a lot of wonderful women in the world and countless numbers are worthy of love. Obviously you can't commit to them all. *Obviously*.

The tragedy of the modern male – so reluctant to commit, so quick to make a break for his precious freedom – is that he will wake up one morning and find that he is committed to none of them.

The Prisoners of Gender

Guardian, 22 February 1990

H EATHER FORMAINI REALLY KNOWS HOW to hurt a guy. Reading her book *Men: The Darker Continent* makes a man feel like he has come home ridiculously late, stinking of the ale house, his brutish paws covered with blood. This is a book about the tyranny of masculinity, the martial law imposed by manhood, the lives and crimes of men – the prisoners of gender.

'Why do men abuse children and use murder as a way of seeking to solve a problem within themselves?' she asks. Well, I know why I do it. 'Why are men so afraid of intimacy? How does a man come to find out or understand who he really is?'

Trumpeted as 'a path-breaking and controversial analysis', it is in fact constructed on a familiar litany of complaints. Formaini is from the All Men Are Rapists school of feminism, which I always thought was about as clever as saying All Women Are Hairdressers. I suspect that the author has attempted to write a kind of Male Eunuch manifesto. She fails not because she underestimates the qualities of men – though most of our crimes are considerably more petty than she would lead you to believe – but because her view of women is so one-dimensional, so crass, so absurdly sentimental. 'To be a woman is to be human,' she swoons. 'Women are so in touch with their feelings . . .'

Does anyone still buy this mawkish crud? Do we still really believe that women are saintly life-givers, in touch with their feelings and their friends, brimming with baby milk and compassion? From the prim bullying of the woman in Downing Street to the kids you see slapped by their shrieking mothers in Sainsbury's, everything would seem to point to the fact that women are as lost, messed up and confused, as capable of cruelty and stupidity, as essentially human, as the next man. Seeing them as the beatific saviours of the universe is a denial of their humanity – as well as being almost inconceivably dumb.

Formaini's quaint view of woman as deity on earth is very much the view from Greenham Common – feminism's Dunkirk, that glorious, mythologised failure – where she won a UN peace prize. I'm sure it went down a treat around the Greenham campfires, but it doesn't work so well here when the language she uses goes beyond healthy cock-baiting into emotional fascism. She tosses around phrases like 'less than human' and then expects to be taken seriously. We need not be concerned about the hurt feelings of all us New Men but rather the effect her heavy-handed use of language has on her arguments, which is to make them redundant.

That's a shame because buried among the dewy-eyed dogma, the mindless ranting by this mullah of the sex war, Formaini makes some telling points about the prisoners of gender. It's true that most men are inadequate at being fathers, being husbands, all the big stuff. When it comes to the important things in life, we are often as useless as a male nipple. 'A man often reverts to the time-honoured system of marrying a woman he doesn't quite love,' writes Formaini, in a telling passage, 'and loving a woman he cannot marry. In this way he can maintain a state of idealism about love and yet never face the reality of it.'

She makes other good points about how men substitute authority for affection in their relationships with their children, how we seek mother substitutes in wives and father substitutes in work. Men are separated from the other halves of ourselves, runs her thesis, and we spend our lives looking for that other half.

This all rings true enough but Formaini soils her soapbox by overselling her arguments. The essential prick-hating nature of her views keeps breaking through. I am stunned by the wrong-headed certainties of her sexual apartheid.

'Men not only spend minimal time with their children, they also see them at their best – when they have eaten, are bathed and sweet-smelling.' I don't know what town – or century – this woman lives in, but around these parts my male friends are constantly tormented by foul-tempered, foul-smelling brats.

Formaini seems to have no notion of the way real men and women live their lives, the constant laughable struggle we indulge in just to get by. Wives, she says, are seen by men as 'women to help them develop and to support them in their comings and goings with warm socks and simmering soup.' Warm socks and simmering soup? Most of the pussy-whipped saps I hang around with wouldn't know warm socks and simmering soup if they came up and bit them on the back of their au pair.

She talks about the way men run the world as though Thatcher, Bhutto, Aquino never happened, about equal parenting as though it could save the rain forests, about war as though men see it like going to the football. She's so 1973.

The ideas for a better future that Formaini proposes – that men should share the responsibility of raising their children and try to avoid killing women whenever possible – seem self-evident to me. *Men: The Darker Continent* stands as an absurd book principally because of Formaini's ludicrously old-fashioned notions about women (see the lyrics of 'I Am Woman' by Helen Reddy for further reading) and their other, lesser halves. You know us – we're macho, we're macho, we don't know our ass from a hole in the ground, we're macho – keeping the women down.

Formaini interviewed 120 men for her book but perusing the re-sults of what she calls her 'sessions with Sam' and the rest, you can't help wondering the value of her extensive research. 'It's just awful that we accept all that masculine shit without questioning where it came from,' says Sam. Quite right, Sam, but have you noticed that the feminist shit can taste just as bad?

Formaini appears to have learned nothing from her sessions with Sam. She blathers on about women being in touch with their feelings and yet when men pursue their emotional impulses, she throws up her hands in horror. It is when she talks of men who stray from the path of righteous monogamy that Formaini reveals herself as a real old-fashioned girl, an alternative puritan, Thatcher with hairy arm-pits.

'For if heterosexual men are seeking their lost part in a woman, what their "screwing around" actually does is further separate them from their feelings.' Have you seen my lost part anywhere? 'It is as though the penis is detached from the body and lives a life of its own.' But the penis does live a life of its own. The penis is quite capable of taking a shine to someone without wishing to go to the supermarket with them every Saturday morning for the next 30 years. That is the secret – and the curse – of the prisoners of gender, and something that Heather Formaini cannot understand or forgive.

The book's last chapter, 'Is There A Future For Men?', contrasts Gabriel, a promiscuous professor who will basically put it in any-thing, with Jim and Daniel, who both work for ecological causes and are faithful to their wives. This really separates the New Men from the Lads as far as Formaini is concerned and the author's message is clear; if men want to have a future, then they'd better keep their politics Green and their fly zipped. As rational debate it's on a par with 'Get on your bike' but then it would be foolish to expect anything more complex from the sad, ranting rump of what used to be the feminist movement.

Performance

Elle, February 1994

S EX IS DIFFERENT FOR BOYS. Women expect a cuddle afterwards. Men want a review. It is no idle sweet nothing when a man asks, 'Was it good for you?' His greatest fear is that one black night you will reply, 'Was *what* good for me?' There are a whole host of things that are crucial to a man's sense of himself. Fighting, driving, making money – a man, any man, wants to be good at all these things. But he would rather be a pacifist, pedestrian bankrupt than an inept sack artist. He will trade his kingdom and everything in it, just as long as he's a good lay.

Why do men fret so about sexual performance? Why do we give ourselves hernias trying to make the earth move? Because sexual performance is *not* like playing the piano – it is not something you learn, get down pat and then do at parties to entertain people. Well, okay, it's a *bit* like playing the piano. With sufficient practice and experience, you can achieve a level of proficiency, learn a few tunes, manage some of the longer movements. But there's a nasty twist. In certain circumstances a man can hammer out Beethoven's Ninth Symphony. And other days the same man can only manage *Chopsticks*.

Naturally, men want to perform well because good sex with someone you love is a beautiful experience. But most of all men want to perform well because they are vain bastards. And insecure. Sexual performance is where a man's vanity and insecurity slug it out, where he discovers whether he is a real man or not quite man enough.

And it's different every time! That's the killer. It's not instant coffee, girls. We don't just add hot water and stir to taste. You might worry a bit about how long it takes to get your engine warmed up and running, but the male of the species is a more fragile creature. Indifference, distraction, anger – his body will cruelly reflect these emotions. You can fake an orgasm but you can't fake an erection.

Sexual performance matters to men of all ages. Even the testosterone-engorged adolescent who, you might think, just wants to get his nasty little end away, cares desperately about putting on a good show. When I was a teenager, it was customary to prepare for a heavy date by having a shave, a shower and a wank – the latter to ensure that the heights of ecstasy were not over before they had really begun. Getting it up and then doing it badly is probably considered rather worse than failing to cut the mustard at all. Most men don't fear impotence. They fear mediocrity. So we aspire to excellence – three times a night.

Drinking too much is, of course, the oldest excuse for poor sexual performance – or no sexual performance at all – and the only acceptable one. But there are a thousand other little distractions that can put a man off his stroke. Anything from guilt to bodily hair – yours, not his – can make a man have a bad match. (Notice how, again and again, I resort to the phraseology of competitive sport!)

I had a friend who loved his girlfriend but pined for some extra-curricular activity. He finally wound up in bed with a girl he liked but found that his sex drive had downed tools. Rain stopped play. The woman did not take it well and neither did my friend. He felt bad about the woman he didn't satisfy, the girlfriend he almost cheated on. But most of all he felt bad about himself: what went wrong?

To me it was obvious – he didn't really want to cheat on his girlfriend. The inability to get it on was all in his head. But it worried him, tormented him, hit him where he lived. And I understood. It would have worried me, too. It would have worried any of us.

Frankly, there are two reasons why every man in the world enjoys being fellated. One is that it feels good. The other is that a blow job relieves a man of the burden of sexual performance. And that probably feels even better. Of course we want to perform well. Naturally we want to blow your minds. Men realise that sex is not static. It is usually either improving or getting worse. Perhaps it is improving because you are trusting each other more, becoming more familiar with each other's deepest desires. Or perhaps it's declining because you have been together a little too long. So, if he puts on a virtuoso sexual performance, a man knows – or at least believes – that all is well in a relationship. Nothing is more reassuring.

'Do you love me?' asks a woman. 'Did you come?' asks a man. Well, if you have to *ask* . . . And, of course, in his sexual performance a man sees a reflection of the passing of time. Sex with a girl of 16 or a woman of 35 . . . is it so different? You tell me. But for a boy of 16 and a man of 35, they are two completely different ways of travel. One is a brief multiple-entry visa, the other is a slow boat to China. Three times in an hour is nothing when you're 17. That passes. The rabbit-like abandon goes but, with the pyrotechnics of sexual performance, we disguise the fact that – in Mother Nature's eyes – we are past our prime. So it had better be good.

Men are pathetically easy to please after the curtain comes down on another performance. A few warm words from you will make his proud, insecure heart sing. But see it from his point of view – he has so many things to think about. Did he do it long enough? Soft enough? Hard enough? Often enough? The business with the tongue – okay was it? And this modern-world intermission where he has to get out of bed to put on a bloody condom ... did that spoil it for you? Honest? After all of that stuff, it is a relief to know that a good time has been had by all. No, but really – marks out of 10 ...

Roses are Red, Valentines are Blue . . .

Guardian, 14 February 1991

WEET, FUNNY VALENTINE – don't you know that romance is just love before it has had a chance to go wrong? And don't you know that if that frail flower isn't crushed in its first flush, then one, five, 10 years later, you will be pushing a pram to Sainsbury's with some human carbuncle (some blowsy frump or beer-bellied lump), thinking to yourself – where, oh where, is my own true love? And they will be right there with you, your own true love grown cold and distant, staring sourly at all the sell-by dates.

Ah romance! There are so many fish in the sea – and all of us so slippery. Romance is dinner with an angel but breakfast with the blues. It always ends in tears. But life is flat, filmed in grubby black and white, until it begins again, until the next time.

Nothing in this world or the next can match the thrill of the *amour fou*, that crazy love we call romance. It's a troublemaker. It picks fights with true and honest love, and romance always gives it a good kicking.

Because romance is not love, though perhaps it is love's opposite, love's neurotic twin sister. Love is a bond built on trust, affection and time. Love uses the front door. Romance, like the SAS, comes crashing through the window brandishing a semi-automatic and wearing a balaclava. We know the ones we love – but it could be anybody inside that balaclava. Yet we take a chance.

Romance is based on a hunch, an instinct. There's a face in the crowd bathed in a golden light. Perhaps he will treat you better than he treated the last one. Romance makes you close your eyes and leap into the dark. You turn your life inside out, hurt the people you love, push your old heart through a mincer for a handful of sweet nothings. Romance makes it seem like a good idea at the time.

All is clouded by romance, blinded by its comfy blinkers, bound by its velvet ropes. It is more exciting than real life. Falling in love – being that happy, that lost, that scared – could be as close to heaven as you will ever get. It is better than drugs, better than sex, better than money – and I'm talking pure drugs, good sex, big money.

Romance makes you feel like a king and act like a jerk. Suddenly Simon Bates has the ability to make you choke with emotion – because every song he plays was written about you. How did Abba know exactly what you are going through?

Romance holds you a hostage to life. In that respect it is like having children – except that parental responsibility follows you to the grave. Romance rarely follows you out of the door. Are women more romantic than men? I think not. Most of the pussy-whipped saps that I hang around with do not dream of hot sex with Kim Basinger, executive relief from Michelle Pfeiffer. No, what they long for – what they miss – is that sense of wonder that means you are falling, falling, fallen. 'I ache for romance,' they say. 'I pine for it.' Romance is what a man dreams of when his wife has turned out the lights.

Romance makes life sweeter but harder, too. Suddenly the road gets rougher, it's lonelier and tougher. Romance – or its absence – is the root of all domestic upheaval. A lack of romance in a marriage will kill it faster than any other kind of scarcity. Even money. Romance is the hard currency of the soul.

No good can come of it. It has to go away or wither and die. Romance is as fresh and immature as Peter Pan, unable to exist in all its green glory in the adult world. Romance wears green tights and a feather in its hat, romance talks to fairies, befriends the Lost Boys. Maybe it metamorphoses into a love that will endure – but that's not romance. And, in our cheating hearts, we know it's not as good. Love doesn't have that burn.

Romance is the fleeting moment that promises forever. You said you would always love me, they say one day, the bitterest pill you have to swallow. Because romance comes with such a solid sense of finality – this may not be the first time but surely it is the last – words like 'forever' and 'no one but you' spring easily to your lying lips. But for ever is a fluid concept in this rose-coloured minefield. It means one thing when a person has a head full of Chardonnay and moonlight, and another thing entirely in the cold grey light of a relationship.

Romance is a faithless lover – a real bitch, a right bastard. It makes life worth living and then – so soon! – it breaks your heart.

Because it fades, it changes, it turns nasty. It never stays the same. We could forgive it almost anything – if only it would stay the same.

And still we climb every mountain, make those furtive phone calls, dream the impossible dream. And for what? For the possibility that you have finally found the other half of your soul – 'That person doesn't exist!' she told me – for the best feeling in the world, that's all, for the promise that it's not all a crock of pain and cruelty and mediocrity. Because romance convinces you that it's a wonderful life. That's why it will wipe the floor with love every time. It tells you exactly what you want to hear, even if it is all lies.

Sweet, funny valentine – romance is not the only thing that matters. It just always feels that way.

Savan Grace

Glenn Savan quit the advertising business to wait tables – and to write his first novel, *White Palace*

Elle, March 1988

ON THE SOUTHSIDE OF ST LOUIS there is a burger joint that makes McDonald's look like Le Caprice.

The White Castle is housed in exactly that – a squat, cubic white castle built in the Disneyland-Norman style. Inside, the red-necked, blue-collared clientele pop tiny, bite-size burgers by the pungent half-dozen. Known with good reason as 'belly bombers' to the fast food gourmets who consume them, these culinary depth charges cost 39 cents each and give your digestive system an experience it will never forget, no matter how hard it tries.

The Taste Some People Won't Live Without, it says on the staff's white hats, and they grimly serve up more pock-marked grey meat in soft buns to the kind of mutants who dine here, who tend to be what you might reasonably identify as hillbillies or white trash but who are known locally as *hoosiers*.

'You know it's proletarian because nobody here would understand the word', says Glenn Savan, the author of *White Palace*, an irresistible first novel whose hero finds true love in a place like this.

Told with outrageous humour and a massive heart, *White Palace* is a boy-meets-slut, boy-loses-slut love story. Its protagonists are Max Baron, a young, good-looking advertising executive from middle-class West St Louis county, and the unforgettable Nora Cromwell, a White Palace waitress and salty hoosier madonna on the far side of 40. Nora is the kind of woman who leaves barbecued pork rinds down the back of her sofa. She reads a book only if it is about Marilyn Monroe. It is not unusual for her to wake up on her waterbed with a murderous hangover and half her perm collapsed.

Max is still recovering from the death of his charming, beautiful wife in a freak car accident two years ago and at first his interest in this sagging siren from Dogtown is strictly carnal. They have absolutely nothing in common and the slumming adman feels exactly the same way about Nora as he feels about burgers at the mythical White

Palace – adorable trash that is fun for a while, but hardly the stuff you want for a staple diet.

'They taste like sin would taste, if you could eat it,' one of the book's characters says of belly bombers, though he could be describing Max's initial feelings for Nora. *White Palace* is a novel in heat. *Playboy* described the book's sex scenes as 'worth a thousand reels of uninspired porn', while *Vanity Fair* told its readers, '*White Palace* contains some of the hottest sex scenes in a contemporary novel since Scott Spencer's *Endless Love*.'

But the odd couple's relationship eventually goes beyond the rolling waves of Nora's waterbed and Savan's novel addresses itself to the Big Question – is there life after sex?

Max Baron finds himself falling in love with Nora. His Dogtown darling ends up showing that what she lacks in sophistication, education and taste, she makes up for in dignity, humanity and pride. There were times while reading this beautiful, moving book that I found myself rating Nora Cromwell the most vivid character to appear in American fiction since Holden Caulfield. She turns out to be quite a girl. Inevitably, she breaks Max Baron's heart.

Like Max, the 33-year-old, Martin Amis-sized (talent *and* height) Glenn Savan was born, bred and worked in the advertising business in St Louis (pronounced Lewis, Missouri way). Savan, a graduate of the Iowa Writers' Workshop, quit advertising a few years back to work as a waiter while he wrote *White Palace*. But before quitting his day job to live in a poor area of south St Louis, he was very much the privileged West County adman of his novel. So where does Max Baron end and Glenn Savan begin?

'Max is much more of a stiff ass than I am,' he says.

And has there been a Nora in your life?

'We have all had our dates and love affairs where we were not totally comfortable and where we would not introduce that person to every sector of our lives,' says Savan, which rhymes with raven. 'But when I was 24 and an advertising man living in Timberlake [a rich young St Louis singles ghetto], I got picked up in a cowboy bar. It was a blue-collar bar where people wore the hats and there was country music. It was pretty scuzzy. I wasn't even on the look-out for anything that night but she grabbed hold of me and I took her back to my apartment and she was . . . just pathetic.'

Why's that?

'She had a cough, a kind of consumptive's cough, and she cleaned toilets in a nursing home for a living. She was the lowest rung of the help in a nursing home. Her grammar was awful – she was basically a hillbilly who had come to St Louis to work. But though she was not really attractive, she was sexy in a kind of trashy way. She was absolutely dirt ignorant – and a great fuck. We must have made love four times in succession.'

But their love was not to be.

'I saw her one more time, two nights later. And in the morning, once her make-up was gone, she didn't look too good. She looked at me and said, "Don't bullshit me, you're never going to see me again. You are who you are, I am who I am, and you are never going to introduce me to any of your friends, never going to take me anywhere." And I just sat there like a speared fish with my mouth open. Because of course she was right. I never did see her again. And that incident really *bothered* me, especially my weak-minded, cowardly way of dealing with it.'

So what exactly is *White Palace* about?

'The mystery of attraction,' he says.

St Louis sprawls on the banks of the muddy, sun-spangled Mississippi. This is the heartland, where women say things like, 'Ya know, Jesus came back because he loved us,' over the Key Lime pie. It is a young country – the bizarre slogan of the Better Burger emporium is *Famous Since 1986* – and for the most part it is a thoroughly middle-class land of drive-in banks, ice cubes the size of your fist and $12,500 to join a good country club. St Louis is a baseball and beer city. Both Anheuser Busch, makers of Budweiser, and the Cardinals are owned by Gussie Busch, the only octogenarian I ever saw wearing a stetson.

Glenn Savan has lived all over this town and its varied locales make a vivid and original backdrop to *White Palace*. There is downtown St Louis, where big business is conducted in the shadow of the towering Gateway Arch ('Gateway To The West'). There are the redneck bars, the fast-food joints and country and western songs of the southside. And over in Dogtown (chosen as Nora's home because of its meaty, evocative name), next to the imposing black hulk of the disused Scullion steel mill, there are the small wooden houses, American prefabs, that were built to house home-coming GIs and their young brides at the end of World War II. Huge, rusty gas-guzzlers squat outside these surly little boxes and a lonesome Stars and Stripes flutters gently on one of the scraggy front gardens of Dogtown.

And in *White Palace* there are also the manicured lawns and the suburban bliss of Creve Coeur out in west St Louis county. This is where Glenn Savan grew up and now we sit in his car outside the dream home where he was a boy. He points to the bedroom window where, like some adult-defying kid in Mark Twain, a Huck Finn or Tom Sawyer of the Kennedy era, he would clamber in and out on various pre-teen adventures. Until he was nine years old and his world fell apart.

'We were playing guns, me and my two best buddies, and for the game to go on after you got shot, which was the best part because it was the most fun to die, you had to lie on the ground for 10 seconds and then get up and shout *new man!* Then the game could go on. Well, I fell wrong and I couldn't get up. The game stopped and I had to be carried back to my house – this house – and it went downhill from there. It took about six months before it was diagnosed as rheumatoid arthritis, for which there is no cure and which is usually degenerative. No hope was held out that I was ever going to walk again.'

For three years Glenn Savan was in a wheelchair. When he was 10 and 11 he went to a school for physically handicapped children. 'I was the weird guy on the block,' he smiles. 'I was the kid in his wheelchair on the sidelines while all the other kids did their normal kid activities. It contributed something to my happiness in solitude, which every writer needs.'

At the age of 12 his condition began to improve. Savan got out of his wheelchair and on to crutches. He returned to a normal school and, though he needed crutches for years and walked with a limp until his last year in senior high school, he slowly began to get better. But it was not until his mid 20s, when the crutches had been thrown away and he no longer walked with a limp, that he was told his illness had been wrongly diagnosed and that the kind of arthritis he suffers from is not degenerative. But he grew up not knowing that, fully expecting a relapse at any moment. This life-warping experience – and his reprieve – has given him the ability not to be cowed by limited expectations. For someone who was told he was never going to be able to live without a wheelchair, choosing to live without an advertising man's fat salary and lush lifestyle to wait tables and write a novel was probably not the momentous decision it would have been for someone else.

'I think my wheelchair experience has something to do with my arrested height,' he grins. 'But I was never worried about being short because during the period when you learn those phobias I was worried about whether I was going to be able to walk that day.'

It has also made him comfortable with his own company. In fact, he is so relaxed about being alone that you can tell it worries him sometimes. He has never lived with a woman, despite being quite a person killer ('After a long weekend, I need to decompress'), and he leaves his answering machine on around the clock, keeping his callers at bay. This need to keep a little distance between himself and the world is especially striking in such a warm, generous and open man as Glenn Savan. He embodies the best qualities of the Midwest and, like some favourite son of J. D. Salinger, he uses words like 'swell', 'gee' and 'baloney' to a charming degree. 'I love kids,' he says. 'Kids kill me.' An all-American guy, we drive out to this fancy West Country restaurant and for an aperitif he orders *coffee*.

White Palace is already making Glenn Savan what he calls 'a lot of dough', and it now seems certain to be filmed. Sydney Pollack, who has optioned Savan's novel, will produce and Griffin Dunne is said to be dead keen to play Max. The part of Nora, which has to be one of the meatiest roles for a woman in years, is still up for grabs. The actress currently being mentioned most favourably down in Missouri is Anjelica Huston.

When *White Palace – The Movie* goes into production, Glenn Savan will get $200,000 which he can put with what he refers to as 'this peculiar avalanche of money' he has already made.

His novel is currently averaging a new print a month, it is on its way to sales of 100,000 in the States and it has been bought by publishing houses all around the world. It is a very rare book that manages to be both so intelligent and so accessible. 'I do a lot of work to make my work look effortless,' he says. 'But I don't believe that quality precludes commercial success.'

It is the first day of fall in St Louis and the city is bathed in the silvery light of tomorrow morning's frost. We are sitting in a West County bar and Savan is talking about his attitude to women.

He is saying that he declined the invitation of his best friend to his bachelor party – the raw American equivalent of the stag night where the cabaret is invariably provided by some dial-a-stripper.

'My idea of fun is *not* sitting around with 20 drunken guys having a woman push her pussy in my face. One on one, that's different.'

How does Savan approach sex on the printed page?

'The trouble with most sex scenes is that they don't reveal character and advance the story. All you find out is, hey, their sex organs function like those of *homo sapiens*! To me, you don't write a sex scene unless it is going to be as revelatory of character as a scene at a dinner party or when he first meets her mother. That first seduction scene in *White Palace* took me a month because I kept saying to myself – *no! no!* It's *not* just cock and pussy!'

We drive across town to Webster's, the free form bar and grill where Glenn Savan waited tables for a couple of years while he was writing *White Palace*. This was where he earned the rent for his dumpy southside apartment (he now lives in swanky Clayton with Ethel the cat), where he played the wise-guy waiter and where he sometimes despaired that he would ever be able to get that book out to the world.

'Hey, big guy,' a black kitchen worker calls out to him as we make our way through the church pews and hanging plants of Webster's. On the TV suspended from the ceiling, the St Louis Cardinals are beating the New York Mets at Busch stadium. We go to the bar and order Mexican beer. I ask the big guy what kind of people you get in Webster's. 'In the two years I was waiting tables here, everybody I ever met came in at some point. You get all types here. The hip, the square, the scuzzballs.' Suddenly a sweet memory lights up Savan's face, that face belonging to a Midwest Dustin Hoffman, a Paul Simon of the plains. 'And I did meet a lot of *very* sleazy women,' he says approvingly.

Travel

Chicago – Boss City

Arena, July/August 1989

THE TALLEST SKYSCRAPERS in the world built on stolen swamp-land; wide, rich streets inhabited by the ghosts of Pottawomie Indians and Italian gangsters; a heart big enough to provide a home for refugees as diverse as Mies van der Rohe and Muddy Waters – surely this Chicago is the quintessential American city.

The myths of the Windy City – a tough town erected on the profits of meat and illegal whiskey, the streets red from the slaughter of the stockyards and the prohibition era – leave you unprepared for the frosty, soaring beauty of the place.

Right in the heart of the heartland, surrounded by the endless prairies of the Mid West, Chicago stands on the icy shores of a lake that stretches into the Northern mists like America's third ocean. If the type of architecture that makes your sap rise is the lofty modern grandeur of downtown USA rather than the majestic rubble of old Europe, then the beauty of Chicago surpasses even the skyline of Manhattan.

Since the great fire of 1871 razed the place to the ground, architects have run free here. Daniel Burnham, creator of the Chicago plan of 1909 – and the city is almost totally a twentieth-century invention – counselled city leaders to 'make no little plans, for they have no magic to stir men's blood'. The world's first skyscraper went up here – not because, as with the island of Manhattan, there was no room to spread out, but just for the hell of it. Louis Sullivan, Godfather of the skyscraper and its most poetical theorist (he said he saw the building as the perfect expression of the American impulse), spent most of his working life in Chicago, defining the look of its glorious downtown area. Frank Lloyd Wright was a homeboy. When the Nazis closed down the Bauhaus, Mies van der Rohe came here. And of the five tallest buildings in the world, three are located in downtown Chicago, as is Helmut Jahn's immense, globular, red and blue, glass and space creation, the Illinois Center ('Romantic High-Tech,' said Jahn of his work, with a lyrical turn of phrase that Louis Sullivan would have been proud of). Chicago is a city that is built to inspire awe and a city that is still being built. Hot, young Helmut Jahn, born in Nuremburg in 1940, was drawn to the Windy City as inevitably as Mies was half a century before him, and the result is a living museum of architecture, a town that can be quite overwhelming, truly shocking in its beauty.

And yet young, dynamic Chicago clings to its grizzled old myths, cherishes its reputation as a mean and violent man's town, relishes all your preconceptions.

One night in Chicago I went looking for jazz at Andy's on East Hubbard Street, just north of the flinty river that divides the town, but all I found there were pictures on the walls of long-dead sax players and, on a TV set hiked above the bar, the Chicago Bulls beating Milwaukee at basketball. So I wandered down the street and stumbled across a bar with ENTER AT YOUR OWN RISK on the door. It was Billy Goat's, the legendary hangout of Chicago's newspapermen – Mike Royko and the rest. I pushed open the door and went down a few steps into a bright, spacious bar where men discussed the twin Chicago obsessions of sport and politics, watched the Academy Awards on TV (best line overheard by a Windy City film buff: 'I really liked dat film – *Wanda Der Fish*') and talked in tough, cynical italics, just like newspapermen in black-and-white '40s movies.

'Where's *Jimmy*? *Bartending* school?'

'Jimmy, he's got *your* problem.'

'What's *dat*?'

'He's in *love*.'

And the next day this year's Pulitzer Prizes were announced and three of journalism's Oscars went to Chicago journalists, these men who talk in tough italics in the bar with a small gold bust of JFK on the wall and a sign saying *enter at your own risk* on the door. Talking tough and winning a Pulitzer is very Chicago. Hemingway was born down the road in Oak Park, and his descendants, these hard men of letters, all seem out to disprove the notion that Tough Guys Don't Write; they seem like a tribe of Papas sometimes, sentimental only about the harsh nature of their city, a city that inspires a hard-boiled rapture.

'Crazy with life,' said Dreiser of Chicago. 'Huge, filthy, brilliant and mean,' said Saul Bellow.

'Hog Butcher for the World,' wrote Carl Sandburg, the town's greatest poet. 'Tool maker, Stacker of Wheat, Player with Railroads and the Nation's Freight Handler, Stormy, Husky, Brawling – City of The Big Shoulders.'

All the literary lions of Chicago – Dreiser, Sandburg, Bellow, plus David Mamet, Ring Lardner, Nelson Algren, Studs Terkel, Mike Royko and, most recently, Vietnam Vet and author of *Paco's Story* Larry Heinemann – are linked by a common muscular intelligence. It is said that when the late, unlamented Mayor 'Boss' Daley was growing up on the South Side, the smell of the stockyards and its daily holocaust was never out of his nostrils, and it seems that Chicago's historic capacity for mayhem, for cruelty and chaos of every kind, is never far from the mind's eye of its greatest artists. It is almost as if the violence of the past inspires, spurs on and inflames the cultural aspiration of the present.

Chicago is a city torn from mud and built on blood. In the 1910–1912 newspaper circulation war, for example, in which hired thugs fought for William Randolph Hearst's *Examiner* and Medill McCormick's *Tribune*, 27 newsstand sellers were shot dead and many more wounded and maimed – this was back when a circulation war meant exactly that. This bloody, mindless past has left a real craving in the city's present for the cultural higher ground, for art and intellect and artistic endeavour of every description. You see it in the great writers that Chicago produces, in the average citizen's knowledge of architecture. And you see it most of all in the Art Institute, Chicago's great museum.

The Art Institute has a school that produced Jeff Koons and a collection that surpasses even the Hermitage in Leningrad, the Met in New York and the Louvre in Paris. Rooms full of Modigliani, de Chirico, Gris and Braque. The finest moments of an artist's period are here – Picasso's big blue 'The Old Guitarist', Robert Rauschenberg's 'Retroactive II', a Van Gogh self-portrait, Pollock's 'The Grayed Rainbow', a screaming Edvard Munch. An entire wall full of Monet's 'Haystacks' and whole bunches of his 'Irises' – this is the truly great stuff, the stuff every Japanese insurance company would pay a fortune to have up on its 40th floor. And there are Cézanne apples, Matisse dancers, Gauguin's natives and even the work of shabby English depressives like Lucian Freud and Gilbert and George. There are acres of impressionists, including Seurat's 'Sunday Afternoon on the Island of La Grande Jatte', and great American paintings like Grant Wood's 'American Gothic' and, the very greatest of them all, Edward Hopper's haunting 'Nighthawks'. A pack of

Chicago skinheads, ugly and clumping inside their tattoos and boots, roam the Ivan Albright room, smacking their lips appreciatively at the huge canvases full of creatures in Hell or the black, mottled flesh of burns victims. The skinheads utter the mantra of teenage America, that endless refrain of adolescent USA.

'That's cool.'

'Oh, that's cool.'

'Yeah, that's *cool*.'

It is an overpowering collection, put together with real passion, and yet I have never seen a good word written about it by visitors to Chicago, as if the place goes against all our expectations of the city. Even writers of some vision have seen fit to put it down. 'It rivals that of the *Jeu de Paume*,' said Martin Amis about the Art Institute's impressionist collection. 'But there is a tangible air of donation, patronage, social power.'

Not like England, Martin! Not like Charles and Doris! Nothing like our Saatchis!

'Huge museums were presently crammed with loot from the older civilisations,' wrote Jan Morris, 'enabling over-educated daughters to swell parental hearts by recognising a Botticelli when they saw one.'

Yet the cultural aspirations of Chicago's first families, the dynasties who created the Art Institute, go way beyond a desire for tax breaks, and those skinheads in the Albright room were not there to collect conversational gambits for dinner party chit-chat. 'In the Twenties kids in Chicago hunted for treasure in the March thaw,' wrote Saul Bellow. 'Dirty snow hillocks formed along the kerbs and when they melted, water ran braided and brilliant in the gutters and you could find marvellous loot – bottle tops, machine gears, Indian-head pennies. And last spring, almost an elderly fellow now, I found that I had left the sidewalk and that I was following the curb and looking. For what?'

For what every Chicagoan looks for: gold in the gutter, fortune snatched from the dirt, the hope that it is possible to transcend an unsatisfactory past, that it will melt away to reveal a bright and shining future. It is the denial of tradition, it is the promise of the New World, and it is the very essence of Chicago – the belief that it is possible to shrug off the soiled and stained rags of the past and discover you are in the presence of magic.

Down in Daley Plaza, in the shadow of the giant Picasso sculpture, there is a small memorial for the men who died in two wars. But

Daley Plaza is a long way from the Cenotaph and this is for the fallen as seen from an American perspective. When you kneel to read the inscription, and are so close to it that you can feel the heat of the eternal flame on your face, you see that the two wars in question are Korea and Vietnam.

Daley Plaza itself is a memorial to the notorious Boss Daley, Mayor of Chicago for 20 years. Daley came to the attention of the world in 1968, when his police force ran riot with nightsticks and tear gas at the Democratic convention, cracking the heads of and blinding Abbie Hoffman, Jerry Rubin and their army of hippy activists, as well as non-participant bystanders as varied as the unknown John Belushi, Winston Churchill, MP, and countless members of the public and press. But in Chicago itself, Daley is best remembered for the political machine he built, a machine that won him five mayoral elections and made the Windy City his fiefdom for nearly a quarter of a century.

'Daley kept his machine in place with an army of patronage workers,' said *Business* magazine, 'depending on the black vote, but he did little to deal with the poverty faced by ethnic minorities. In fact, his imaginative version of town planning carved up the city's South Side with six-lane freeways, hemming blacks into overcrowded ghettos. However, many businessmen refer back to his era as a time when things got down – no matter how – and the city remains a product of his vision of a vibrant downtown.'

It is Easter in Chicago, and Daley Plaza is graced with a large crucifix, scattered palms and a sign saying *He is risen*. Just around the corner is a poster urging *Daley for Mayor*. Boss Daley died in 1976, but his son, also Richard Daley, is also a politician, and when I was in Chicago he was running for Mayor.

Vote Daley Mayor, say more signs. *Get Drugs And Guns Out Of The Schools*. The Daley name is an emotive one in Chicago, the years of quiet corruption of the Boss and his machine inspiring Mike Royko to amend the city's motto, *I will*, to *I will (if I don't get caught)*.

But, by almost all accounts, this latest Daley is a very different man from his father. Boss Daley – who told his cops 'Shoot to kill' during the 1968 race riots – would admittedly take some beating. But this Daley does not have the same unthinking racism as his father, he spent years nursing one of his children when the child was dying of spina bifida, and he is supported in his campaign by no less than Chicago's favourite Nobel Prize winner, Saul Bellow.

'An altogether distasteful and ugly business,' was Bellow's description of the Mayoral contest after one of Daley's opponents accused Jewish doctors of injecting black babies with the AIDS virus. And yet every election in Chicago is to some extent a distasteful and ugly business because the major issue is always the same – race. Chicago's electorate is divided along racial lines: 42 per cent black, 42 per cent white and the rest Latinos. It is the great irony of the city that in this great ethnic melting-pot, this town of immigrants in a nation of immigrants, the refugees from Sweden, Poland, Ireland, Germany, Italy and the rest all eventually became 'white'. But the other half of the city, the blacks who came to Chicago from the Southern states to escape the poverty and bigotry of their rural homelands, these refugees from America itself, never managed to cross the tracks to the economic promised land. Chicago kept its promise to everyone except the Americans who came here, the blacks who remain trapped in the South and the West Sides.

There are obvious and startling exceptions to this rule – sport, music and even politics remain passports out of the ghetto, and there is a black middle class in Chicago that simply does not exist anywhere in England – but the ugly fact remains that if you are born in the South Side, the odds are that you will also die there.

Chicago is a Democrat's town (the Civil War swelled its Yankee coffers just as it devastated the South) and the Mayoral race is between Daley and black independent Democrat Timothy Evans. The Republican, Edward 'Fast Eddie' Vrodilyak, might just as well be representing the Monster Raving Loony Party.

Almost all the votes that Daley and Evans receive will be cast along racial lines, and what will decide the election is who will woo the Latinos and the few floating voters and who will inspire the larger turn-out of their supporters at the poll. This in turn will be decided by the size of the candidates' campaign funds. Daley has money. Evans has none. Things start to look bad for the black independent candidate when he pays a campaign visit to Cabrini Green – also known as Beirut, Death Row, The Graveyard and DMZ – and while he is walking through Chicago's South Bronx he is suddenly forced to take cover as, from the top of the projects, gangs of youths begin to stone him.

But at least Evans has the most famous Chicago politician on his side. Jesse Jackson works tirelessly for the black candidate even when it becomes clear that he is fighting a losing battle. By any normal political standards, Jackson would be expected to support the official candidate of his party. But it is inconceivable that Jackson, who once asked Boss Daley for a job in his administration and was offered a job operating a toll booth, could *ever* support a man called Daley. This is Chicago, where you are forever stepping into old and bitter feuds.

'We all share this big old chocolate egg we call the earth,' says Bob Hope on his Easter special, his dead eyes woodenly following the autocue. 'But more than a religious celebration, Easter is when every nation on earth checks in for a little R and R.'

Some of Chicago's most glorious R and R – rest and recreation, an evocative old 'Nam term – is to be found around midnight in the blues clubs on Rush Street.

Chicago was the end of the rainbow for the countless number of blacks who made the journey up from the South. It is where they could run no further – this part of the States is called the North Shore, as clear a natural border as the east or west coasts – where they had to look the American Dream in the eye. It is of course the city of the blues, where the greasy gravitas of that music became as much about savouring life's small sweet pleasures as it was about tasting its defeat and despair.

Chicago was also, if not the home of jazz, the place where much of its early output was first recorded. Most recently, the city has spawned the now ubiquitous beat of House music, the product of young Chicagoans like Marshall Jefferson.

There are blues clubs all over Chicago, as omnipresent and integrated into the fabric of the city's life as pubs in London or cafés in Paris. The one I found was long and thin and featured a band called the Blue Lights. Their singer was as long and thin as Clint Eastwood and, in his crisp white jacket and snap-brim fedora, as cool and urbane as David Niven. He was an old black guy of 60 or so and he growled the fleshy sacrament of the blues.

'*Another mule been kicking in my stool*,' he groaned, and, later, almost smiling, '*I love to dip my dipper in somebody else's dipping.*'

The four-piece band kicked up a storm behind him and he told the story of willing women living down the hall, of how he loved to gorge himself on forbidden fruit. He agonised about the infidelity of women and the impossibility of being faithful. He sang non-stop about fucking, about every possible permutation of ecstasy and heartache, every joy and treachery, every act of betrayal and frisson of delight that a man could ever know. The waitress brought more beer. This, I thought, is the blues.

I stepped back out on Rush Street in the early hours, consumed with exhilaration, until a black man around the same age as me stopped me with an apologetic smile.

'Brother,' he said, 'can you spare 35 cents for something to eat?'

Reeling with guilt, I gave him my loose change, a pathetic handful of nickels, dimes and quarters. I was still feeling bad about it the next day when someone – a New Yorker – tried to throw some light on the divided heart of the city.

'You have to understand,' he told me, 'Chicago is a southern town.'

'Sir!' the conductor declared to Charles Dickens in the 1860s as their train rattled into the outskirts of Chicago. 'You are about to enter the Boss City of the universe!'

The railroads – like the stockyards and the steel mills – are silent now, and the bicoastal businessmen who commute between New York and Los Angeles do so without ever having to set foot in Chicago. Yet, seen from the top of the Hancock Center, when the lights of the city make it look like God's airport, or down among the frenzied, sweating greed of the commodity markets in the Board of Trade building, or looking at the material heaven of Michigan Avenue's Magnificent Mile through the smoked-glass window of a stretch limo and a highball haze, it still looks like Boss City.

'Chicago has Pullman braggadocio,' said Jan Morris, 'swagger of brass and green liveries, swank of cheroot, wink of deal.' Two businessmen in from the coast sit in the luxurious lounge of the Mayfair Regent hotel, sipping cocktails and discussing deals.

Outside, Big John, the Hancock Center – all black and tapering, criss-crossed with diagonal steel braces like gigantic kisses – glowers down on the wide, white, roomy opulence of Michigan Avenue. This is where the sight of a bum still draws stares and where those bums do not have that raw, crazed helplessness you see among their sad tribe in New York, or the sullen, simmering violence you sense among their kind in Washington, that Lebanon on the Potomac.

In downtown Chicago, under the awnings of Cartier and Tiffany, Saks and Bloomingdale's – where later today Joan Collins will autograph bottles of her new perfume, Spectacular – the misery of the projects ('As close to hell as you can get without dying,' someone said) seem light-years away, instead of within walking distance. Now the brilliant sunshine is breaking up the ice around Lake Michigan, and under the huge blue Mid-Western sky Chicago seems at peace with itself. American dreams are made of this; for all the Paloma Picasso jewellery in Tiffany and for all the 30-buck bottles of perfume being shifted in Bloomingdale's, this is still the heartland of Middle America, where the frontier began and where it is still possible to feel that pioneer's shiver of excitement when you sense all of the country stretching out before you.

There is an easy, informal grace about the citizens of Chicago, a friendliness that is so unforced and genuine that you will miss it long after you have flown home. For all its impressive retail outlets, it remains a place of honest hedonism and innocent pleasures, a baseball and beer town, where you root for the Cubs and feast on American cuisine at its robust best – spicy deep-pan pizzas, Gold Coast chilli dogs, steaks at Arnie's on State Street ('The great street' – Frank Sinatra). Some of the culinary aberrations – the 'incredible edibles', as they are billed – are almost as much fun as the good stuff, such as 'The Wunderbar – Cheesecake On A Stick Dipped In Dark Chocolate, Ready To Enjoy Right From The Freezer' or 'Croissant Of The Day'.

And as State Street winds south ('I just want to say: they do things they don't do on Broadway, hey!' – Frank Sinatra) and it takes on the down-at-heel shabbiness you see in the worst parts of Broadway, this is where you find some real fast-food treasures, burger Valhallas full of the chunky '50s red-upholstered swivel chairs and curving silver soda-fountain bars you find in swish retro joints in London, but in the downtown Chicago area they are done *without irony*. This is the real thing. But best of all, even better than the eye-watering architecture, there are the people. It is easy to meet people in Chicago. The city has something you do not see in stiff-assed old Europe, and you probably call it humanity. There is an openness about the people, a warmth and friendliness that is a reflection of all that is best about this country, a touching confirmation of all of America's highest hopes for itself.

'The people in Chicago are polite,' sniffed Jan Morris. 'When they are not rioting.'

The myths of Chicago – chatter of machine-gun, thud of nightstick, ghetto on fire – persist perhaps because it is all so close. Out in the wealthy suburb of Cicero there are plenty of arthritic octogenarians wheezing over their flower beds who less than half a century ago were getting rich on the lush pickings of prohibition and prostitution. And just over a century ago, this is where the term *underworld* – as in a subterranean, criminal netherworld – was invented.

In the days before the fire the nineteenth-century boomtown was sinking into the swampland on which it was built, so they raised the entire city, building by building, foot by foot, and in the warren of rooms and passages below a small, psychotic Yorkshireman called Roger Plant presided over Chicago's first criminal empire, giving refuge to thieves and killers and criminals of every description.

'There were rooms for assignation and procuresses,' wrote Herbert Asbury, 'dens where young girls were raped by half-a-dozen men and then sold to the bordellos, cubicles which were rented to streetwalkers and male degenerates, and hidden rooms used as hideaways by every species of crook.'

Just over five feet tall yet full of fury, this Roger Plant apparently had a sentimental streak. He named his underworld Under The Willow, after a tree that he was particularly fond of, and historians report that the pint-sized felon would water his beloved willow by drinking from a bucket of whiskey and water and then pissing on it, urged on by his laughing, drunken cronies. It died.

'This is a frontier town and it's got to go through its red-blooded youth,' said a real-estate developer of the time. 'A church and a women's Christian Temperance Union never growed a big town yet.' With the death of Boss Daley, Chicago finally outgrew its red-blooded youth, but you feel that the city is still hauling itself from the bloody swamplands of its past.

Tough-looking cops, perhaps the grandchildren of the cops who cornered John Dillinger in an alley on the North Side or who took graft from that syphilitic czar Capone, tour downtown in white cars with *we protect and serve* emblazoned on the side. These cops all look 50 – a hard nut, lived-in, no-soda-in-that 50 – and their squad cars emit strange, unearthly beeping noises as, disappointed with the crime-free streets of clean and rich downtown Chicago, they bark apoplectic commands at recalcitrant motorists.

'*Now* you can move your car, pal – read the *sign* – no right turn, *pal*!' Meanwhile the cultured citizens of the Windy City queue peacefully for the big Robert Mapplethorpe retrospective at the Museum of Contemporary Art, an ironic choice of exhibition for such a racially conscious city. Elderly Chicago matrons tour large white rooms where huge black cocks dangle from the walls.

'Obviously Mapplethorpe had a fetish with the black male,' murmurs a guide.

No kidding! There are some beautiful monochrome portraits of Patti Smith and Cindy Sherman, some powerful self-portraits, including one of Mapplethorpe posing with a death's head walking stick just before his death (plus the slapstick – Bob with the bullwhip jammed up his ass), but the artist's message is ultimately his obsession with the *schlong noir*. Only the glossy technique and reverential presentation pull it from the leering maw of hard core, only Mapplethorpe's winning way with light and composition distinguish the work from pornography.

When you jump on the 'L', the elevated railway that runs 30 feet above the streets of Chicago, it is probably wise to refrain from thumbing through your Robert Mapplethorpe catalogue. The L was crowded, but it was quite a while before I saw any other white faces and they belonged to a pair of wary cops, sauntering cagily along an opposite platform. The best way to get to the South Side is to take a cab, and then you see other black images – innocent and bright and human after Mapplethorpe's clinical exercises – starting to appear on the billboards beyond the borders of downtown. There are black models, 40 feet high, advertising hair products and goods for the happy home in a neighbourhood where over half of the households are run by single women on welfare and the most dangerous form of transport is the elevator. There is a billboard for Arsenio Hall's chat show, Hall grinning, dapper, lean and wry, set to join Tyson and Eddie Murphy in the pantheon of contemporary black heroes. And painted all over the side of some low-rented warehouse there is: *God bless Mayor Harold Washington – the right choice for Chicago – vote Democrat.*

But Mayor Washington – Chicago's first black Mayor, a man of real vision and passion who could possibly have healed the deep and still livid wounds of the Boss Daleys days – died in office of a heart attack two years ago. His successor, the sad Mayor Sawyer, was not strong enough or popular enough to hold his administration together, and now the black population's hopes are fading fast with candidate Evans. The ancient and massive exhortation to vote for Harold Washington looks like a memorial to hope.

'The ghetto takes its revenge,' said Sandburg, but nothing happened to me when I was down on the South Side. The violence of the projects is mostly turned inwards on those who least warrant it, with the drugs and the gangs as its cheerleaders. Drugs and gangs can never seem glamorous or fun again, not after you have glimpsed these projects. The gangs are not whooping troupes of hijinks and male bonding, they are, in this city, the Vice Lords and Disciples, murderous tribes that take over your home so they can conduct their business, and they shoot each other – and anybody else who is passing – in municipal basketball courts. And as for drugs, all those harmless recreational joints and lines of your younger days are a world apart from the abject misery they inflict on the projects. Drugs and gangs come home to roost with a vengeance in the projects of America. I walked quickly in the ugly shadows of those buildings, where the illegitimate children are known as trophies, through eerily empty streets, past old men burning garbage in oil drums to keep warm, and I walked past miles, literally miles, of automobile junkyards, endless rusted pastures of scrapped cars, seemingly all the dumped autos of Middle America's freewheeling past that have now been replaced by economical little Jap numbers. And in the distance you could see the matchless beauty of downtown Chicago's skyline, sated with steely grandeur, and the silhouettes of the projects looked like cruel travesties of its glory. And at dinner that night someone – I discovered later he was another Pulitzer Prize-winner – quoted another of the alternative mottoes that Mike Royko, city sage, had come up with for Chicago.

'Where's *mine?*'

I took a ride uptown to Lincoln Square, one of what they call 'the neighbourhoods', a hard-working blue-collar community where some people are Swedes, some are Greek, some are German and everyone is an American. Mostly they were getting by; there were well-kept lawns, the *Trib* waiting in the letterbox of the picturesque houses, indulgent grandmothers taking their shining-faced charges to video stores. It was all a long way from both the lush spendour of Lake Shore Drive and from the rusty steel pastures of the South Side. Americans getting by – there were Illinois State Lottery and *we accept food stamps* stickers in the windows of the small shops, there was normality everywhere. I longed to get back to a more vivid Chicago and turned a corner past a sign screaming *Bagel Nosh presents – incredible edibles* and then I saw it, right in the middle of the road, a brown Chevrolet sitting right on the roof of a red Corvette. The drivers were gone. I stared in awe.

'Weirdest darn car wreck *I* ever saw,' a local man said, snapping a photograph.

'Can I ask you who you will be voting for?' I said.

He shot me a quick sideways glance. 'Rich Daley,' he said, squinting through his viewfinder at the beautiful car wreck.

* * *

'Jeez, not many taxis around,' said Joel Murray, brother of Bill, on the stage at Second City, where Belushi began. 'Must be some kind of Muslim holiday.'

And the next day a Palestinian cab driver took me to O'Hare where I caught my flight home, learning later in the week that Richard Daley had romped home as Mayor, but that during his acceptance speech the talk had been almost exclusively of reconciliation. In triumph, Mayor Daley seemed to be quoting not his father but Harold Washington. Maybe he even meant it.

And I remembered walking the windy streets of Chicago just before I left, seeking some eloquent symbol of the horror, the horror that is out there beyond the rich splendour of downtown, and of finding it on the wall of a dark tunnel close enough to the the lake to hear its whisper. An outraged cry from the heart, writ large, black on white. *I need your love*, it said.

Japan – In the Sticks

The Sunday Times, 20 January 1991

A S I RODE THE Kinki Nippon Railway from Kyoto to Nara, I suddenly understood how Japan rose from the ashes of 1945 to build the most potent economy in the world.

The long, clean carriage was full of every kind of *Nihon-jin* ('Japanese-person'). There were high-school kids in their distinctive uniforms – the girls dressed like sailors, the boys in those lapel-less suits sported by the early Beatles. There were shockingly beautiful *oh-eru* ('OL' – standing for Office Ladies), young women with hair down to their waists who will work for the great Japanese corporations until they meet the 'sarariman' (literally 'salaryman') of their dreams. And there were the sararimen themselves, the men in grey suits whose dedication to company and country built the backbone of the economic miracle. All *Nihon-jin* life was there.

And as the Kinki Nippon line rattled south, it was as if a spell had been cast over the train. Because the whole carriage – students, office ladies and sararimen alike – closed their brown eyes and slept: every one of them. It was then I understood their secret. These people just work harder than everybody else.

Travelling beyond the borders of Tokyo presents *gaijin* (literally 'outside-persons' – anyone not fortunate enough to be Japanese) with problems they do not encounter in the capital. Every subway stop in Tokyo has its name written in Roman as well as Japanese characters. But Tokyo is a sophisticated, cosmopolitan metropolis and this helpful habit stops at the city limits. By the time you get to the Kinki Nippon Railway, all the signs are in Japanese and it is every *gaijin* for himself.

You might learn to speak some Japanese (it's about as difficult at Italian) but you are not going to learn to read Japanese (about as easy as walking on water). There are thousands of different symbols in Japanese writing and three different writing systems, one for words and two for syllables. Basic literacy is incredibly hard work there, and it ingrains an aptitude for learning that helps make the Japanese the most highly educated people on the planet – and so the lost traveller will often find himself often relying on the kindness of *Nihon-jin*.

What you have to do is look very worried, a little frightened and, if possible, name the location where you would like to be, punctuating your wish with a wistful smile. The Japanese smile all the time. They also nod and bow a lot. The nodding is to encourage the person they are talking to, the bowing is to show respect, and the smiling is for embarrassment, nervousness, happiness – almost anything. It is very easy for an enthusiastic *gaijin* to overdo the bowing. But you can never overdo the smiling.

'Nara, *sumimasan*?' ('Nara, please?') I smiled at an Office Lady as Kinki Nippon came into a station that could have been anywhere, and the carriage awoke, the spell broken.

'*Hai*! (yes)' she said with that glorious briskness that you hear only in Japanese.

Like a fool I believed her. The Japanese are always kind when directing lost *gaijin*. Sometimes they are even accurate.

I never did find out the name of that town, but you don't wait long for a train in Japan and Kinki Nippon was soon depositing me in the ancient capital of Nara. We disembarked, leaving one lone *sarariman* on the train, still sleeping like a baby.

There is real magic in Nara. Between AD 710 and 784, this was the first capital of Japan and some of the shrines and temples of 1,200 years ago are still standing today. Nara is the only place in the world that can make Kyoto (which didn't become the capital until as recently as 794) look like Milton Keynes.

Many of the town's treasures are located in the lush pastures of Nara Park, where more than 1,000 sacred tame deer wander among the visitors, gently butting your behind with their lovely heads if they feel you are giving too many of your rice cookies to some other deer.

It was a stormy day so the *soba-ya* was crowded. *Soba-ya* are distinctive blue collar joints – noodle restaurants, serving piping hot bowls of buckwheat noodles and vegetables in a steaming tasty soup. Copious slurping is the order of the day.

The sign on the wall requested payment up front. For all of Japan's reputation as a wallet-breaking destination, it is possible for the traveller to live here cheaply. You can eat yourself into a coma in any *soba-ya* and it will never cost you more than a few pounds. Yet more yen are saved by the fact that there is no tipping in Japan.

Taxi drivers, waiters, bell boys – you don't tip any of them. And almost everything is done with love and pride. On the train back to Kyoto, I was just about to nod off when a girl in a pink uniform came down the aisle handing out *oshibori* (hot wet towels) for all the weary passengers. The Kinki Nippon Railway. They're getting there.

I spent my first night in Kyoto at a *ryokan*, a traditional Japanese inn – an exquisite, low-slung building of wood and paper, where you are so desperate not to commit a *faux pas* that you find yourself slipping out of your shoes while still only halfway up the gravel garden path.

The *ryokan* maid chuckles gently at these anxious *gaijin* antics and shows you to your room. This is the closest you will ever get to the classic Japanese sensibility. You sit cross-legged on the floor to be served tea, soup and candy by the maid, in a room where the floor is made of *tatami* (mats made of soft rice straw woven inside rush grass); the sliding walls of creamy *washi* rice paper open on to a stone garden. In the corner of the room there is the sacred *tokonoma* alcove containing a scroll and a flower arrangement. Apart from the huge Sony TV, a room in a *ryokan* would have looked like this five centuries ago. In Japan, the eternal truths are not open to interpretation or negotiation.

When staying at a *ryokan*, you take off your *gaijin* gear, put on a *yukata* – a light cotton kimono – and keep it on until you leave. You make your way through paper corridors to the *ofuro*, the Japanese bath. The Japanese use baths for soaking, meditating, relaxing – for everything, in fact, apart from washing. Washing has to be done *outside* the deep wooden bath tub – sitting down, on a low wooden stool. This is very important to get right as the *ryokan* is the home of communal hygiene. The sexes are separated, but the men and women use the same bath.

I can't pretend I wasn't a little nervous about jumping into a bath with a bunch of other guys, but I just muttered a manly '*Konnichi-wa*' (hello) and it all seemed perfectly natural.

My *ryokan* dinner was an artfully arranged, beautifully prepared banquet of miso soup, salmon, pickles, rice, tofu, wafer thin fish called nohoni and mushrooms the size of small apples – eaten sitting on the floor and lovingly served by gentle smiling women in kimonos. As I ate, my futon was being silently unfurled in the next room. The bedding would disappear in the morning while I was eating breakfast.

The traveller encounters this lavish hospitality all over Japan.

They spoil you rotten in a *ryokan*, of course, and in the impossible opulence of a fine hotel such as the Kyoto Grand, where they pipe Mozart into the sauna. Even in business hotels, where there often isn't room to swing a raw fish, for around £10 a night you will get a TV in the room, a bath and a crisp, clean *yukata* on the bed.

In many ways Kyoto is a typical busy Japanese town. *Omawari-san* (policemen – literally 'Mr Respected Walking-About') patrol crime-free streets (for every crime in Japan, there are 250 in the United States). People ride bicycles on the pavement, vending machines sell everything from Diet Coke to sake, a million little silver balls rattle in the Pachinko amusement arcade. There are restaurants with plastic replicas of meals in the window, newborn babies with luxuriant black Beatle cuts, tipsy salarymen buying 'Manga – Comic For Business Boys' in the railway station.

But Kyoto also has 2,000 shrines and temples, and no matter how many of them you see, you feel that you are missing something. 'Though in Kyoto, I long for Kyoto,' said Basho, Japan's greatest poet. Too true, Basho.

You cross the city's dry river and enter its wooden back-streets, with their infinite tangle of electrical webbing above the houses, and if you walk all day then Kyoto slowly starts to reveal itself. You soon come to learn that the temples are Buddhist and the shrines are Shinto and that most Japanese manage to incorporate both religions into their life.

At Ryoanji Temple we shuffled in stockinged feet and stared at the legendary Zen rock garden with its promise of enlightenment. At Kinkakuji we saw the heart-thumping Golden Pavilion, the three-storey temple covered in gold leaf that inspired Yukio Mishima's story of a temple burned down by a monk maddened by its perfect beauty.

But the greatest sight of all is Kyoto itself. You discover temples, gardens and shrines not marked on any map – incredibly beautiful places of worship where the believers always made me reluctant to reach for my camera.

I left Kyoto on the beautiful bullet train (known as *Shinkansen* – 'new trunk line' – in Japan) – a cosmic phallus within which a constant wagon-train of trolleys selling food and drink comes trundling down the aisle and the vendors bow upon entering and leaving a carriage. The speed and comfort is incredible – the sensation is closer to British Airways (business class) than British Rail. Outside the window, Japan's wheatfields and the purple majesty of distant mountains flashed silently by.

I had developed a noisy crick in my neck and that was how I met the Buddhist monk. He was sitting next to me sporting a shaven head and a blue business suit – a corporate Friar Tuck who, and after listening to me loudly snap the crick for a while, suddenly grabbed me by the neck and started to massage me, without even asking. I blushed hotly. Then he started on my legs. The monk told me he had been a doctor in the navy before devoting himself to Buddhism.

As the *Shinkansen* was pulling into our destination, a Western hippy girl lit up a cigarette next to a No Smoking sign. A middle-aged man walked up to her and angrily slapped the sign. She turned her back and continued to smoke. You rarely see displays of temper in Japan – harmony is everything, courtesy is everywhere – and his anger subsided immediately. He caught my eye and we smiled at each other, both of us embarrassed and ashamed. He probably thought – and I would agree with him – that Westerners had already dumped enough toxic waste around here. We were coming into Hiroshima.

At Hiroshima station there was a bewildering labyrinth of sushi restaurants. My Buddhist monk and I sat cross-legged on the floor of the one called Aji, poured each other's beer, as is the Japanese way, and ate raw fish made in heaven. My monk refused to let me pay my way. He pointed me in the right direction for my hotel and then he was gone forever.

I got lost immediately. It's not easy finding your way around when the streets have no names, only numbers. But two high-school girls – one skinny and giggling, hand over her mouth, the other chubby and competent – took me to the door of my business hotel.

Hiroshima is a bustling, lively Japanese city, teeming with people and neon. But, of course, it can never be just another city. Down by the banks of the Motosayu river, the skate-boarding kids play in the shadow of the atomic bomb dome – the former Industry Promotion Hall, the building above which the nuclear bomb exploded at 8.15 am on 6 August 1945. A gaping wreck of twisted metal and concrete, it is the only building left standing from the attack that completely flattened Hiroshima and killed – or began to kill – 250,000 people.

The dome is an effective memorial to those people, as is the cenotaph containing all their names in the Peace Memorial Park. Most effective of all is Hiroshima's Peace Memorial Museum. The catalogue of grief and horror documented in the graphic photographs, is unforgettable – upsetting beyond belief.

You can see why a lot of this material has never been released in the West. One day, in the summer of 1945, the Allies made Hiroshima resemble a concentration camp in hell. And no cause is that good.

Thirty minutes from Hiroshima is Japan's most beautiful island, Miyajima, and after seeing the museum in the Peace Memorial Park, you are more than ready for it. Miyajima is like the best dream you ever had.

You catch a train from Hiroshima to Miyajimaguchi and then take the ferry to Miyajima itself, a hilly green island where wild monkeys squawk in the tall trees and tame deer wander the streets. There is a Shinto shrine on the beach which is one of the *Nihon Sankei* – the country's three most valuable and beautiful sights. At high tide, the base of the shrine disappears and it appears to be floating on the sea.

I started up to the summit of Miyajima, realising that I had never been anywhere that smelled so sweet. There is a cable car to take you to the very top, and from there you can see New Hiroshima City in the distance, white and peaceful on the other side of the big blue bay.

And later, at night, there would be squid boats in the bay, all of them burning the incandescent lamps they cast across the waters to attract their catch. The lamps of these squid boats are so impossibly brilliant that even astronauts orbiting the earth can see them. Up in the heavens, they say, it is what you notice first about our planet – the whole of Japan, traced in a special light, the brightest light in the world.

Ghana – Heat and Faith

The Sunday Times, 5 August 1990

T HE ANTICIPATION of my first trip to Africa was tinged with an atavistic dread. My arms burning, I worked my way through the doctor's list of exotic vaccinations – meningitis, rabies, typhoid, tetanus, cholera, yellow fever and hepatitis in the rear – feeling that I was about to travel with Club Malaria to the original White Man's Graveyard.

Formerly the Gold Coast, a British colony, Ghana was famous for its exports of gold and ivory, infamous for its exports of human beings. Gold, ivory and slaves were branded before being shipped out. The forts and castles of the slaving industry still stand on the West African coastline, memorials to unimaginable cruelty in places of phenomenal beauty. Many of the governors who ran these places are buried there, dead from malaria in their 40s.

This ancient fear of fever is definitely a drawback to travelling in Africa. Because no matter how many shots you have (the Ghanaian authorities insist only on a yellow fever certificate, though your GP will insist on more), nothing can prevent your AIDS angst. Tragically, the HIV virus is endemic to the African continent, where it is known as 'the slimming disease'. It is possible to bring your own supply of disposable syringes to deal with medical emergencies but then the authorities are likely to assume that you play lead guitar for a pop group and body-search you accordingly.

It was an old Africa hand called Bob Ashworth who really allayed my fears of catching something nasty in the bush. Bob is the affable Lancashire man who owns Insight Travel, a new company formed to promote host-based holidays in the Ashanti region of Ghana. 'Don't be a tourist,' say the brash brochures. 'Be a guest.' The idea is that you stay with a host family, get to know the people and see their country while treating their culture with respect. It's not like East Africa where you spend the day taking photographs of the wildlife, then go back to a four-star hotel and tell the man from room service to bring you a strawberry daiquiri. Insight offers Africa – in your face.

The idea is that you spend 10 nights in the home of your host family, spread over 15 nights so you can take off on your own and see some more of the country. Ashworth spent six years in Africa, and he knows and loves the place. I was shamed by photographs of his small sons frolicking in the West African sunshine without any obvious medical assistance.

Insight does all it can to prepare you for Africa, though nothing can truly equip you for the continent. The friendliness of the people, the physical beauty of the place and its mind-boggling poverty are all overwhelming.

The roads make quite an impression, too. When I arrived in Accra, the Ghanaian capital, just before dawn on a Monday morning, I soon realised that I wasn't going to die of some terrible disease but would be killed in a car crash instead. It seems that if an African doesn't drive at 70 mph smack in the middle of the potted country roads then he is announcing: 'The menfolk of my tribe are all pitifully endowed.'

Insight travellers spend their first day and night in Accra, recovering from the overnight flight – it's not exactly jet lag because it's the same time in Ghana as it is in England – and from their first sight of the Third World, which leaves the senses reeling.

Many Ghanaians have tribal scars cut into their cheeks. They attract each other's attention by hissing loudly. Hissing at someone is quite okay, nobody gets offended. Ghanaians greet each other with elaborate handshakes and often you find yourself shaking hands throughout a conversation – at the start, at the end and also if someone says something particularly amusing or apposite. Sometimes you even hold hands between handshakes.

Ghanaians are both ferociously friendly and very polite. I ordered a Coke in a bar and the waiter produced a packet of straws, holding them out with the formality of a wine waiter for me to choose one. Everywhere you go you see the courtliness of poor people.

Women walk barefoot to the market, plump, sleeping babies strapped to their backs, fantastic loads balanced on their heads. There are flame trees and beggars by the side of the road. The flame trees are fantastically red, the beggars are horribly mutilated. They aren't beggars because they've drunk too much lager – they have twisted limbs shrivelled to the size of pool cues, decaying faces, or they are blind from a disease called *oncho* (caused by the black flies that swarm around fast running rivers). They walk and crawl by the side of the road where the open drains run, and wish you a long life.

Over a lunch of bean stew with chicken and friend plantain, I told my Ghanaian companion how shocked I was by the poverty. I saw no rubbish in Africa. Only an affluent society produces rubbish. Children make toys from tin cans, bottles are used again and again, plastic carrier bags are ironed and sold as luxury items in the market. Environmentalists by necessity, they have been recycling for years.

'This isn't Eastern Europe,' said my friend. 'We don't want all the things you have in the West. We want food, clothing, water, electricity, education. The basics.'

You learn fast in Africa. The next day I set off for Kumasi, home of the Ashanti and my host family, and I learned that there are no bus timetables in Ghana. The buses leave when they are full. Ghanaian full. That's very full.

The bus station resembled the evacuation from Dunkirk. There were vehicles of every size and shape, from clapboard lorries known as mammy wagons emblazoned with slogans – 'I Thank God', 'Live is War', 'Sooner or Later' – to 20-year-old taxis known as smokers because of the kamikaze speeds they reach. The taxis all had cracked windscreens and Dutch or German number plates. People were wearing Western T-shirts with incongruous slogans. There were small boys in 'I Ran the Aspen Marathon 1973' shirts, and little wizened old men with garish heavy metal shirts that boasted of their appetite for sex and drugs and rock and roll. They are living in our cast-offs in Africa, surviving on what we would consider garbage.

The place teemed with life. Outside the bus, girls with trays of bread and bottles on their heads strolled around. Inside the bus, music blasted somewhere above top volume on an exhausted stereo, barefoot merchants wandered up and down the aisle and the temperature rose to that of a microwave in hell. I was sodden with sweat, convinced that we would never leave.

A mad crippled beggar got on and made a long speech. At the end he walked down the aisle and everyone gave him some money. When I gave him some everyone smiled shyly at me and said thank you, as though some kindness had been done to them. A travelling salesman got on next and made a long ranting commercial for the sachet of powdered medicine he was brandishing. It was Third World hard sell. A few people heckled and everyone else ignored him. It was the Ghanaian cold shoulder.

Our final passenger – a man carrying four boxes of peeping, fluffy yellow chicks – climbed on and the bus groaned into life. People banged on the side of the bus in farewell. It cost 1,000 cedis for the four-hour bus ride to Kumasi, less than £2 (almost everything costs nearly nothing in British terms) and I got to watch Africa unfold before my eyes.

A smiling young preacher in a shirt and tie jumped on, stood behind the impassive driver and suggested we say prayers. The passengers closed their eyes for a moment, then everyone sang a song called Thank You Jesus. It went: 'Thank you Jesus, thank you Jesus, thank you Jesus, thank you Jesus, thank you Jesus – oh yeah.'

Africa's passion for Christianity starts to trouble you after a while. How can people with so little believe so much? You are left asking all the old theological questions that have tormented man through the ages – like if God really exists, then why didn't He install decent plumbing?

'My Lord is Good,' they sang, raising their sweet, rich voices, and it was beautiful. They kept up the prayers and hymns for two hours. I was a captive audience to the heat and faith and noise and gentleness of Africa.

As we chugged north we came to lush rainforests where 1,000 shades of green were broken only by the vivid red splash of the flame trees. By the side of the road were wrecks that turned my stomach – crushed mammy wagons, burnt-out cars, taxis crumpled under the wheels of lorries. There were small villages of wooden shacks and tin huts where the only lavish building was the church. And in all the villages, there was always one hut with a sign outside saying: 'Beauty salon.' Goats strolled through red dirt living rooms. There were children everywhere.

When I arrived in Kumasi I was met by Abena Gyamfi, who runs Insight in Ghana. Nobody had any trouble meeting me in Ghana. 'Tony will be the white guy,' I could imagine them saying. Abena picked up my bag and lugged it up a hill to a cool, dark bar. We had an Ashanti beer and caught a taxi. Copious use of the horn was in order.

I stayed with the Yeboah family in a house straight out of Karen Blixen's Africa. Mr Yeboah was the local celebrity teacher and everyone knew him as Owura – the master. Recently retired, his subject was Twi-Fante, the language of the Ashanti (English is the official language of Ghana but it is everyone's second language after Twi, Ga or Ewe, depending on their tribe).

They gave me fruit from their garden and water that had been boiled and cooled. Worried about my European stomach, they had boiled me a fridge full. Mr Yeboah opened the fridge door with a flourish. The water was kept in ancient Lucozade bottles, old jam pots, recycled containers from every corner of the larder (my stomach stayed strong and true all the time I was in Africa). There was also a large bottle of beer. They bought me a bottle of Ghanaian lager every day and always produced it after dinner. They were two of the kindest people I have ever met.

That night Mary Yeboah prepared a feast of fish, rice and fried plantain. There was also a touching bowl of Heinz baked beans in case I didn't like African food. I was moved by the sight of the baked beans but said I loved African food and that, as I saw it, baked beans were no match for fried plantain and *fufu* (a sticky yellow dumpling made by pounding plantain and cassava together with a long wooden pole). She finished laying the table and disappeared into the kitchen. I asked Owura if she was joining us.

'I'm an African,' he said. 'I don't eat with my wife.'

At first I thought he was having me on. He wasn't. She stayed in the kitchen. 'This is my office,' she told me. Kumasi is closer to London than New York, but it suddenly seemed a very long way from home.

My room had mosquito nets on the window and a huge fan above a big brass bed. I was very comfortable. I led a life of spartan luxury. There was no running water in the house but all the buckets you required. I found I could manage to make my toilette, including a daily shampoo with Vidal Sassoon's Wash-and-Go, in just under three buckets. The morality of travelling in Africa, of having fun in the midst of poverty, began to seem amazingly simple – they need the hard currency and we need our eyes opened.

The Yeboahs fussed over me constantly; they treated me like a pallid member of the family. Mr Yeboah taught me some Twi, Mrs Yeboah taught me how to make *fufu* (my Twi was more impressive than my *fufu*). Insight is ready to organise trips of all kinds but you find that among the Ashanti, things take on a momentum of their own.

We caught a *tro-tro* (a public transport truck) to a market that stretched to the horizon, a riot of heat and noise and dust where vultures like large, filthy black rags flapped and clawed at something they had found in a ditch. Tourism is practically non-existent in Ghana and the traders and their clientele marvelled at a *buroni* (white man) in their midst. I was offered water and marriage.

The best thing about Ghana is the people. Everyone treats you with a tenderness that I haven't found anywhere else. It is astonishing that this late in the century something approaching love can still exist between strangers. They say you go to East Africa to see the animals and to West Africa to meet the people. After a couple of weeks you start to feel like a very small village child when you see another *buroni* – *hey everybody, look at the white guy.*

I went to a funeral where 2,000 people dressed in the traditional garb of mourning – red togas for family members, black togas for everyone else. The man they were burying was a big-shot business-man, so there was a grand turnout. I offered my condolences to his three wives and the local chief. Despite the obvious grief of the dead man's family, funerals in Ghana are a raucous affair – they are always held on Saturdays, the bodies packed in ice until the weekend – and everyone got a big laugh out of the sight of a *buroni* in a toga.

Later that night we went dancing at the legendary Hotel de Kingsway, the home of 'high life' music for the past 40 years. It was a typical African evening. The taxi ran out of petrol on the way to the club and when we got there, the 'high life' was playing at a level that made your ear drums weep. Dancers in togas grooved around, fresh from the funeral. At midnight I was dancing with an African girl in a club where I was the only white man and – apart from feeling incredibly funky – I felt safer than I would at closing time in the Rat and Trumpet back in England. Africa is very good at making you confront all your notions about race.

One day Mr Yeboah drove me to his home village of Himan in his battered VW Beetle. We drove down roads as bumpy as ploughed fields that cut through the tall grass, steep tracks of red mud that had been baked as hard as stone. The Beetle wheezed gamely as we passed women with metal buckets on their heads going to collect water from streams and men with machetes coming back from the fields. Everybody waved, everybody smiled. In Africa they smile at strangers. We passed one village that had water and electricity and another that had none.

'Then why don't they move to the other village?' I asked Mr Yeboah.

'Because it's not their village,' said Owura.

We were going to Himan to see the fetish priest. I wanted to see a witchdoctor in action and though, as a practising Catholic, Mr Yeboah didn't go along with all this *juju* business, he was quite happy to make the introductions.

Himan was another red dirt village with no water or electricity.

There were stone houses with tin roofs and scraggy chickens in the yard fighting each other with psychotic politeness. Who would be a chicken in Africa? Girls asked when I was going to marry them and I said: '*Ohchina*' (tomorrow). A hawk swooped low over the village and a huge laughing crowd of children followed us to the witchdoctor's shrine.

In Africa, children attach themselves to you without wanting anything, or at least nothing apart from contact. Still, I had brought a large bag of sweets with me and bringing it out almost started a toffee riot. Maybe the next time those children see a *buroni* they will follow him expecting candy instead of plain human contact and I will have been responsible for killing some of the sweetness in them. But the alternative was keeping all the toffees to myself.

I had met the fetish priest once before. On that occasion he had been a shy young Rasta toying diffidently with his totems and potions. Now, allegedly possessed by the gods, he was a changed man. I took the customary two eggs, bottle of schnapps and 1,000 cedis into his shrine and there he was, sitting on a raised dais surrounded by his acolytes. He was smeared with white powder, wearing a tattered coat of many colours, and chain-smoking Benson & Hedges (a big status symbol in Africa).

He stared at me as if we had never met and wiggled his eyebrows mysteriously. He took one of my eggs and dramatically threw it out of the shrine. It smashed messily on the red dirt. He was imperious, arrogant – a man possessed. Through a nervous interpreter (Mr Yeboah had slipped off to see some relations), he gave me a list of things I must not do. No adultery. No stealing. Then he said he would give me a potion that would protect me from the jealousy of my enemies. I told him I would appreciate it.

The drums were beating outside. The fetish priest came out of his shrine to dance; now, possessed by a different god, he had slipped on a grass skirt. All this wasn't being laid on for my benefit. It was a festival to placate the gods that is held every 40 days. The drums beat from morning to night, the sun beats down and the priest is taken over by the spirits of various gods. Two-year-old children danced like James Brown. The effect on a dehydrated *buroni* was almost hallucinogenic.

The *juju* man strutted before the drummers, puffing heartily on a B&H. The god he was possessed by was a little on the testy side. He grabbed a fantastic looking girl by the hair, swung her around and dashed her to the ground. She picked herself up off the red earth and started to dance with him.

'He always dances with the prettiest girls in the village,' smirked Mr Yeboah, that old sceptic. 'It's purely coincidence.'

I said an emotional goodbye to Mr and Mrs Yeboah, Owura and Mary, on a big blue Sunday morning at Kumasi bus station. It was time to go to the coast and have other adventures before returning home. I was groggy from a bad night's sleep, but then I always had a bad night's sleep in Africa. Someone was always beating the drums as they watched over a corpse or pounding *fufu* or playing 'high life' at maximum volume. But Africa was worth it.

Slaves of Milan

Arena, May/June 1988

T OURISTS SKIP MILANO. It is first thing on a bleak Monday morning in the Eurolounge at Heathrow, and nobody here is going to Northern Italy to see the sights. Just to underline this impression of high powered, international commerce ready to get out there and generate some serious lire, Ian Rush walks into the Eurolounge just as the flight to Milano is starting to board.

'Hi, Ian!!'

'Hi.'

His skin has a sickly, poor boy pallor, the complexion of someone who had a fishfinger childhood, and he has a sad, hangdog expression that only lightens up when he sees a friendly face. Then he seems shy and touched. He has the brightest eyes I have ever seen, huge moist blue searchlights, and these beautiful Bambi peepers shine from his unhealthy face like jewels floating in a sea of suet, reflections of the sporting genius of his soul.

It is the morning after the fifth round cup match between Liverpool and Everton and Rush is flying economy with his wife of six months on a British Airways Boeing 757 to Milan. From there he will be whisked off to nearby Turin, home of Gianni Agnelli, the owner of Fiat, Juventus and Ian Rush.

Rush has not had an easy time in Italy – his lack of goals and Italian taking their toll – and he does not look happy to be going to work now. As our plane passes over the black Alps and their sun-dappled, snowy peaks, Rush starts to pick a scab on his right ear, just above the lobe. By the time we are on the ground and in the coach taking us to the terminal, the melancholy striker's ear is pouring with blood. He dabs at the wound unhappily with a piece of caramel-coloured kitchen towel.

He is met inside the terminal and whisked quickly through customs, a man who never dreamed that becoming a lire billionaire could be this hard.

* * *

Milano sprawls at the foot of the mountains, shrouded in Alpine mists and the pale sunshine of Lombardy. 'It is prosaic and winterish,' Henry James wrote of the city, 'as if it were on the wrong side of the Alps.'

The Milanesi would like that – they like to boast about their big-cocked work ethic, and they love to compare their city to New York. 'For Italians,' says the writer Gregorio Magnani, adapting Sinatra, 'if you can make it there, you can make it anywhere.'

Tired of southern sloth, thousands came to the city to work (though they head for the nearby lakes and mountains at the week-end). This is the town where they never hold their carnival on a working day. The town where the traditional '*Buon Giorno*' (good day) is often replaced by '*Buon Lavoro*' – do good work. Captains of service industries bolt a small, black, potent cup of coffee standing up in a bar and tell you, with paranoid relish, what southerners say about the Milanesi. Things like, 'Why should we work when we have the slaves of Milano?' and 'Roma eats while Milano works'. You have not experienced just how virulent a north-south divide can be until you have heard an Italian talk about his country's two nations.

Terroni is what northerners call southerners, and it is an epithet guaranteed to start a fist fight in any bar south of Florence, loaded as *terroni* is with all the fear and loathing and atavistic dread of a term like *nigger*. 'Oh, *terroni* is bad,' someone told me. '*Terroni* is very bad . . .'

But though the Milanesi are far from being lazy Latins pinching bottoms and loafing amid the sun, sea and pasta, and though they are always telling you that their country has two borders – the Alps and the Mediterranean – and that they are on the wrong side of both of them, Milano is a totally Italian city. This is, after all, the home of the glamorous *Made In Italy* label and Milano, as she is, could exist in no other country. Under that misty, industrious surface there lurks a peculiarly Italian passion. You feel it out at Linate airport when the baggage handlers stage another wildcat strike and all the foreign businessmen have to waddle down the windy runway with their own suitcases. And you feel it in the heart of the city when a soldier on leave asks you for directions and then, realising that you are a foreigner and do not speak Italian, he laughs and *hugs* you.

But most of all Milano feels Italian at night, especially when it is after one and, in a striking display of civil anarchy, all the traffic lights are switched to amber. That is when some charming slave of Milan will tell you that everything in this town is business, and all anyone thinks about in his office is *moda, moda, moda* (fashion) and

– yes – he has to be in the offices tomorrow morning but first you *have* to see this Brazilian bar or transvestite club or Hollywood (pronounced 'Ollywood), and as he comes up to another amber light, he guns the motor and slams his foot to the ground.

Definitely Italian.

SOME GRAFFITI DI MILANO: 'TIMBERLAND ARE BEST'

Now, whatever way you look at it, that sure beats 'Gooners Run Tottenham Yids', and it says a lot about the city. The *paninari* (sandwich boys) posing with spotty machismo in Italy & Italy (imagine McDonald's with cold quarter pounds and cod gold Roman columns) are obsessed with America and *moda*. But even at their dumbest – and all these ageing *paninari* think that enough nights in a Burghy bar will turn them into Tom Cruise – the Milanesi have a certain grace. 'Timberland Are Best'. You almost expect them to round it off with 'discuss'.

Actually, fashion fans, I can exclusively reveal that the sandwich boys are moving away from their Republican flyboy look and getting into a mode of *moda* that is derived from our own fair land. Downtown in Milano, near where the *pans* roam Wendy and Burghy, Quick and Italy & Italy, there is currently a proliferation of shops selling what can only be described as green wellie chic; hunting, shooting and fishing clothes, which run the gamut from heavy mock-Church's brogues to the most chinless, tweediest togs imaginable. This is all symptomatic of the way young Milanesi – unlike, say, the young people of Paris – fail to cherish and love their own culture as much as it deserves. They will grow out of it of course – the million lire suits at Giorgio's store on Via San Andrea are always only a block or two away.

Milan is a city built in a series of concentric circles which echo the borders of the city walls down through the centuries. You buy a metro ticket for 700 lire (35 pence) from a newsstand creaking under the weight of publications that are mostly concerned with AC Milan, clothes, hard core porn and horoscopes – football, fashion, fucking and the future, the great loves of the Milanesi – and then it is a clean, fast ride to the town's geographic and historic heart, the fabulous Duomo.

The Duomo – which means simply cathedral – is one wild church, the third largest in the world, a statistic that does nothing to convey the insane grandeur of the place. This Gothic extravaganza, the biggest on the planet, juts into the cool blue city sky like some mad eruption of faith – a massive white marble temple exploding with a forest of well over one hundred thin marble spires, another hundred leering giant gargoyles and a bewildering array of thousands of statues. Begun in 1387 and finished some 500 years later, the cathedral's construction has inspired an old Milanesi saying '*Lungo come la fabrica del Duomo*,' which means something is taking as long as the building of the Duomo.

Poets through the ages have struggled to convey the mad, heroic beauty of the Duomo. 'It is the most princely creation that mankind has ever taken from thought to deed,' said Mark Twain, while even the normally po-faced Henrik Ibsen was moved to write, 'Whoever designed that work ought to create a new planet and launch it into space.' Emilio de Marchi was suitably moist-eyed and Italian about the Gothic marvel. 'It's our Duomo,' he said. 'It's the church of our families, it's home, it's huge, it's all marble, it's beautiful, ornate, splendid, it's one of a kind.'

It is also a church that is still used, very much in working order. In the cool shadows inside, among the massive white columns and the infinite stained glass windows, Milanesi businessmen in their lunch hour kneel before the Madonna and child, make the signs of the cross and clasp their hands in prayer. One of them – wrapped up against February in a deep camel hair coat, squat and heavy bearded, like a company man Martin Scorsese – catches my eye. He looks like the archetypal hard nosed, go-getting Milano corporate cowboy. The sight of him – with his head bowed, his lips muttering in supplication, not worried if he gets the knees of his million lire suit messed up – is strangely moving. After long minutes lost in prayer he eventually rises and checks his watch. Five past two. Time to get back to the office.

Maybe he had time for a slug of *espresso* standing up in some bar before he got back to his desk. This is a city that is fuelled by ambition and coffee beans, and within sight of the Madonnina di Milano, the beautiful golden statue that crowns the Duomo's glory, there are literally hundreds of bars serving the need of coffee society.

Milan is the home of the 60 second coffee shot. *Cappuccino* – which is known by its pet name of *cappuccio*, or *cappucci* in the plural – is only drunk at breakfast. '*Spruzzo di cioccalato?*' means, do you want cocoa powder sprinkled on your *cappuccio*, to which you must reply with an excited, '*Si, si! Grazie mille, signorina!*' After your breakfast – which will consist of *cappuccio*, a *brioche* and a *panini* containing ham, cheese and something unexpected – I always had a fried aubergine you would die for – drinking the frothy stuff is not really on, though the Milanesi are far too sweet and cool to make a big deal out of it if you insist. Instead there is an infinite variety of coffees to bolt at the bar or linger over at a table (though the Milanesi are not that big on lingering). Take it *liscio* (straight and strong) or have a *caffe doppio* (double espresso). Have a *caffe ris-tretto* (extra strong), a *caffe freddo* (cold), *caffe fiordipanna* (with ice cream) or a *caffe corretto* (with cognac or grappa). You can take it in so many ways, but in the end there is only one way to take it. Going to the office, coming home from work, diving into a bar for two minutes on your way from A to B – drinking coffee is not a sedentary occupation – there is only *espresso*, knocked back standing up at the bar. Taken habitually, quickly, needed more than wanted. Small cups, smaller measure. Get it down, get out of there, get on with your life. *Buon Lavoro, amico.*

Money is on the streets and in the air. Memories of Italia as the hungry exhausted nation it was immediately after World War Two can be confined to the history books next to images of a bombed-out and broke Germany.

This is Italy after *Il Surpassimento* – literally 'the surpassing' – meaning that the country's standard of living has now overtaken that of both France and the UK. Milan is the slick engine of Italy's economic recovery. When the city made the cover of *Time* last summer the magazine reported a staggering increase in Italy's growth rate from 0.5 per cent in 1983 to 3.5 per cent a year later, settling down to a still impressive 2.7 per cent 18 months ago.

Unlike the UK, Italy has built up its service economy while keeping its traditional manufacturing industries very much intact. So Milan is the centre of the fashion, marketing, telecommunications and advertising (there are 680 agencies in the city) industries, while also finding room just down the motorway for steelworks, car plants and a huge chemical manufacturer, Montedison, a company with 70,000 employees that is quoted on the New York stock exchange.

'The city gives birth to more businesses than babies,' says Socialist mayor Paolo Pilliterri.

You've come a long way, *bambini*.

Milano is where you see the best looking people in the world trying to look the richest. They are pretty convincing, especially down in the Quadrilatero D'Oro, Golden Rectangle, the central area bordered by the wide, lush Via Montenapoleone (known as Montenapo

– the Milanesi are big on affectionate abbreviations) on the west side and the narrow opulence of Via Del Spiga on the east. These two streets – the Rodeo Drive and South Molton Street of Italia respectively – are formed into the Quadrilatero D'Oro by Via Manzoni on the north side and Corso Venezia on the south side. In this small, rich area, which would be easily swallowed by Soho, you will find the greatest concentration of label power in the world. This is where Stendhal's dictum that 'Milan is a wealthy republic dedicated to art and pleasure' really stands up and crows.

Montenapo has jewels from Misani and Faraone and a couple of Gucci's. There are furriers here – the women of Milano love their furs to a degree that would be morally and financially unthinkable in London; sable and mink with enough zeros on the price tag to make you go cross-eyed. Corso Venezia is for silver, china, crystal and gold, while Ettore Sottsass Jnr's Memphis outfit is on Via Manzoni. On Via Del Spiga, that rich man's alley, there is Ferre, Fendi, Lancetti and Versace. The men with their names on the labels are here too – Gianni Versace lives on the nearby Via Gesu, and Giorgio Armani, whose four shops are all in the neighbourhood, resides very comfortably on the Golden Rectangle's adjacent Borgonuovo.

This is the place where the look you see all over this town reaches its most perfect expression. It is the monied, high gloss look of the women of Milan, the lovely Milanesa, where the fashion plates melt to flesh, and blood and looks and lire walk hand in glove. The Milanesa share a concept of beauty. They all want to look this way and in the Quadrilatero D'Oro they do it to perfection.

The Milanesa look is mostly legs and fur – a boxed mass of some ritzy animal skin and taut, pencil thin legs in shiny dark tights click-click-clicking on high Fuck Me heels. They have expensively tailored black hair framing the faces of knowing angels and their brown eyes are often hidden behind shades. What they look like of course is *models*. Not the models you see flying into moda mecca at the airport or the models – sulky, skinny, droopy girls – checking into the Hotel Diane or the models out at Porta Genova. No, the Milanesa are a classic glossy fantasy made pampered flesh. The models the women of Milano look like are the ones in the magazines.

The real thing head out to Porta Genova where Fabrizio Ferri and Flavio Lucchini have their sprawling Super Studio, the largest complex of photographic and TV studios on the planet. This is the true, glossy heart of the fashion industry. Under a sky that is filled with a network of black tram lines like giant spider webs, tall thin girls from across the planet cross a small bridge with their portfolios in large, flat leather cases, their 'book', that touching begging bowl of beauty.

An infinite procession of heart thumping beauties – and more than a few ugly ducklings, the models who are 'different' or 'unusual' – cross that bridge in search of work. There are shy French ones, ballsy Americans, overpainted English roses – the more fly models come to castings clean-faced, that is, without make up – and they all head out to the endless acres of light and space at Super Studio where there is always more work and the smell of fresh emulsion paint in the air.

Fabrizio Ferri, who is a photographer as well as co-owner of Super Studio (the other owner, Flavio Lucchini, is a publisher of *moda* titles like *Donna* and *Mondo L'Uomo* – between them these guys have got it sewn up) flicks through a young designer's portfolio, quickly skipping over *The Face* cover of Isabella Rossellini. Fabrizio is looking at the book with his wife and Isabella is an old flame.

Sometimes in Milano you feel you are being suffocated by the fashion industry – *It's only frocks!* you want to scream. But out at Super Studio, in the belly of the *moda* beast, you realise that it is always much more than that. Out in this self-contained world there are 20 studio options, some of them interlocking, it is like a massive pre-war movie set, bustling with people and props, action and money. The sickly sweet smell of paint and cosmetics are every-where, and there are rooms the size of warehouses full of shoes and clothes and people pulling at them, high black rooms blazing at one end with a blinding artificial light in which a man is fanatically pol-ishing a tiny spot on a brand new car, and – in this industry where beauty is a raw material, where looks are a commodity, a talent, a skill – every minute more flesh for fantasy arrives.

'Like a meat rack,' someone observed, but the girls arriving in twos – models always run in pairs – for calls at Super Studio seemed to me to be far too human, too vulnerable, too painfully diffident to be mistaken for sides of beef. Anyone looking for a meat rack in Milano has to go to the Cimitero Monumentale after dark.

The Cimitero Monumentale is the massive, neo-Gothic burying ground of the bourgeoisie of Lombardy and along its high, imposing walls is the traditional hunting ground of the prostitutes of Milan. But the whores who ply their trade along the perimeters of this giant graveyard are transvestites, many of them in the middle of the long, painful, plenty-lire process of changing their sex.

On the Via Censio, what looks roughly like a girl is disgorged from a big white van. The *Mafioso* are in everything here and a low ranking wise guy sits quietly in a nearby parked car as the tart – a crossover between the genders – totters across the street. She is wearing an unbuttoned fur coat, high heels and a heroin glaze. Beyond her there are close to three miles of whores along the wall of the graveyard and a slow wagon train of kerb-crawling Fiats.

Most of the tarts are dressed, despite the temperature hovering around the freezing mark, in only the regulation fur and heels. I take my companion's word for the fact that most of them have tits *and* a cock. I never quite understood the sexuality of the men in this city. The best looking women in the world – the Milanesa not the models – are in this town and yet all the sex for sale is by these sleazy 'tranny' mutants. Maybe Milano men, some of them anyway, like the best of both worlds, someone suggested, while another companion predicted that, with its deadly combination of homosexuality, smack and rubber free sex, Milano is ripe for an AIDS epidemic to match the one in the city to which it likes to compare itself.

Slipping away from the tranny run, we drop into a bar for a late drink. It is in the early hours now, there are only a few people in the joint but Milano still does it right. The vodka comes in a frozen glass, the cognac comes in a warmed glass, and a Marguerita is served with a salted rim. Still looking at the world through a grappa haze – the traditional unholy trinity of apple grappa, honey grappa and the killer pepper grappa – we race home through the amber lights.

There are more trannies on a couple of the TV shows – big ugly buggers fooling no one – selling hard core videos with nursery school plotlines (the chance meeting *à trois* on the beach seemed to be a particular favourite) with all the stilted banality of the local car salesmen you see selling second hand autos on local television in the States.

When I fell asleep around four, what looked like a girl was rubbing her butt with a balloon, there was still heavy trading going on in the shadows of the Cimitero Monumentale and I was finally starting to understand the desperation with which the Milanesi bolt down their early morning *espresso*.

When it is morning in Milan you ingest your *panini* and *brioche* without ever letting your fingers touch your breakfast. Everything comes tucked up in a small paper napkin that must always be kept between fingers and food. Businessmen delicately dab their lips, drink their *pronto caffe* with heaped spoonfuls of sugar and run for their train.

Milano was the home town of Mussolini's *Fascisti* – the party was founded there in 1919 – and though there is no plaque on the lamp posts where partisans strung up and then beat to pulp the bodies of Benito Mussolini and his mistress, the unlucky-in-love Clara Petacci, there is a huge, fabulous butcher's shop called La Prima – the first, the prime – at the nearby Loreto metro, where the endless sides of prime beef hanging on hooks serve as an ironic reminder of the bloody fate of both *Il Duce* and Italian Fascism. The most permanent reminder of the city's blackshirt past is the gigantic Stazione Centrale, the building designed – as is the way with dictators through the ages – to inspire awe. It is the city's major railway station and still in full working order – even if these days the winged horses the size of small office blocks on top of this Olympian ideal look a little laughable.

Italy is a country forever stumbling on the rubble of its past. All over Milan there are the bomb craters of construction work and signs boasting of the building of the town's third metro line – 'The Third Line Advances!' Except that the third line is advancing at snail's pace and has been doing so for years because the construction work keeps unearthing more priceless archaeological ruins.

Up in the misty streets of Milan the girls in fur click by on their heels and their younger brothers or sisters exchange Burghy-flavoured kisses in the middle of the Galleria. It is real teen tongue-down-your-throat passion, for one of the many fine things about the Milanesi is that they have no shame. They heavy pet in public, they double park, treble park, sideways park, and even the haggard masturbators buying their wet sex, anal sex, Ilona Staller sex, hard core wank rags from the newsstands do so with no furtiveness and stand in the street examining their purchases with frowning interest.

Milanesi outbursts are always inventive, curses tending to invoke images of despair and pain. There is, *Non rompere le balle* (don't break my balls), and that old standard, *Mi stai sul cazzo* (you're on my prick), plus the three little pig curses – *Porca Madonna* (pig Madonna), *Porco Dio* (pig God), and, best of all, *Porca Miseria* (pig misery).

They are big on hand gestures. The undersides of the chin quickly brushed with the back of the hand (don't break my balls), the same gesture executed slowly (a Lombardy shrug) or the forearm quickly chopped with the side of the hand (let's go, *amico*).

In more reflective moments, the Milanesi murmur the word, '*Bo*', which is not so much a word as an existential gasp, a philosophical shrug of the soul. '*Bo*.' One time my taxi – yellow cabs only here in the Big Olive – swung round the corner into a misty, lemon coloured street that was paralysed with traffic.

'Bo,' my driver said quietly to himself, meaning we come from dust, we return to dust, this is a brief intermission, that's the way it is. 'Bo.'

Milan is too Italian to truly emulate the pressured, cooking atmosphere of New York, though the city does sprint at around the same pace as dollar belt cities like St Louis, Chicago or Houston, places where people come for days at a time to do business and get out again, cities with a lot of visitors and a zero rating of tourists. But for all its Lombardic work ethic, the Big Olive has a delicacy, an easy grace about it that exists on all levels here from the garden of the Hotel Diane where Paulo Roversi, a 16 million lire a day fashion photographer, meets Nino Cerruti to discuss his new catalogue, all the way down to the tiny bars on Corso Garibaldi where street sweepers and builders drop in for a mid-afternoon liquor or a glass of Sassela Valtellina.

And down in the Piazza La Scala, where the souvenir stalls are selling small golden replicas of the Madonnina, La Scala ashtrays and Ruud Gullit hats (a red and black AC Milan baseball cap and dreadlock wig combined), you can pick up your copies of the pink daily sportspaper, *La Gazzetta Dello Sport*, and the glossy monthly, *Forza Milan*! (come on/go for it/let's do it, Milan), where students of the British game are surprised to find – among the usual action shots, match reports and profiles – a series of photographs of star players, the cream of world football, hard at work in their kitchens. For one of the most popular features in this AC Milan club magazine are players' recipes (Mario Bortolazis' *Quaglie Con Riso* – quail in rice – looked particularly tempting). No wonder some of our boys find it hard to settle out here.

And when you are leaving Milano, when you are on the road to the airport somewhere between the pale mountains and the hazy, lire-crazy Big Olive itself, it suddenly hits you how you are going to miss this place.

And you think of tonight, when you will be back home, and how the bridge at Porta Genova will be empty but the garden of the Hotel Diane will smell of campari and soda, and of how they will soon be heading for the pink and white neon of Le Tre Gazzelle on Corso Vittorio Emmanuele for a 60 second *espresso* hit. And of how, much later, the drums will be beating at Leoncino – 'the little lion' – the secret Brazilian club down a dark flight of stairs on Corso Garibaldi, and of the whores lining up for a couple of miles by the walls of the Cimitero Monumentale, and when you remember what it is like in the early hours hurtling towards a string of locked amber lights you think to yourself . . . *ah, Forza Milano . . . Bo.*

Hong Kong – Bright Lies, Big City

Arena, July/August 1990

> '*She came through the turnstile and joined the crowd waiting for the ferry: the women in cotton pyjama suits, the men with felt slippers and gold teeth. Her hair was tied behind her head in a pony-tail, and she wore jeans – green knee-length denim jeans. That's odd, I thought. A Chinese girl in jeans. How do you explain that?*'
>
> Richard Mason, *The World of Suzie Wong*

EX TOURISM MAY BE morally reprehensible but there's no denying it's a great way to meet girls. The foreign devil in the Far East is confronted by the potent myth of the Oriental woman. There's just no getting around them out here. Your first taste of the Far East is overwhelming anyway – nothing in Europe or North America could prepare you for this assault on the senses – and nothing is more overwhelming than the beauty of the women.

The *gweilo* – white ghost, foreign devil – and the Oriental woman have been an item from way back. This has been one of the most popular private obsessions of the Western male. From Pierre Loti's book *Madame Chrysanthemum*, the story of a French naval officer who had an affair with a Japanese geisha in the nineteenth century, to its spin-off, Puccini's *Madame Butterfly*, through Richard Mason's *Suzi Wong*, right up to Schoenberg and Boubil's *Miss Saigon*, the Oriental woman has been celebrated, mythologised, idolised down the ages. Synonymous with sexual licence – and a kind of battered, world-weary *amour fou* – she has sold airline seats and theatre tickets, her promise has put a spring in the step of generations of sailors on shore leave and GIs on R and R. In the best book about Hong Kong, *Hong Kong: Epilogue to an Empire*, Jan Morris writes of this ancient fever.

'From the beginning Hong Kong seems to have been more prurient even than most such colonial settlements, partly because of the climate perhaps, partly because European males have always been attracted by nubile Chinese females, partly because the early settlers were often men of vigorous appetite and flexible morals, and partly because the air of Hong Kong seems to suggest that in sex, as in most other things, anything goes. Even in High Victorian times, it appears, English gentlemen might acceptably flirt with Chinese women, as they certainly might not with African or Indians. The London *Graphic* reported with amusement, in 1872, the response of an Englishman disembarking in Hong Kong when a pretty Chinese girl asked if she could wash his clothes for him: "Yes, and me too, if you like, my duck of diamonds!" '

When William Holden met his true love and duck of diamonds Suzie Wong on the Star Ferry, their first conversation tried to establish if she was 'Good' or 'Bad', because there is nowhere quite like the Far East for putting that ancient Madonna/Whore divide between women. The great big grey area of morality that we have in the West just doesn't exist out here. Leaving a dinner party in Hong Kong one night I started placing innocent goodbye kisses on the cheeks of the women present and three Chinese girls backed up against the wall, shaking with embarrassment and fear, as if I were a Japanese soldier approaching them with a bayonet in one hand and my cock in the other. There are girls out here – impossibly slender, the blackest hair, the brownest eyes – who can break your heart at 50 paces. As is the Chinese custom, they adopt English names for use in business or in their dealings with gweilos and the names they choose are invariably golden oldies like Irene and Mabel and Janet. You see some phenomenal, Bambi-eyed beauty and discover later that your heart gave an extra beat for a girl called Doris.

Aesthetically, these women can't be beat. The *cheong sam* – high-neck, slit to the waist, tight as skin – could only ever be worn by a girl from this sweet corner of the world. Thin, delicate, leggy, they make you sigh with pity for the great lumbering Western brood mare with her scalped legs, sagging breasts and hair coloured by a bottle. Emotionally, it is easy to misread them, to mistake their charm for total passivity. The Oriental woman is capable of revealing a toughness that her myth rarely mentions. Marriage is never far from a good girl's mind and if a gweilo is reluctant to embark on what Shelley called 'the longest journey', then the Chinese girl is quite capable of spitting in his eye as she walks up the aisle with another guy. Hong Kong is a place of enormous wealth – a teacher here who asked her class of five-year-olds where leather came from received the answer 'Gucci' – but you always feel that this is life lived without a safety net. There are few laws, no welfare state and a future that contains the People's Liberation Army. The women are tough because they have learnt they have to be.

And then there are the other girls, the bad girls, the bar girls, who are often Filipino because there is a very strict economic apartheid at work in Hong Kong. The Japanese are at the top and the Filipinos are at the bottom (both Okinawa and Manila are only a few hundred miles away). The Japanese buy and the Filipinos sell.

They swarm over you when you arrive at that kind of bar because they earn a commission on every Hong Kong dollar you spend. You can pay a bar fine and take a girl out. You can take two, three, five, all of them out if you want. How are your moral brake pads? How big is your credit card limit? In Hong Kong you have to beat off your wildest dreams with a big stick, and you soon realise what warm, sweet-natured girls these Filipinos are. You soon find yourself saying things like, 'Boy, I hope you don't meet too many *creeps*.' Watched over by a smiling, gold-toothed fat old *Mamma-san*, they slip you free beers and offer you one on the house. Hearts of gold. Truly.

'Bangkok,' one of them chanted at me. 'Manila, Hong Kong.'

'How did you get here?' I said.

'Someone signed a contract at home,' she said, 'and so here I am.'

And rumour has it that if you paid that bar fine and stumble with your duck of diamonds out into Hong Kong's frantic neon glow, you would later watch her sitting naked on the edge of a hotel bed, talking in Cantonese into the phone as she calls the card company for authorisation of payment. Then they say that from a bag also containing her stage clothes and a gross of industrial-strength condoms she would produce one of those metal machines that they use for taking the imprint of a charge card. So they say. All major credit cards accepted. Very efficient. Very Hong Kong.

Hong Kong is God's Chinatown. There's an ecstatic feel to the place, heightened by the knowledge that the place has seven more years to go. It smells of money and sex, duck soup and avarice. When you are in Hong Kong, it seems a crying shame that one day you will have to die. Whatever it is like after 1997, it will never be like this. 'The kingdoms of the world lay before us,' Jan Morris wrote in a 1974 piece called 'Anglo-China', describing the view from Hong Kong's highest point, Victoria Peak. 'The skyscrapers of Victoria, jam-packed at the foot of the hill, seemed to vibrate with pride, greed, energy and success, and all among them the traffic swirled, and the crowds milled, and the shops glittered, and the money rang.'

Crowded Hong Kong, jam-packed with nearly six million people, all of them – merchant banker, Wanchai bar girl, Chinese baby, Japanese businessman – howling out for life, howling out for more. Nowhere in the history of mankind did people ever live as closely together as this. Lines of tower blocks sweep unbroken across the skyline. Washing dries on a million verandas that are crowded with potted plants, vegetation to placate the Gods who are very touchy about *feng shui* (the Chinese law of placement that keeps the balance between all things). Sometimes one of these potted plants falls from up around the thirtieth floor and, if your luck's out to lunch, you're a dead man.

The tropical weather arrived early this year and Hong Kong was hot, rainy, humid and shrouded in the mists of the South China Sea. Technically Hong Kong is a colony containing 235 islands, most of them uninhabited rocks, plus a rugged tip of the Chinese mainland. In reality the place is known as a 'territory', which is what they used to call untamed land in the United States and seems totally appropriate in this frontier town that somehow manages to combine a sophisticated, metropolitan glamour with an edge of Oriental anarchy.

Life in Hong Kong is focused on the water front, the Fragrant Harbour (*Heung Gong* in Cantonese) that gave the place its name. On Hong Kong island itself is the corporate grandeur of the Central Business District – I. M. Pei's Bank of China glitters in the mist, Norman Foster's Hong Kong and Shanghai Bank gazes balefully down at the withered rickshaw boys. Behind Central (formerly Victoria) on this steep, crowded island is the small Chinese area – supermarkets, restaurants, temples, shops, houses – and beyond that Mid-Level, the lush apartments where the gweilo expats make their home. At the very top of the island is Victoria Park and the folks who live on the hill, the rich Anglo/Chinese you read about in the *Hong Kong Tatler* ('*Suns Shine* – The marriage of Mr David Sun and Miss Christina Lee was a spectacular occasion. Their wedding attended by 1,000 distinguished guests was followed by a cocktail reception in the Grand Hyatt's ballroom. More than 4,000 roses, lilies and lilacs were flown in to decorate the hotel.'), living out their lives in fantastic lofty splendour, counting down the days to Year Zero.

The best hotels hug the harbour and from your plush suite at the Hilton you can gaze across the foggy Fragrant Harbour at Hong Kong's other half, Kowloon, the bustling tip of the Chinese peninsula, only a dollar ride away on the legendary Star Ferry that constantly shuttles between Hong Kong island and Kowloon. On the Kowloon side you find Hong Kong's cosmic shopping malls, its Chinese residential areas and the heart of its nightlife. Bars, clubs, restaurants, markets, teahouses, *daipaidongs* (fast-food street stalls), all of them roaring well after the witching hour, all of them nestling comfortably in Hong Kong's rampage of endless neon (the place is addicted to neon). Beyond Kowloon are the New Territories, which contain 90 per cent of the territory's land mass, though little of its action. And beyond that is Red China.

In Hong Kong – and Kowloon and the New Territories all count as Hong Kong – there are still buildings going up, there are still hotels and banks being built where multinational corporations are consulting the *feng shui* geomancers to ensure that the gods are pleased with the construction. You can be forgiven for thinking that it is business and pleasure as usual in Hong Kong, that the place is looking towards the future with complete confidence. This is far from the case. 1997 – the Year of the Ox, the year Hong Kong reverts to Chinese rule – has been breathing down the neck of Hong Kong ever since 4 June 1989, date of the Tiananmen Square massacre in Peking. I met a 29-year-old Hong Kong Chinese who works as a PA in one of the largest merchant banks and she was furious that all her friends – repeat *all* her friends – have already left Hong Kong for Canada, Australia and the United States.

'You can't understand the fear if you are protected by a passport,' she said, adding that I should tell the provincial racists of England not to worry about being swamped by millions of Chinese. 'Do they think I would go to *Yorkshire*?' she snorted elegantly with a contemptuous toss of her black mane. 'I was born under the British flag – but they will not give me a passport.'

It is estimated that 99 per cent of Hong Kong's doctors want to leave before 1997 – 'Only after they've been paid,' said one gweilo cynic – but I met a young lawyer from England who had fallen in love with the place and planned to stay even after the Reds roll in. That's Hong Kong's greatest contradiction – it was built for commerce, it is run for profit, and yet there is a deep and abiding, profound love for Hong Kong in the hearts of many of the people that live here, whether Chinese or gweilo. The young lawyer is from Newcastle. He can speak perfect Cantonese, he studies the martial arts, he loves a girl who flies for Cathay Pacific. And he couldn't stop playing that old Doors song, 'Roadhouse Blues', Jim Morrison's voice singing the blues deep into the Hong Kong night.

'The future's uncertain and the end is always near ... save our city ... right now.'

But it doesn't look like anything can save Hong Kong from the great British sell-out. In the bookshops a work called *How To Emigrate* was doing good business, information about visas – that insurance against life under Peking – was everywhere. You are going to have to catch Hong Kong while you can.

The British presence in what the men of Empire used to call 'Honkers' is minimal. Hong Kong is a British invention, but it has always had a Chinese heart. Of the six million or so residents, only about 120,000 are not Chinese, and these expatriates are drawn from every corner of the globe. There are only minimal reminders that Hong Kong represents the eleventh hour of the British Empire. There are the turbaned Indian doormen everywhere from fancy hotels to clip joints, giving the place a faint tang of the Raj, there are the throwback schoolchildren in their old-fashioned caps and blazers and, up on the steep hills behind Central, a wet, dead-looking Union Jack hangs limply above Victoria prison on a mountainous road called Old Bailey Street.

Wander a few blocks off the well-worn gweilo tracks, and you are soon reminded that you are deep in Asia. Just behind the glittering corporate skyline of the Central Business District there is a winding street called Hollywood Road, named not after Tinsel Town but a small, leafy village in Merry Olde England. At the far end of Hollywood Road is the Man Mo Temple, the oldest temple in Hong Kong, a place of worship for both Buddhists and Taoists, and by far the strangest and most alien place I have ever entered in my life (Chinese religion is a heady brew of Taoism, Mahayana Buddhism and Confucian ancestor worship). At the gate a small herd of ancient female beggars pounce on the visiting gweilo, jostling you with their palms outstretched, their corrugated faces impassive, always completely and utterly silent. But after you get past the beggars, everyone ignores you.

The Man Mo Temple is dedicated to two Gods – Man, who is the god of Literature, and Mo, the God of Martial Arts and War. Man takes care of civil servants and statesmen and Mo is worshipped by the police and the Triads. At the far end of the temple, through an atmosphere choked with incense and paper burning in huge stone drums – this turns out to be symbolic money drawn from the 'Bank of Hell' for use in the afterlife – you can make out the two black Gods sitting on their altar. Man wears red robes and Mo wears green.

Through the temple's thick fog you can see two sacred brass deer (representing longevity), other smaller altars for lesser Gods and figures symbolising the Eight Immortals who protect the temple from evil. Red and gold are everywhere, the colours dominating the Chinese temples as much as they do in a Chinese restaurant or at a Chinese wedding ceremony. Red and gold represent wealth and power. Even at their most spiritual the Chinese – born Capitalists to a man – are protecting their status and taking care of business. The excited worshippers, bobbing their heads and burning their Bank of Hell money, the profusion of sacred images and the lung-clenching, mind-warping perfumed smoke all combine to make the Man Mo Temple a powerful, almost hallucinogenic experience for a gweilo raised in the polite faith of Christianity. You stumble back out into Hollywood Road just when you were starting to sway on your feet. It's a long way from sharing a cucumber sandwich with the vicar.

You will see a shrine to Mo, God of the art of war, in every Hong Kong police station. The police need all the help they can get. The drug that is destined to be the crack of the Nineties, called LA Glass or Ice, is being cooked up in Taiwan and South Korea, and Hong Kong is the great gateway to the West. This Ice stuff is supercrack, paracrack, causing an almost immediate seven- to ten-pound weight loss, provoking days without sleep, violent mood swings from feelings of God-like omnipotence to suicidal depression, hallucinations, psychosis and paranoia.

An even more insidious threat is posed by the Triads, as deeply integrated into Hong Kong life as the Mafia in Sicily or the IRA in Ulster. The Triads feature in TV commercials where law-abiding Hong Kong Chinese are invited to report intimidation to a confidential telephone number. Though the women and babies of Hong Kong can be shockingly beautiful, these community gangsters – their hair worn in long rats' tails at the back, their eyes and mouth setting into three mean razor cuts when they get mad – are no oil paintings.

The Triads are big on blades, low on efficiency. The week I was in town there was a mass carve-up that went badly wrong. Some people were meant to be taught a lesson – nothing more – and a few of them ended up bleeding to death. Recently a man was meant to have a tendon in his leg cut, was slashed too deeply and ended up crippled (they say the inept knife-man was executed). The Triads delegate a lot of work, often to non-members who are anxious to impress, and this is when things go wrong. A Scottish lawyer of my acquaintance told me they often hire kids, or ship in some paddyfield psycho from mainland China, get him to make a hit or do a job, and then ship him back home with £20 in the pocket of his Mao jacket.

A cop that I ran into – and there is nowhere like Hong Kong for seeing life's great parade, you are constantly mixing with cops and lawyers and whores and sailors, and feel like you are walking through a Damon Runyon story – told me that morale in the police force is low because after 1997 they will be viewed as the arm of imperial oppression by the Communists. He was a gweilo, reluctantly planning to head home, and he said that it was far worse for the Hong Kong Chinese cops, who fear for their future in the territory, but who, like most Hong Kong Chinese, don't have the status to get out before the fall. And he predicted sparks flying when the 14 K Triads and the People's Liberation Army eventually meet. The razor-toting hoods of Capitalism and the murderous enforcers of Communism – a real clash of cultures, not to mention haircuts. Europe may feel outside of history now, but in the Far East all the old conflicts are still raging.

Yet you always feel safe in Hong Kong. In New York crime is random, in London crime is mindless and in Hong Kong crime is commercial. Criminal activity, like so much else, is profit-motivated. You wander narrow foreign streets, black as the grave or violent with neon, at all hours of the day and night, and you never feel threatened. Of course it is possible to get into big trouble in Hong Kong, but it's not on the set menu.

Just like Manhattan – the place Hong Kong is spiritually twinned with – the Fragrant Harbour relishes its reputation for toughness and an excessive desire for gain, but just like New Yorkers, the people of Hong Kong are capable of boundless generosity, touching and unexpected kindness. Within minutes of your first meeting, people are inviting you into their homes, onto their boats, and into their lives.

I stood on a Mid-Level veranda with another foreign devil, looking at the spangled mountains of tower blocks as the smell of his Chinese girlfriend's hot pot came from the kitchen. The night before, we had taken his company's junk to an idyllic island called Lamma, a two-man crew steering our multi-racial party to the best fish I have ever tasted and sailing us back to Hong Kong at midnight, the harbour glittering like a good dream. It was hard to believe – and too cruel to bear – that it would all be long gone in ten years. I told my gweilo friend that this place was too good to lose, too sweet to let go. The Hong Kong Chinese should all come to England. My gweilo friend told me to forget it.

'I'm not being cruel,' he said, 'but for all the cosmopolitan, educated Chinese here, there are many more who were peasants on the mainland not so long ago, and they would never feel at home in England. We should certainly allow more into England – but Hong Kong is China.' He pointed out the shallow pool of water outside the tower block directly below us. 'That's the Hopewell Centre. Because it's round, it has bad *feng shui*. So the architect had to put the pool of water there to counteract the building's roundness and give it good *feng shui*. See?' he said, as his girlfriend called us in to dinner. 'Hong Kong is China.'

What will be left in 1997? Sometimes I think a few million pea-brain Reds in green pyjamas are not enough to crush the spirit of this place. But when you see the numbers and the quality of the people leaving – specifically the Hong Kong Chinese who do not have the insurance of a foreign passport, who do not have the luxury of being able to head for Kai Tak international airport if the going gets tough, the ones that are leaving *now* – then it is hard to see how it can possibly survive in anything remotely resembling its present state. Beautiful and loose, this is Hong Kong, and when the money goes, she goes too. By the time the Communists get here there could be nothing left, or at least nothing worth having.

When the tropical rain stops you step outside the Hilton where the trams rattle under towering silver banks and the clouds hang low over golden skyscrapers, you walk down to the Star Ferry, where another plane load of doe-eyed Filipino girls has just arrived, and catch the boat to Kowloon for dim sum ('little hearts') at the Kar Luen Lau ('spring moon') in the Peninsula hotel. Trolleys with small morsels of steaming food in bamboo baskets trundle past tables full of women who lunch – rich, glossy Hong Kong Chinese women from Rolls Royce heaven on Victoria Peak (there are more Rolls Royces here per head than anywhere in the world). Their men are out chasing the Hong Kong dollar but their daughters are with them along with the odd, middle-aged gweilo broad, looking intimidated in the face of all the unapologetic wealth of the ladies from the Peak. They drip jewellery and seem like a peculiar strain of Mid-Atlantic women, glossy Oriental amazons combining Anglo class-consciousness and American materialism. They say things like, 'Marriage? I have had many offers,' and 'He must have a private jet,' and 'Are you going back to Emporio?' Naive gweilo that I am, I was shocked by their lack of sympathy for the Vietnamese boat people who languish in the squalid camps of Hong Kong.

'Forget all that talk about Thai pirates . . .'

'They only come the last few miles by boat . . .'

'The girls arrive in nail polish!'

'And there are gangsters in the camps . . .'

Hong Kong's heart hardens at the mention of refugees from Communism. There are six million of them here already. And runaways from other shades of oppression too. On Sunday the small park near the Star Ferry Pier fills with thousands of Filipino women – maids, domestics, cleaners, bar girls, anything menial, anything where you spend a lot of time on your knees – getting together on their one day off. In a place that springs so many sights on you – from the moment your plane comes screaming in through the skyscrapers to land at the inner-city airport, to the moment you look down on Babylon's endless beauty from Victoria Peak – this is one of the most stunning.

It is an army of Filipino women, spilling out of the park onto the elevated walkways between the office blocks and shopping malls. They sit on the ground in the rain, laughing, chatting, shouting – they make this phenomenal high-pitched keening noise, like a huge flock of exotic birds – and they swap photographs from home – the things they left behind, pictures of lost men, lost children, faces squinting in the Filipino sun – they eat canned meat and rice, they read magazines with titles like *Love and Hororscope*, they play hopeful, spunky tapes on cheap cassette players. Women singers seem to be especially popular. They grab each other excitedly, brown eyes flashing, while Jody Watley and Madonna sing for this scattered tribe, this Filipino diaspora, under the imposing shadows of the Hilton and the Hong Kong and Shanghai Bank.

'Only boys who save their pennies make my rainy day . . . for we are living in a material world.'

And they dance, they shriek, they shout to be heard above their own noise, they organise impromptu markets, they comfort each other. And of course it wasn't fair, it wasn't fair that they had fled the poverty of the Philipines and all they had to show for it were the worst jobs Hong Kong could offer, all they had were mats on a stone garden, meat from a tin can and each other. It wasn't fair, but they didn't seem to mind. They were having a raucous good time and I realised that all the testimonies to the Filipinos that I had heard from old Far East hands, all that sentimental talk about their sunny, optimistic natures in the face of life's cruel ironies, I realised that it was all true.

When I came off the Star Ferry later that night the stone garden by my hotel looked like a garbage bomb had hit it. It looked like the aftermath of a Cup Final or a festival, it looked as if a whirlwind of revelry had blown through the place. And among the torn scraps of *Love and Hororscope* magazine, and the empty cans and plastic spoons, there were still a few tiny Filipinos lingering in the park. But they didn't look so happy any more. Because they had nowhere else to go. You see it all the time here.

Saturday night in Hong Kong. It is possible that there are places where you can have a better time out on the town – but my travels have yet to take me there. Hong Kong steals your wallet when you arrive and 10 days later shows you where you can get everything for free.

'A few of us are going to have a curry,' said my Scottish lawyer friend. 'Want to come?'

He made it sound like a takeaway from the Taj Mahal on Holloway Road, but naturally it turned out to be a huge party on the upper reaches of Mid-Level in honour of the head of his firm, fresh off the plane from London. A crack team of white-suited chefs from the sub-continent served the best Indian food I have ever tasted. The visiting taipan told me that his company would stay in Hong Kong until the Communists made it impossible for them to stay. My friend and I slipped off into the night.

We jumped in his yellow jeep, picked up the lawyer from Newcastle and headed for the cross-harbour tunnel. The road to Kowloon was slick with rain. 'It's so easy to overturn these jeeps,' said our driver, putting his foot down. We steeled ourselves with drinks at Canton Road's Hot Gossip, the Mecca for Hong Kong nightlife, and walked across to Club Volvo.

Club Volvo is certainly a trip. It has nothing to do with the car of the same name, a fact that has caused the Scandinavian motor manufacturers considerable grief, and their five-year battle to change the club's name is back in the courts again. This being Hong Kong, however – where rules are left unmade rather than broken – they have been having trouble doing anything about it.

Imagine Buckingham Palace turned into an upmarket knocking shop and you are on the way to picturing Club Vulva – sorry, Volvo. It is a huge, palatial expanse of temptation. You walk through the door and are met by about two dozen beautiful Chinese girls wielding torches, one of whom escorts you half a mile through the dimly-lit, gaudy interior to your table. It is also possible to be driven to your table in a little golden, custom-made replica Rolls Royce, and you soon get used to the sight of this car steering Japanese businessmen to their table past acres of chrome, mirrors and women. There are getting on for a thousand 'hostesses' in Club Volvo. Their look is feather, boas, high heels, satin dresses – they dress like the Pointer Sisters.

As soon as you arrive at your table you are joined by an equal number of hostesses. There is a clock on your table and this is switched on. It records the time and drink that you and your smiling escorts so carelessly consume. The fine for damaging this clock is HK$50,000 (around £5,000).

The girls come from Macao, Peking, Mongolia, the Philippines, the New Territories and even one or two from Hong Kong. You can talk, dance, you drink, but basically the relationship is one-directional. You are expected to take them home. They always ask you what hotel you are staying at, it immediately says something about your status and character – like asking what star sign you are. On the little menu, the bar fine – 'escort service charge' – is listed right there alongside the price of beer and cognac. When it became clear that we were just passing through on our endless night of revelry, they turned off the light on our table. It means you are not a player.

We moved on to China City, which was a little less regal than Club Volvo, though almost as huge. These Pointer Sisters soon realised that we were just three gweilos who were already in love with good girls who happened to be elsewhere, but it was okay. Because after a while you realise that these are regular girls – if you wanted to, you could get them to go to the movies or dinner with you, though it would probably not be a smart move. Because then maybe you would go to bed, and maybe you would fall in love – and then definitely the black moment would come when you would wonder what your brown-eyed darling was getting up to at work tonight.

So we went back to HG's – Hot Gossip – where Rick the manager explained to me why nowhere else in Hong Kong has the allure of this place. 'Because the Cathay Pacific girls come here,' he said. 'And the gweilos come because of them.'

At five o'clock in the morning we were in a maelstrom called Boobs, a reeling expat bar that defies the Hong Kong dawn, and I pulled on my Tsing Tao beer wondering what would happen to the Rolls Royce in Club Volvo when the Communists come.

And it occurred to me that, apart from Club Volvo, which is something else, everywhere we went we got in for free. The Scottish lawyer jerked his thumb at the Geordie lawyer.

'He has big face,' he said solemnly. It's a Chinese thing.

Someone back home had told me that one of the best views of Hong Kong harbour was Kowloon side in the bar of the Regent hotel. So on my last night in town I went alone to the Regent and sure enough there it was – behind giant glass walls that reached from floor to ceiling, the Fragrant Harbour shimmered in the South China Sea, this beautiful offspring of greed and love, always held by Asia, forever dreaming of the West.

And as I was leaving the Regent I heard some ghostly music come faintly from down an empty hall. The sound was so low that at first I thought I was imagining it, still a little scattered from Saturday night, but I followed the music all the way down the hall until I eventually came to a private party in full swing. It was a reception thrown by the Vancouver Property Exhibition for the Hong Kong Chinese who were planning to make their new lives in Canada and it was a potent reminder that there were probably some fine views on the Titanic.

Soviet Union – Tales from Tashkent

Arena, January/February 1988

YOU KNOW YOU ARE GETTING OLD when the Red Army starts looking young. Passport control at Moscow airport is staffed by spotty, 17-year-old soldiers, all these skinny kids in drab olive green uniforms and scuffed jackboots who are presumably considered too weedy for some of the other activities that the Russian army are currently engaged in.

Like the country they serve, these boys are badly clothed and touchy beyond belief. You stand in a glass box scored with height measurements and watch one of these pock-marked faces twitching with suspicion on the other side of the screen. The unknown soldier checks the height you allege in your passport with what the glass box decrees, he sceptically paws your visa, he endlessly compares your passport photo with your face.

The paranoia at passport control is contagious and, before they let you out of there, you find that you are sweating. The casual, unthinking oppression gets to you in the end and something inside you feels as if it is suffocating. It is a feeling you never really shake off in the Soviet Union.

Moscow's distinguishing feature is the delicate touch of Stalin's town planning. Georgian Joe may have been moved from Lenin's side in Red Square but the mark of his heavy hand is everywhere. This is a city built to inspire awe and ease troop movements. Eight, 16, even 32 lane roads are commonplace, and it is said that a car that is only a gleaming dot on the bleak horizon when you start to cross will mow you down before you reach the other side.

This coarse megalomania, the Russian tendency to a grotesque grandeur, is reflected in the infinite tower blocks, those monumental rabbit hutches of equality. In his brilliant *Among The Russians*, Colin Thubron wrote of 'the gigantism of a people troubled, in their most secret selves, by fear of inferiority – a nation which centuries of Tartar domination held back from Europe.' Even the massive blocks of flats look unsure of themselves, for Stalin's skyscrapers are topped with neon advertising hoardings – the only kind you will see in the USSR – for the Communist Party. 'The Aims Of The Party Are The Aims Of The People', 'The Soviet Union Is The Source Of Peace'. Banal, gaudy and all over the place, these commercials for that nervy bully the State soon became as easy to ignore as a Marlboro billboard.

Down on the Arbat, touted by Intourist propaganda as the St Germain of Moscow, there are young women in cheap shoes and plump housewives pushing 40 with *glitter* around their eyes. The women here have a concept of glamour that belongs to an insane air stewardess.

In the metropolis of the common man, this pleb mecca, the shabby sometimes rubs shoulders with the surreal. Two big soldiers, their dumb faces frowning, stare at a street artist's abstract paintings while holding hands (holding hands with your friend here is like buying him a drink in the west). Like Slavic streetwalkers, old women and girls of eleven strut around in fishnet tights – not to look like steamy Siberia-bait but because tart hose was all that came in with the last shipment of tights.

Women trudge through the rain in their indoor slippers, huge fluffy balls and nylon rabbit's ears splattered with mud and grime. You see queues waiting for hours outside restaurants that are half empty. And although this is a land totally starved of western culture, one stall on the Arbat is inexplicably selling a bizarre memorial plaque to Creedence Clearwater Revival with John and the lads in suitably heroic pose.

Among the young women you are jolted by sudden outbreaks of beauty. There are brown-eyed blondes, pale blue-eyed brunettes, girls with Estonian colouring or Tartar cheekbones that turn your head around. But the old women are squat and rough, hell's grandmother, short, bossy, cubic, built to suffer and survive. These burly little *baboushkas* shriek at foreigners who exchange a kiss in public. There is a puritan streak here, which is ironic in a country where divorce is rampant and where the Russian woman has an average of five or six abortions (the favoured means of contraception for the comrades).

The few old men who survived Lenin's famine, Stalin's purges and Hitler's invasion stagger slowly through the streets with chests full of war medals. These are red and gold, lavished with ornate hammers and sickles and stars. They are the only flamboyant thing in the streets of Moscow, worn on the sad rags of men who can barely walk. If history has made the old women of Russia strong then it has all but finished off the old men.

Muscovites live lives of surly patience. They are capable of the distracted bad manners you find in New York – the snarled word, the casual shove – and yet they become docile lambs when it is time to join a queue, and it is nearly always time to join a queue in Moscow. They queue to see Lenin's pickled corpse, they queue for watermelons, sweet ice cream and tours of the Kremlin. It is no accident that roubles look like toy money. They are as difficult to unload as Monopoly dosh.

Now that the Politburo have decided to stamp out alcoholism and have imposed what is virtually prohibition, you cannot get a drink outside of the underground bars and Intourist hotels. They can blow up the planet but they can't let you have a cold beer.

The people are nostalgic for a materialist, consumer society they have never known. They join queues when they do not know what they are lining up for. When the black market suddenly opens up shop in some quiet corner, the most useless garbage takes on an exaggerated appeal to the deprived locals. A selection of small, brass, totally useless signs of the zodiac provokes excitement of almost Beatlemania proportions. There are no names on any of the shops other than that of the product that is sold (subject to availability) because the proprietor is the people. On the pitiful shelves of the department stores you find gnarled grey chickens, dusty, sickly sweets and a few lonesome bottles of sulphuric mineral water. A panic breaks out in the people's bakers when it is realised that there are more customers than loaves. Everywhere the shops feel like six o'clock on Christmas eve.

In the book stores you will find more Gorbachev than Tolstoy and it is easier to find a statue of Chekov than one of his books. Not only do they ignore our great writers, they piss over their own culture too. This squalid standard of living, this permanent abuse of the human spirit, is mocked by the heroic gigantism of the city.

Down in the Metro there are huge, laughably Olympian statues of poetic looking soldiers, contemplative footballers, sensitive farmhands and thoughtful factory workers. In their big shadows the black marketeers approach you for hard currency, denim and music.

'Where you from? You speak English? Perhaps you haf something to sell? I can gif you a *very* favourable rate. Or I buy your jacket? I can gif you a *very* warm jacket in return. You haf cassettes perhaps? I already haf half of "Joshua Tree".'

The tragedy of all this unfulfilled craving is that it makes life's little trinkets – Levi's, U2, money that is actually worth the paper it is printed on – take on a desperate importance. You realise with a shudder that the unrelenting tack of Oxford Street would look like the promised land to these poor saps.

You see soldiers everywhere in this peace-loving nation. Ask the Russians about this and they will cite the 20 million dead, the human cost of victory in the Great Patriotic War, when Mother Russia's womb was ravaged and avenged. The scars will never heal, the wounds will never be allowed to slip from the collective memory.

Never mind the Hitler–Stalin pact. Never mind that the Great Patriotic War started in 1941, a couple of years after World War Two. Never mind the millions of Russians who had already been murdered by their countrymen. Never mind the way that Russia helped turn Poland into an abattoir and the rest of Eastern Europe into her own dowdy patio. All that is drowned out by the screams of the 20 million that echo down the century. They excuse everything . . .

At the Intourist hotel there are no shortages. The sad, joyless food is in plentiful supply so that, though you are never satisfied, you are never hungry. These Intourist hotels are where the action is – with your dollars or yen, your deutsche marks or pounds, you can get a drink in the hard currency bar or hang out at the Intourist nightclub. But on our last night in Moscow we decide to see midnight in Red Square so we step out of the hotel, past the State bouncer who is there round the clock to keep out the locals, and into the lean, hungry streets where the only thing in plentiful supply are representatives of the Red Army and, of course, *that face*. That face is blank and smug, smooth domed and pointy bearded. You see it on buildings and banknotes, statues and stamps, reproduced in busts available in a choice of black or grey in the Berioska shops for tourists, that face that appears everywhere. The next morning we flew east.

Soviet Central Asia is the baked heartland of the USSR, a vast region of mountains and deserts that shares its borders with Iran, Afghanistan and China. Temperatures here stay at well over 100 Fahrenheit all through the summer months, maturing the crop of the cotton plantations where the people, Uzbeks and Tajiks with broad, Oriental faces, bend their backs picking the white gold that brings the area its wealth. 'The very nature is on a par with the majestic people's achievements,' says the wonderful brochure. 'As for the mountains, they are the highest, and as for the rivers, they are the most tempestuous.'

The five Soviet Republics here are a mere 60 years old, though they have a history of commerce and violence that stretches back a thousand years. The Silk Route caravans passed through here but so did the hordes of Genghis Khan. 'The flames of the massacre spread far and wide,' recorded a thirteenth century historian, 'and evil covered everything like a cloud driven by the wind.'

Razed to the ground by the Golden Horde, Samarkand was rebuilt and later became Tamerlane's 'Pearl of the East', the capital of an empire that reached from Central Asia to India, Syria and Iran. In the fabulous Registan Square, which is still magnificent enough to tighten the muscles in your throat, Tamerlane declared wars, displayed loot and the heads of his enemies, and generally out-Mongoled the Mongols.

On the wide, white streets of Dushanbe, where the girls in multi-coloured silk dresses squat in the shade like exotic birds, we find the mark of more recent violence. Under one of the black pill box hats that most of the men wear, an ancient face lined with sun and time cracks into a toothless grin. The old man points to his right foot, which is no longer there.

'Fascists!' he says cheerfully, miming the Nazi soldier squeezing the trigger of the rifle that blew his foot off 45 years ago. 'Fascists!' he laughs, shrugging philosophically. 'Fascists!' We cross the street and turn to see him waving, friendly but forlorn, like a child who wants to make friends.

Dawn comes very late out here and when the sun is at its highest in the middle of the afternoon, the impossible heat hits you like a mugging. You retreat to a teahouse and drink hot green *chai* by a still green pool, surrounded by the local men sprawling on huge beds. The women are at home in the yellow stucco homes looking after big, riotous families and the atmosphere in the teahouse is like a sub-tropical gay bar.

This is a male dominated society and, like two of the neighbouring countries, the people here are Muslims. Everywhere you see the two blues of Islam, the light sapphire and darker cobalt representing the sea and the sky and the union of man and heaven. But partly because of prompting from an atheistic State and partly because of the easy going hedonistic nature of the people, Soviet Central Asia is not a hotbed of fundamentalist Islam. Most of the Mosques are preserved as museum pieces now and when the sun goes down, the boys in the teahouse are ready to party.

You see packs of them trying to fight their way past the State bouncer on the door of the Intourist hotel so they can get to the dancefloor of the nightclub and shake their Uzbek booty with glamorous comradettes from East Germany and Hungary. The band plays on – bizarre covers of modern Motown like *'Billie Jean iz not my luffer'* and *'I jerst called to say, I luff you'* – while the local cops try to persuade them to leave quietly.

Moscow distrusts these people. They are warm, open, anarchic, nothing like the stiff-assed drones you find avoiding your eyes on the streets of the capital – and their numbers are growing. While the white Russian woman is having her pregnancy aborted in Moscow or Kiev or Leningrad, the brown-eyed Uzbek or Tajik woman in Dushanbe or Tashkent or Samarkand is giving birth again. The population of the Soviet Central Asians (you soon learn not to call them Russians) is growing at more than double the rate of their pale comrades in the west of the USSR. Soon ethnic Russians will be outnumbered by Soviet Asians – some Western analysts believe they already are.

Moscow fears it will one day be swamped. The fear of the darker skin, The Other, is compounded by the fact that Uzbeks and Tajiks, though historically a warrior people, are reluctant to butcher Afghans – fellow Muslims – in the war being fought so close to their border. In the dark bars and cool teahouses, rumours abound of Uzbek soldiers who have been executed for refusing to fire on Afghans. And for the people of Soviet Central Asia, Russian is only their second language.

It is nothing like Moscow. Yet in the town square you find the inevitable statue of Lenin. And in the middle of the afternoon when you can feel the desert heat hitting you in waves and the sun seems to fill the sky, Lenin stands in the square in his peaked cap and long trench coat, absurdly bundled up against the elements, with one hand raised as if to hail a taxi. He looks a long way from home.

We drive up past Varzob to the brown, snow capped Parmir mountains, where snow tigers and bears roam the place they call the roof of the world.

'The twin peaks are called Mount Communism and Mount Lenin,' says the inscrutable Intourist guide.

'What did they used to be called?'

The po-faced State mask slips and for a moment she looks embarrassed. 'Well, Mount Communism was once called Mount Stalin but it was changed in the Fifties.'

'No, I mean what were their original, historic names?'

'There were *no* previous names,' she says, the expressionless face of the Party hack once more intact behind her dark glasses.

On our way back to town we stop off at a small mountain village where sturdy, barefoot children demand 'bon bons', with the laughing violence of the young beggars of Napoli and tear chewing gum from our hands. Nobody asks us for U2 records.

On the hot, bumpy ride back to Dushanbe the Intourist guide (never far from your side in the Soviet Union, where they like to keep you on a long leash) starts to open up and talks with that casual, brutal candour that sometimes breaks through the Russian veil. 'In theory all the Republics of the Soviet Union have the right to secede if they want to.' A hard, cynical smile. 'Anyone can be independent. But if they want to live somewhere other than the Soviet Union then they will *really* find themselves living somewhere else.'

Soon her husband, an engineer, will join the Communist Party, she says. He will join the Party for the same reason everyone else does. 'He needs the card to get ahead,' she says, sounding every inch the lower middle class climber.

Back in Dushanbe we go to the town's museum where there are snow tigers and bears, expertly stuffed and striking dramatic poses. There are also less well preserved exhibits, like the big snakes rotting inside milky bottles of formaldehyde and, incredibly, the desert rats and mountain vermin that have been matter-of-factly killed with a bang on the head and then stuck on the museum's wall, their small, furry bodies still hunched as they must have been at the moment of death. It was that combination of the grotesque and the hilarious that you only find in Asia, and it reminds you yet again that this is a country that spans continents, and your mind swims at the insane immensity of the Soviet Union.

We fly to Tashkent where the desert heat is cooled by the presence of a thousand fountains. Tashkent is the King's Cross of Central Asia, that great crossroads that everyone has to pass through at some time. This is the ancient city that looks like a new town. It was torn apart by an earthquake in 1966 and rebuilt over the space of just two or three years in one of those heroic bursts of energy that the Soviets summon up in moments of supreme crisis.

In the hotel's noisy, cavernous restaurant we make friends with a gang of Uzbeks who stroll into the kitchen with a proprietorial air and order plates of chicken and salad.

'Notting-ham Forest,' one of them says. 'Liver-pool.'

'Moscow Dynamo,' I say. 'Dynamo Kiev. Moscow Spartak.'

'Boo-by Charlton.'

'Lev Yashin,' I tell him. 'The Cat.'

We laugh and he bangs the table, ordering champagnesky.

The Uzbeks bought us our champagnesky and I gave away my Levi jacket, and it was very easy to pretend that everything in the world was equal, easy to pretend that we would one day meet again.

The faces on the party hoardings change when you get out east. The smiling, fair-skinned Slavs you see on the billboards in Moscow make way for heroes of a more oriental hue. Radiant cotton pickers and ecstatic factory workers beam down at you on the road to Khiva, but they don't do justice to the Uzbeks, a people whose looks run the gamut from full-blooded Mongol to aquiline Mediterranean. After one glass of champagnesky too many, you can see the beauty of the whole world reflected in those faces. I asked an Uzbek why some of his race looked Chinese, some Italian, others French or Japanese.

'They all look like Uzbeks to me,' he said.

There is a burnt, timeless beauty about Khiva, though the holy places of Islam have been desanctified now and remade into museums extolling the eternal glory of communism. In one cobwebbed corner there remains a photograph of Stalin. His dark Georgian features smirk slyly, as if pleased his denounced presence is still visible in the more remote areas of the Soviet Union, as if the people can never truly get their greatest saviour and persecutor out of their hearts.

Before leaving the hotel the next morning, there is an interview with a journalist from a local radio station. He is an Uzbek but the hurt, confused nature of his questions can be found all over the Soviet Union. What holds this massive country together is a naked terror of the rest of the world.

'Why do you never believe we want peace?' he says, his brown eyes blazing.

'They don't understand about the 20 million in the west,' I say into his bulky old tape machine. 'They don't understand how that mountain of corpses makes you sick.'

Tears in his eyes, he embraces the life out of me before I leave, as if we have made some kind of breakthrough, as if I understand. The most frightening thing about the Soviets is their conviction that *they* are the good guys.

We fly to Bukhara where the lights of the hotel's rooftop disco are visible from the alleys of the adobe shanty town. From the square where they once threw heretics from the top of the towering minaret (after wrapping them in a sack so there was not so much mess to clear up) you can just about make out the hotel's houseband striking up that old Soviet favourite. '*I jerst called to say – I luff you.*'

We come back to our hotel room to find our Arab cleaning woman listening to Prefab Sprout on the Walkman. She is a nubile young woman in an advanced state of decay, aged somewhere between 25 and the grave. She indicates that she has had ten children then mimes the fact that two of them died. She lifts two fingers and then, in a graphic imitation of dying, rolls her eyes back into her head and lets her tongue loll from her mouth, capturing the suffocating finality of death more eloquently than the Westerner, with all his cosy notions of eternity, ever could. We gave her the Walkman.

Down on the cotton picking collective farm, the Soviets ply you with all that dry, undigested data that passes for hard information in this country. The farm has a population of 11,000 with a workforce of 3,000 whose children go to one of the farm's four schools. You stare across the fields of cotton stretching to the horizon, thinking about the other collective farms where the managers burned the warehouses to the ground to cover up the fact that they had not reached the quota demanded by the State. We ask our hosts about it. They say it never happened.

'There were no warehouses burnt.'

But people were sent to jail for the crime.

'It never happened.'

The children of the cotton pickers put on a show for the foreigners. They wear Uzbek national dress, the girls in the multi-coloured silk dresses and the boys in pill box hats, and ooze State sanctioned cuteness. This is the Olga Korbut school of charm. They are unhappy looking little mites, totally devoid of the dark energy of the kids running around the sandy streets. Their dancing parodies the gender stereotypes – macho little men scowling, vampish little women simpering. They chant songs about the glory of the bald old fish on the wall.

'Lenin – Lenin – Lenin,' they peep. 'Bo – bo – bo.'

'Great dancing, cute kids,' a droll American scrawls in the visitor's book. 'See you on Broadway.'

Bukhara was where I saw a man with a picture of Lenin tattooed on his chest. It looked as crass and brutish as a Union Jack t-shirt at closing time.

And Bukhara was where I got sick, finally coming down with the Genghis Khan's Revenge that had always been lurking in the water and which the local tourist literature had warned me about.

I stumbled groaning onto the sleeper to Samarkand. The thought of all those nukes ouside the window of our cabin did not settle my stomach (you know you are travelling through a militarily sensitive area when the Soviets make you travel at night).

The man in the samovar held a small, passive songbird in one brown fist and poured hot green *chai* with the other. He stroked the bird's tiny head and smiled metallically.

The *chai* pulled my stomach together and I awoke near dawn as we were pulling into Samarkand. I staggered out to the rattling, luggage-strewn corridor, peering out into the darkness for my first glimpse of the Pearl of the East.

'It is a very long way from civilisation,' a smug Russian was saying with that snobbery that strolls casually into racism. 'Civilisation being Moscow,' she added ludicrously.

Samarkand, Tamerlane's dark age capital of the world, is straight from *Tales from the One Thousand and One Nights*. Here you see Islam, that most austere of religions, at its most flamboyantly beautiful. At the Registan three massive madrassahs, medieval temples of learning, face a square flanked by four slender minarets, all of them inlaid with the geometric tiles of sapphire and cobalt, the two blues of Islam. All over the city there jut from the skyline crops of gold domes, blue domes and fluted domes, shining in the heat of the afternoon as they shone five centuries ago, and in the cool refuge of the mosques, where there are man-sized niches in the wall to indicate the direction of Mecca, you can find whole ceilings of an intricate stalictite design – alluding to the cave where Mohammed wrote *The Koran* – inlaid with acres of gold leaf.

The heavy hand of the Soviet Union is never far away. Back at the hotel is the hard currency bar where the lights are kept low as if something shameful is happening, the TV flickers with images of the war across the border. The Soviet news broadcast shows the heroic struggles of its boys against the animalistic Afghan rebels, who are filmed pumping a few kilos of lead into a couple of dead bodies. We drink the German beer we have bought with American dollars and the report on the TV goes on forever, as the Soviets show their brave conscripts, the cruel enemy, the grateful population, and come up with everything they can to stop themselves thinking of Vietnam.

Our last port of call in Soviet Central Asia takes us to Tashkent a second time for a reception in our honour at the Vatan (motherland) society. In an airy boardroom reeking of polished wood and privilege, there are girls in Uzbek national dress and a picture of Mikhail on the wall. We are plied with green *chai* and black grapes and souvenirs of our stay in Uzbekistan. Our urbane host is a silver-haired gentleman of about 60 whose job description on his business card is The People's Poet. His lavish generosity to his guests is matched only by his stumbling subservience to the State, that abstract concept residing in a grey city thousands of miles away.

'Ask me some questions,' says The People's Poet. 'Anything you want.' 'Do your people like Gorbachev more than other Soviet leaders of recent times?' The People's Poet stares dumbfounded at his soft, hairy hands, loathe to place his current leader above the bland KGB hack Andropov or the corrupt, cumbersome Brezhnev, reluctant to make any statement that could imply even the mildest criticism of the State.

'If you ask this question then you know he is popular,' says the People's Poet. 'All our leaders are popular with the people. Ask me something else.'

'How does Islam fit into a secular society?'

'I can best answer that by reciting one of my poems,' he says.

On the night flight to Leningrad you are woken up at three in the morning by a blonde, hammock-breasted air stewardess grimly pushing a trolley containing a pile of drab tack. A depressed-looking fluffy toy. Some batteries. A nail file. A small hammer.

'What's this?'

'Souvenir trolley,' she grunts.

So you turn over with the worn jackboots of the soldier snoring behind you stuck in your back and you try to get some sleep. There is nothing else to do. Aeroflot does not show movies.

A mist is coming from the Neva, Leningrad's awesome river, and it covers the city's pale lemon buildings making them look ghostly and distant, like mansions in a dream.

Formerly St Petersburg, the capital of all Russia, this pastel coloured city and home of the Tsars was rejected after the revolution and given a new name by the Bolsheviks. But it still feels like Europe's last gasp before the dark, infinite sprawl of Asia. Peter the Great's 'Window Of The West' still combines a French aesthetic with Russian bombast, and it is still what Jan Morris called, 'A Cleopatra among cities'.

Inside the opulence of the Winter Palace, the Hermitage creaks with the work of Pissaro, Picasso, Matisse, Monet, Renoir, Gauguin, Van Gogh and Delacroix. And in the wide, wintry streets you also find wonder piled upon wonder, for this city is built on marshy soil, and it will not support tower blocks.

It feels like Paris or Venice, replete with the Russian love for the vast, which was how Peter the Great conceived of it in his feverish, visionary mind. 'Bathed in the lost harmony of Europe,' Colin Thubron wrote, 'it symbolizes the paradoxical leaning of Russia towards the west, spurred by an atavistic dread of China and a centuries-old longing for civilized recognition.'

Peter the Great carved his city out of this soft, life-sapping soil three centuries ago. Six feet seven inches tall, Peter was a paranoid, barbarian genius who single-handedly dragged his country into the industrial age. Peter founded the Russian navy, taught himself a dozen trades (he made his own huge boots), threw tantrums, got paralytically drunk, beat up members of his court, married a peasant girl and – like a caveman craving civilisation – invented Russia's greatest city on these northern marshes. Thousands of the men and women enlisted as forced labour died of disease or drowning. Russians have been dying for this city by the sea ever since.

The huge green sweep of the Piskarevskoye Memorial Cemetery is not covered with gravestones. It looks like a well-tended field intersected with stone pathways. Only when you walk through Piskarevskoye do you realise that it is a collection of mass graves.

Below every one of the small headstones dotted sparsely across the field, there are buried thousands upon thousands of men, women and children, nearly 500,000 in all, not quite half of the 1,200,000 Russians who died in the Battle of Leningrad in 1941 to 1944. During those three years Leningrad suffered ten times the death toll of Hiroshima. Ten Hiroshimas. This is what the *glasnost* and *perestroika* of Mikhail Gorbachev have to compete with. But how can you ask this country for openness, trust and rational thought when – nearly 50 years on – it is still reeling with the memory of the 20 million corpses?

'The Fascists burned the foodstores,' it says inside the memorial.

'Leningrad was besieged for 900 days and nights. There were 250 artillery attacks lasting nine hours each . . . the children drank boiled salted water at school, there was nothing else . . . the people died from bombing, famine, disease and fire . . . when the snow melted in the spring of 1941 the streets of Leningrad were covered with thousands of frozen bodies . . .'

This vast understated cemetery has the feel of the concentration camp about it. Your throat closes and chokes on the scale of that blinding, incomprehensible waste. You can't take it in. Nobody will ever take it in.

And framed in a glass case at Piskarevskoye there is an invitation to a party at Leningrad's Astoria Hotel. It is to the Nazi Chiefs of Staff from Hitler. The party at the Astoria was to be a celebration of the fall of Leningrad. But the city did not fall and there was no such party. 'The people were stronger than stone,' it says underneath. 'They overcame everything.'

As we prepare to leave, two tall young soldiers, some kind of guard of honour, are rolling out a shabby red carpet. Some US Congressmen are in town and the Russians want them to see this. It is as if they think that then the Americans will *understand*.

The guide from Intourist, an organisation said to have close links with the KGB, takes us to a Berioska shop down by the bay to squeeze the final few hard currency banknotes out of us before we fly home. I slip away from the strong vodka and blankly-smiling dolls and walk down to the quay. Out on the choppy grey sea the white sails of a dozen yachts dip in the end of summer breeze. Across the Bay of Finland you can just make out a thin sliver of land, bled of all colour by the bad weather and the flat white sky.

Later they will search me and my luggage at the airport, they will read my address book and examine some paperbacks as if they were weapons, and when all this is happening I will be very glad to be getting out of the Soviet Union.

But alone at the bay I think of the people it takes to make ten Hiroshimas, I think of the shabby red carpet at Piskarevskoye, and my eyes are streaming in the cold, Baltic wind.

Houston – True West

Arena, September/October 1990

N THE HEART OF THE LAND where the ice machines hum, Houston rises from the flat Texas prairie, 'the golden buckle of the sunbelt' and the greenest city I ever saw.

Houston started as a scam. In 1836 two slick New York con men called the Allen brothers pitched their tent here, staked a claim and advertised the baking, mosquito-infested marshland as a verdant Eden to the folks back home. The gullible souls who came out west were finally rewarded for their faith in 1901 when oil first burst from a gusher called Spindletop. The duped American dreamers had got very lucky indeed.

'The central symbol in *Giant* is oil,' wrote David Dalton of the classic Texan movie, 'a colossal metaphor for money and sex, a power that can transform men. Jett Rink erects his one derrick and, as it erupts like a liquid libido, it embodies the mystery Freud called, "a boiling cauldron of seething excitation".'

And that's what they built Houston on. The Lone Star State, the only state in the union that was ever an independent republic – from 1836 to 1845 it really was a whole other country – became the perfect expression of America's ability to transform men.

Like all the great western legends, it was founded in a raw reality. The Texan myth boasted of a life of panoramic grandeur, limitless and free, where very tough, very rich men retained a curious innocence, as if in deference to those first settlers who were skinned by the Allen boys. The character James Dean played in *Giant*, the poor boy whose child-like belief in Texan soil is rewarded with unimaginable riches, was based on a real wildcatter called Clem McCarthy. 'Clem McCarthy was a big, beefy, brash man,' wrote David Dalton, 'as simple, wild and huge as his home state.'

They built this place on the heroic stuff that John Wayne movies are made of, and yet it all seems very close. Driving in from the airport you are struck by the shocking newness of everything. As all the mirrored skyscrapers of a town built from oil dollars twinkle in the gloaming, you can feel the ghosts of Clem McCarthy and the other wildcatters breathing on the back of your European neck.

'In Houston,' said my Texan friend with characteristic dryness, 'if it's got a second coat of paint, it's an antique.'

Even history happened yesterday. First settled by the Spanish, the area later became part of Mexico and gained independence in 1821. It was then fought over for years. This is where women were women and men were cowboys.

Down the road from Houston is the Alamo in San Antonio, where, in 1836, 150 men fought 4,000 regulars from the Mexican army. They were wiped out, but in the rematch a few months later General Sam Houston defeated Santa Anna's army at San Jacinto, 20 miles east of what is now downtown Houston. Sam Houston became president of the Texas Republic, the Allen brothers named their town after him and the Lone Star State flew its flag over the big country.

The Texan flag is one white and one red horizontal bar held by a vertical blue bar containing a solitary white star. You still see it everywhere in Texas. It is certainly more familiar down here than the Stars and Stripes. You come to believe that Texans regard the rest of America as a watered-down version of their home state. 'This is Texas,' people are always telling you, as if that explains everything.

Texan pride lives and breathes in Houston. Businessmen in Hugo Boss suits walk tall through the Galleria shopping mall wearing Tony Lama cowboy boots, remembering the Alamo in the corporate world. Houston enjoys its reputation for hospitality – 'Where y'all from?' coo little old ladies, 'Where y'all going?' – and ostentation (a baby in lush River Oaks was given a Rolls-Royce for being born). Houston cherishes its brash, big-hearted mythology and in doing so makes it real.

And yet Houstonians are torn. While many of them can't get enough of epic Texan lore – that oil-soaked, blood-sodden tradition of Clem McCarthy, Sam Houston and Jim Bowie – other Houstonians are a little embarrassed by this shit-kicking heritage. Houston is a sophisticated, cosmopolitan metropolis. There's the Rothko Chapel, the de Menil collection, the Alley theatre. At the Museum of Fine Arts there are Monet water lillies and haystacks. You will see fine examples of Braque's Cubism and Brancusi's work in bronze. You will get your fill of Matisse, Degas, Cezanne. And yet Houston carries the weight of the west on its shoulders.

'Go to the Alamo in San Antonio,' an emotional husband and wife told me in a dark and drunken bar. 'And then you will understand Texas.'

More urbane, sober Houstonians tried to talk me out of the pilgrimage. 'It's only a *wall*,' one said. 'What do you want to go and look at a *wall* for?'

Though my urbane companions pointed me in the direction of the serenity of the Rothko Chapel, during those early days in Houston my heart pined for the blazing heroism of the Alamo. This is the land where it is still legal to carry a gun on the passenger seat of your car but not under the dashboard, where the only bad weapon is a concealed weapon. I was anticipating good men with fast guns. Cowboys. So when the Shopping Mall Vigilante appeared just down the road in Dallas, he confirmed all of my preconceived notions about Texas.

Tom Broom, aka the Shopping Mall Vigilante, was a quietly-spoken white Caucasian male who parked his car in a shopping mall just in time to see Eddie Edwards, a 41-year-old black male, shoot Demetria Taylor, Edwards' 28-year-old former girlfriend. Broom then saw Edwards finish her off, killing Taylor by shooting her in the head.

Getting out of his car, Tom 'What's In A Name?' Broom pulled out his Magnum and ordered the fleeing Edwards to halt. When he didn't stop, Broom shot him. Edwards died, Broom went home and the Shopping Mall Vigilante was born.

For a while – as with any mythic crime buster – the identity of the Shopping Mall Vigilante was a secret. 'Thousands of ordinary Texans are hailing him a hero,' said *People* magazine.

Broom didn't want the mantle. 'I'm no Charles Bronson type,' he told the press shortly after he turned himself in to the police. The Shopping Mall Vigilante seemed genuinely tormented by the killing. 'I knew I had to turn myself in,' he said. 'I have decent values. I'm sorry I killed a man.'

The Shopping Mall Vigilante was soon being portrayed as a peace-loving victim. It turned out that he had been carrying his Magnum after he had been mugged while delivering pizza and having his 1988 Mustang stolen within the space of a week. 'I love my gun,' he said wistfully.

Controversy raged around the bespectacled head of the Shopping Mall Vigilante. In New York or Los Angeles, it was said, the case would have lasted for years, making a small army of lawyers rich men. But not here. 'There's not a court in Texas that would convict this man,' they said.

And so it proved. The police released the Shopping Mall Vigilante without bringing charges. The District Attorney's office pressed for a murder indictment. It went before the Grand Jury but never got to trial. The Shopping Mall Vigilante walked away a free man without having to face a jury of his peers. Eighty-five per cent of more than 10,000 Texans polled by the *Times Herald* said that the shopping mall Vigilante had acted correctly.

'That's a Texas reaction,' sniffed the Assistant DA.

Well, I thought, this *is* Texas.

And this is Texas too. From the Spindletop lounge, a revolving restaurant and bar on top of the Hyatt Regency hotel, you can look down on the skyline of downtown Houston as it turns before your eyes. The Spindletop is named after the first successful oil well. Houston's first ejaculation of wealth beyond all imagination, but as locals struggle to point out the names of the buildings and who owns them, you get a sense of Houston's fluctuating fortunes. They can tell you that Philip Johnson did this and I.M. Pei did that, but it is difficult to remember who owns all those buildings, because in recent years they have changed hands so many times. Houston, where so many fortunes have been made, has also seen many more lost.

For most of the twentieth century, Houston just kept on getting richer. The oil town became boom town in the Seventies and Eighties, when the global energy crisis stuffed Houston's pockets, and cowboys as rich as sheiks walked the Galleria. Then the oil market crashed. The economic Alamo came on 31 March 1986, when the price of oil went below $10 a barrel, a sickening fraction of what it had been in Houston's heyday. Banks went bust, millionaires went bankrupt, good men stepped from thirtieth-storey windows.

But Houston is fighting back. If the late Eighties were the Alamo, then the early Nineties are San Jacinto. The town may have taken a few body blows in recent years but it is still one of those American cities that makes Europe look like the Third World. In River Oaks, Houston's Beverly Hills – though built on oil not celluloid – there are plenty of people prepared to pay a cool million just for a patch of dirt. Stretch limos purr downtown, the restaurants are full and valet parkers grab the keys to the Taurus when you pull up outside your destination. And all through the night, the ice machines hum.

You can still see a few bitter vestiges of the traumas of 1986. It sometimes reveals itself when you broach one of the great American topics of today – the growing number of Hispanics.

'Hell,' said my Texan friend. 'Back in '81, when we had all the money, we should have *bought* Mexico and made them all speak English.'

I didn't know if he was putting me on. He didn't know either.

The proximity of Mexico seems like an exotic bonus to the visiting gringo who likes eating enchilladas, guacamole and fajitas – all that baby food from hell – or dancing with black-eyed beauties from Loredo at clubs like the Mansion on Waugh. But there's an underlying pathos to the relationship between Mexico and Texas, as there is bound to be where the end of the First World meets the start of the Third World.

'Where are you from?' Jan Morris asks the maid in her hotel.

'I'm not from nowhere,' the girl replied wistfully. 'I'm from Mexico.'

And the Mexicans head north because they have nothing to lose, nothing to leave behind. Jan Morris wrote of the poignancy of the bridge at Brownsville, Texas, the bridge that divides the United States from Mexico and marks the global divide of north and south. 'Only a certain sad excitement attends the bridge itself, with all its mixed emotions – this is after all one of the supreme boundaries of the world, the boundary between the richest society ever established, and the world of poverty, frustration, ill-health and ignorance which, starting just over there in Mexico, extends in so ominous a swathe from here to Bangladesh.'

You see the Mexican presence constantly. It can be touching, colourful, alarming. At a restaurant called Vargos on the edge of town the bill arrived bearing the waiter's name.

'*Your server was Jesus*,' it said.

It is a better life here, but it's a hard life, too. The Mexican girl you danced with has three jobs and she sends money home (the world is divided between girls who are sent money by their parents and girls who send money to their parents). Back in Loredo she worked in a bank. Here, among other things, she's a hat-check girl. The man dragging the hotel swimming pool with a suction pump attached to a broom is, of course, a Mexican. And everyone you see waiting at a bus stop – in this driving society, this land where the car is king – is Mexican, dog-tired domestics waiting for a bus in a city that really doesn't have too many buses. These small, scattered tribes of maids, cleaners and pool men always made me think of that cruel, true line in Richard Rayner's *Los Angeles Without A Map*, when a carload of youths (Hispanics as it happens) drive past a bus stop and shout two words at the sad sacks waiting for a ride – 'Asshole losers!' In Texas, waiting for a bus is an admission that life has got you licked.

In downtown Houston on a hot Saturday morning, you see that this is a driving town through and through. The streets are empty as Houstonians cruise in their air-conditioned cars or walk in the labyrinth of gleaming tunnels in downtown's subterranean shopping mall. The big end may have fallen out of the American car industry but you still see names of impossible glamour purring down Main Street, names carved in chrome – Buick, Chevrolet, Lincoln Continental, Suburban Silverado (the most popular station wagon in Houston) – and glinting in the sunshine of the South West.

The highest building in downtown Houston is the Texas Commerce Bank, built by our old pal I. M. Pei. At 75 storeys it is so high that it sways. The bankers who work here are conservative gentlemen and they are obliged to obey a 23-page dress code, a veritable Koran of corporate dressing. The building is meant to be closed to the public on the weekend but, hell, this is Texas where they hate to say no to a stranger. When the security guard sees that we are not crack-crazed psychos he lets us take the elevator to the 75th floor, where, with just a glass wall separating you from eternity, you look down on Houston, with its verdant pastures growing between massive skyscrapers and homely-sounding roads that go on for miles.

From the top of I. M. Pei's beautiful monster you can see all the manifestations of Texan expertise of which the locals are justifiably proud. There's the sprawling Texas Medical Center, the most advanced medical complex in the world – heads of state and petrobillionaires in need of heart surgery wouldn't be operated on anywhere else. You can see the Galleria, the golden mall where women who received $20 million divorce settlements kill time with gold cards, making the good life live and breathe. And at the end of town, squatting on the horizon like a figment of Steven Spielberg's imagination, you can see the Astrodome – sunk into the ground, completely covered, blessed with a space-age dome – which was built back in the Sixties as the first sports stadium of the future.

And somewhere out there – just out of sight though never out of mind – NASA, the Lyndon B. Johnson Space Center, focal point for the nation's manned space-flight program. Skylab and the Space Shuttle are choreographed from here, as were the Apollo moon shots. This was, and is, the home of Mission Control, those banks of computers and blipping lights and shirt-sleeved men, laconically directing

America's space flights. With typical – and enviable – Texan openness, the men in Mission Control will allow you to wander free
among all their technology and even brief you for half an hour.

NASA has moon rocks, space suits, real rockets. Children wander
under a picture of President Kennedy and his quote from 1961: 'I
believe this nation should commit itself to achieving the goal, before
the decade is out, of landing a man on the moon and returning him
safely to earth.' You did it, Jack. Now American kids gasp at the
hardware of outer space, marvel at all their country, or their state,
or their town has achieved, exclaiming in a strange tongue that is all
their own.

'Cool,' they say.

'Neato Mosquito.'

'Can you grab that?'

These kids all know the first word spoken on the moon. 'Houston,' said Neil Armstrong, his voice crackling down to Mission Control. 'Tranquility base here. The Eagle has landed.' Most postcards
of Houston's dramatic skyline feature a full yellow moon, shining
above the city as though it were a lush outer suburb of Houston,
home of the right stuff.

And in the shadow of the Texan Commerce Bank, which falls over
all those verdant pastures that soften the business district, you can
see another Houston phenomenon getting underway. It's that annual
fiesta of fun, the Houston International Festival. Over the next ten
days somewhere between one and two million people will throng the
streets of Houston checking out shindigs of every kind. Every year
the Houston International Festival celebrates a different country and
this year it's the Brits.

Some big names are in town to perform, talk, give workshops,
shake hands and hang out. Kazuo Ishiguro, the Booker Prize winner,
is flying in, as is Lindsay Anderson, the film director, Courtney Pine,
the jazz man, and those hard-working royals, the Duke and Duchess
of Kent. There is a comedian who distorts his face with rubber
bands, someone who plays jazz on the bagpipes and, opening the
show with a spirited rendition of the Abba classic, 'Money, Money,
Money', the band of Her Majesty's Welsh Guards (who stunned
Houston by being the biggest party animals since Led Zeppelin came
off the road).

The Festival covers 20 blocks of downtown Houston. There's music, theatre, food – the 'Cornish pastries' (some things the locals got
a little wrong) turned out to be very popular. It's mostly a celebration

of the arts that sweetens the bonds of commerce, but not all of the International Festival is imported from Merry Olde England. If Noel Coward plays and a 'banger on a stick' don't really fry your onions, then the cosmopolitan whirlpool of Houston has something for all tastes. There's Tex Mex music, Cajun delicacies like shrimp on a stick (which no doubt provided the inspiration to impale the bangers), women from Vietnam with a Texas accent selling Thai food.

It was touching to see all those Texans wearing the Festival's official T-shirt, an exploding Union Jack that looked as though it had been designed by the ghost of Jackson Pollock. I was moved. But for a moment I was afraid that my vision of Texas would be distorted by their rampant Anglophilia. How could I know the true taste of Houston with my mouth full of jam scone, banger on a stick and Cornish pastry?

I needn't have worried. I was among people who would not let me loosen my grip on the real Houston.

'Some hide,' muttered my companion as one of those spectacularly tall local girls walked by, one of those cosmic amalgams of hair, teeth and legs – especially legs – that you only see in Texas, where you see them all the time. 'Some hide,' he coughed. It was a compliment.

Texan girls! Let's meet some Texan girls.

'Do you know how to tell a bought tit?' demanded my companion, making reference to the wonders of cosmetic reconstruction.

My reply was in the negative.

'Bought tits don't bounce,' he said. 'Bought-tits-don't-bounce!'

Cosmetic reconstruction – *not* surgery, bub – is very big in Texas. If the American Dream is about anything, it is about transformation – and nothing can transform so radically as the surgeon's knife. Many women down here crave that blade, they long for it to cut away their unwanted nodules and bumps – God's little errors – they crave the perfection that only its cold, razor-sharp steel can bring.

And the women that yearn for the moment when they lay prone on the surgeon's table – *take me*, doctor! – are not the sagging old hags that European cynics would lead you to believe. Far from it. Many of them are very young, many of them are very beautiful. Some of them are rich, some of them will get the money somehow. Some of them look perfect already. Perfect. But not in their heart, not in the mirror.

In the *Houston Chronicle*, two of the city's best-dressed women – it's official – discussed with Linda Gillian Griffin, Fashion Editor, how they had improved on what the Almighty had given them. 'Best-Dressed honorees Laurie O'Connell and Judy Weiss say cosmetic dentistry and surgery have changed their lives,' said the caption under a picture of two ladies who looked like they were from *Dallas* (the soap rather than the city). *They get right help at right time*, said the headline without a trace of sneering.

The glossy veterans of cosmetic reconstruction display a light-hearted pride in their encounters with the surgeon's scalpel. Having your face fixed is an acceptable topic for restaurant conversation. After a while you emerge from your European prejudices about frozen features and mutton-dressed-up-as-Victoria-Principal and begin to see their point. What *is* wrong with wanting perfection? It only starts to seem obscene when you meet a gorgeous 23-year-old who wants a chin implant, a nose job and her breasts inflated. It only starts to seem dubious when you realise that most of these customised women would be dissatisfied with perfection, too.

The end of the rainbow for most Houston women is the River Oaks Country Club. This is some joint, the Versailles of Texas. Membership of this social Valhalla is exclusive, elusive, expensive. If you don't belong – then you don't belong. It stands at the end of River Oaks Boulevard exactly the way that Buckingham Palace waits at the end of the Mall, though in truth it makes the Queen's pad look a little dowdy.

Your roving *Arena* correspondent was invited into 1600 River Oaks Boulevard as the guest of the good people from Cartier, who were attending a fashion show in the ROCC. The place was crowded, but there were only a handful of men present. Glossy models stalked the catwalks while the best-dressed women of Houston scrutinised the clothes and each other. They bossed around waiters called José, they merely nibbled at their tossed salads. They sparkled with jewellery and hairspray, their legs taut on tall heels, their mouths painted a ripe red. Some of them were real Texan beauties, but there was more money than sex in the air. They radiated wealth, they shone with divorce settlements that could clear Third World debt ('I'm just a single parent,' an icy blonde who had landed a $20 million settlement told me later). The Cartier ladies apart, there was a skeletal, anorexic gloss about many of the women. Only the very rich can look this hungry. Their petrified hair framed frozen, cheek-boned faces.

'The Darth Vader look,' said my expatriate pal.

A woman tottered by with her reconstructed nose in the air. She was wearing a diamond the size of a grape. 'Another air stewardess who hit the big time,' said my friend. 'Those women rarely miss. They can smell a custom-made shirt at 50 paces.'

The last *Oprah Winfrey Show* had been about the battered wives of rich men. But the *grande dames* of Houston, those coutured powers behind the petro fortunes, are among the richest women in Texas and I would like to see anyone try to mess with them. To be among them when they are out on the town – sipping white wine spritzers, buying clothes and bitching – is an impressive sight. And all this theatre of riches was being played out first thing on a Monday morning.

While the opulent rooms of the River Oaks Country Club play host to the women of Houston, the men also have a few places where they can get away from it all. The Men's Club – motto: *'Dulcedine Cupior'* ('I am desired by sweet affection') – and Rick's – motto: 'Get your kicks at Rick's' – are both the kind of establishments where you walk in and realise how sober you are.

These are topless bars, but with a Houston twist. The name of the game is Texan table dancing, cock teasing raised to a fine art, where half-naked – three-quarters naked, nine-tenths naked – girls cavort in the faces of men who remain seated, brows beaded, gasping for air.

At first it looks like the most decadent thing this side of the Weimar Republic, but after a while seems curiously innocent. No bodily fluids are exchanged, only dollars ($20 a dance). No flesh is touched. Oh, the odd nipple might brush the trembling nose of some heavy-lidded oil man. The occasional hard little ass might graze against the quivering crutch of an executive from the Texas Commerce Bank. But the girls are in control. The penetration is all in your wallet. There are black whores in lime-green hot pants on Main ('They could have Houston Police Department badges secreted about those bodies,' said my friend. 'Entrapment is considered OK here'), but the doyennes of the table dance are business women, artists, athletes. They stand with their backs to you, bend double and smile at you from between their legs. They have good reason to smile.

These girls earn between two and three thousand dollars a week. They all look like Texan blondes – even the ones from Chicago and Manhattan. Some of them dream of going to LA and being the next Paula Abdul. Others, the slightly older ones (mid-twenties) are content to stay in Houston and keep fit. Though 'keep fit' doesn't really say it, 'stay perfect' is more like it. Cheat time. Never age. Stay perfect.

'If you run 50 miles a week,' one of them said, 'you can kiss your menstruation goodbye.'

'This one,' said the DJ in the Men's Club, slapping on some metal dirge about surviving, 'is for all you Vietnam veterans.'

The air is thick with dreams in the Men's Club. Men with perfect female bodies in their face close their eyes and dream of being blown by Pfeiffer, girls with perfect bodies dream of making it as a choreographer in Tinsel Town. It's some American scene in here, all these people grasping for something that is just out of reach, some classic American scene. You feel that you are right at the yearning heart of that old American dream. Eyes scan the dark and crowded room while perfect – truly perfect – bodies perform inches from their face. You see again that dissatisfaction with perfection, the eternal longing for more.

A blonde that looked like Jean Harlow gave a guy her home number. But he didn't call her. He thought he might meet someone better.

The next day we were driving through the 4th Ward, Houston's black ghetto, improbably sandwiched between the mansions of River Oaks and the skyscrapers of downtown. It is one of those neighbourhoods where you only see black faces on the billboards, where everywhere you see the slogans of faith. *Jesus is Lord.* I had seen the same slogans on the South Side of Chicago, but Houston had none of the Windy City's northern urban squalor. The squalor here, right in the heart of the fourth largest city in the States, was southern and rural. There were ramshackle wooden houses with porches that looked straight from the backwoods. There were scrawny dogs, timeless ragged kids, impassive old men. *Now hiring friendly people*, said the sign in the window of the Taco Bell on South Main.

'Here in Texas,' said my friend, 'new money is 24 hours old and old money is 48 hours old. Wildcatters who were chewing tobacco and discovering oil a generation ago now own Rembrandts and Matisses. There's not really old and new money here. There's only new and slightly used.'

Christie's, the auction house, came to town at the height of the oil boom. They are gone now, but perhaps they will come back as Houston builds a more enduring affluence. It is said that when they arrived Christie's approached a ridiculously rich oil widow and asked her how best to cultivate the art market in Houston.

'Don't say you've got more class than us,' she allegedly said. 'Because everyone's got more class than us. And don't say you've got more money than us – because nobody has.'

She was too hard on Houston. The city has an embarrassment of cultural riches, and many of them can be found on a peaceful street of grey and white wooden houses, where a boy on a bicycle should be throwing newspapers onto the long, clipped lawns. The de Menil museum is here, the incredible private collection of Dominique and the late John de Menil, formidable Texan collectors who spent 40 years and incalculable millions assembling a collection that reaches from the Paleolithic to the present, from ancient Egypt to the East Village. On the same quiet street is Barnett Newman's broken obelisk, built in honour of Martin Luther King and standing in a reflecting pool outside the entrance of the Rothko Chapel.

Mark Rothko was asked by John and Dominique de Menil to create a sacred place, a non-denominational place of worship. As you sit in the Chapel's calm, octagonal interior, surrounded by the dark shades of Rothko's work, the modern marriage of art and money recedes and, once again, art is synonymous with religion.

On Saturday night Houston takes off its stetson and lets its hair down. At the Yucatan Liquor Store blondes who look like Basinger and brunettes who look like Cher dance on the bar under the stuffed swordfish and Christmas lights. Sometimes they are joined by men who look like Meatloaf.

Ecstatic boys scream things like, 'I've got fucking sweat coming out of my ears!' and, 'There's no business like monkey business!' These young Americans swig Mexican beer from the bottle. They tell jokes to girls with teeth from a toothpaste ad. 'Do you know the difference between Burger King and a blow job? No? Want to have lunch tomorrow? *Hahahaha!*'

The Yucatan is teeming with young humanity. Packs of them stumble in, dad's Cadillac outside, like over-privileged youths straight out of Bret Easton Ellis. Their look is strong on beach credibility. They have tans, pumped-iron pecs, pearly teeth. They look like beach bums, surfer jocks. They grab a Mexican girl and head for the dance floor, where a giant screen looms over the action broadcasting the game between the Houston Rockets and the Minnesota Timberwolves. The DJ plays a country and western song. 'I've been looking for love in all the wrong places,' it goes, 'looking for love in too many faces.' And the whole of the Yucatan knows the words and sings along.

At the back of the Yucatan there is an ice house, the Texan version of a roadhouse, one of those blue-collar, clapboard drinking joints where there is always a woman in the corner who looks as if she's just stumbled out of a Hank Williams song.

The ice house behind the Yucatan is called the Grapevine Lounge and in its murky depths a man with 'Vietnam Vet' on his baseball cap pines for the love of the stout, dark-haired barmaid. He is here most nights, longing for her love, though he sees her flirt with everyone. He brings her chocolates, she doesn't eat them but instead casually passes them around to the other men in the dark bar. They taste pretty good.

The vet knows she isn't interested but, after a day spent scraping the wipe-outs off the freeway (this vet is what they call a wrecker), he will be back tomorrow night. It's the kind of mad optimism that you see all over Houston.

The wetbacks who polish your Suburban Silverado until it gleams, the Texas table dancers in Rick's, the old oil men checking in for heart surgery at the Texas Medical Center: I came to believe they are all plugged in to the same almighty source. The lovesick veteran in the ice house, the country club siren under the surgeon's knife, the Mexican girl who just met a boy in the Yucatan that she likes. They all share a belief that things are going to get better, that soon they will be transformed.

There's a storm blowing in from the Gulf, but tonight Houston is warm and calm. The ice machines hum, the limos purr and outside the bankrupt furniture store on Main is a sign saying, CASH IS KING. This sure isn't Europe. That feeling in the air is not *I can't* but *I can*, not *I was* but *I will be*. That seems to me the shining glory of Houston, of Texas, of America – this stubborn refusal to be held by the past. Nothing can beat it.

And on the peaks of Houston's downtown skyline you can see the red lights of the helipads, flashing in twilight's last gleaming like the promise of tomorrow.

Polemic

The Tattooed Jungle

Arena, September/October 1989

ROTTWEILERS JUST CAN'T HELP acting on impulse. After the early summer's rampage of the killer mutts, the nation finally woke up to the fact that there are an awful lot of dangerous, dumb, ugly animals in our midst and that many of them own very large dogs. Rottweilers tore a baby from its cot, they left a five-year-old needing 21 stitches, they killed an 11-year-old girl in Dundee. Naturally enough, the dog owners were *hurt*. Oh, Rambo loves kids. My Psycho wouldn't hurt a fly. Napalm has a heart of gold.

'Rocky bit the vet but he asked for it,' said Arthur in the *New Statesman*. ' 'Cos he stuck a syringe up his arse.'

A word you find cropping up again and again in Arthur's conversation is *respect*. Rocky is a pussycat; just treat him with respect. All the indignant owners of these misunderstood pooches – the playful Pit Bull Terrier, the kind-hearted Alsatian, the peaceable Rottweiler, the gentle Dobermann – are very big on respect. Sick and tired of being pushed and pulled by the elemental forces of the naked city – another burglary, more smashed glass on the pavement and another car radio gone – they want a little respect around here, and their combination bodyguard, burglar alarm and stiff-dick substitute will ensure they get it.

It is symptomatic of the long spiritual decline of the working class (and having this kind of dog is as working class as fishfingers and Ford Escorts) that they see owning an animal that is capable of killing a small child in a few frenzied minutes as a suitable way to win the respect of their fellow citizens. Thirty years ago the grandmothers of the Arthurs of this world would get on their knees and scrub their front doorstep clean every morning. They wanted respect. Today Arthur's dog – or one just like it – will squat blank and drooling on somebody else's doorstep and shit all over it. He only wants respect.

The working class has come a long way in recent years, all of it down-hill. They no longer look like the salt of the earth. They look like one big Manson Family. There never *used* to be all these people drinking Tennents – always those cheap and potent bruise-blue cans of Tennents – in the street at nine o'clock in the morning. Lager at dawn, that macho valium. And there never used to be all these fat tattooed slobs, dressed for the track and built for the bar, leaning out of the window of their van – those rusty white vans – and screaming with rage, 'Yew carnt! Yew farking *carnt*!' as they cut you up and mow down a Lollipop lady.

They are the reason you prefer to avoid Indian restaurants at closing time. You see them at the post office on Monday morning, at the football ground on Saturday afternoon, at every pub – those manly troughs – at any time. They belch and fart and threaten their way through life. They are the lager vomit on the Union Jack. They turn the city into a tattooed jungle. They spoil everything.

The trouble with the working class today is that they are such peasants. Something has died in them – a sense of grace, all feelings of community, their intelligence, decency and wit. Socialism is finished here because it is no longer possible to feel sentimental about the workers.

They love their country – eat shit, you Argie sheep-shaggers – but they don't care enough about the street they live on to bother binning their rubbish. My skip overfloweth. These people make the city streets look like a toilet in a Turkish prison – Rambo steamingly defecating, Little Wayne tossing away his crisp packets, dad's tattooed arms working away on his motor, dumping his derelict big end in the nearest rose bushes when it no longer functions. The way they foul the streets in the tattooed jungle is positively Elizabethan. In fact everything about these rich serfs in their velcro-welded sneakers and boulder-rubbed denim is a throwback to the bad old days, the days when being born on the wrong side of the tracks meant you would always be a dumb prole.

They are the real class traitors, betrayers of the men who fought the Second World War, those men who fought for Churchill but voted for Clement Attlee. But in the tattooed jungle they have no sense of history. The true unruly children of Thatcherism, they know their place and wallow in their peasanthood.

Two years ago I sat in front of a pack of them at Wembley when England played Holland. These well-heeled oiks were perfect emissaries of the *prole nouveau*. They were not particularly young (all over 30), they were certainly not poor (they lounged in the best seats consuming an abundance of booze, spliff and even what they called 'blow'), and yet, with their racism, their mindless desire to consume to excess, and especially with their farting, they were quintessential tattooed jungle, real radicals, the Mujahadin of yobbism. One of them kept elaborately breaking wind.

'Kentucky *Fried*!' he declared every time, and the others roared.

But being born at the shabbier end of the social scale should never be enough to make you a farting philistine.

At a gallery in New York in the '50s, a rich female collector commented admiringly on the manners of a young unknown artist called Jasper Johns. She said that Johns – born in Georgia, raised in North Carolina – must be a member of the southern aristocracy. The painter soon put her right.

'Oh no,' he said casually. 'I'm trash.'

In the tattooed jungle they are happy to advertise the fact. Say it loud: I'm plebeian and proud. All notions of social mobility or cultural aspirations are well suspect, squire. They cling to all those bogus clichés about the working class – that they have no airs and graces, that they lack pretension and are honest, loyal, humorous and hardy – all that sentimental bullshit that leads nowhere but to some poor Indian waiter being insulted on the Holloway Road or some little kid being slapped by the vegetables in Sainsbury's.

'Do as you're *bloody* told, Kylie!'

They sour everything they come into contact with – even on that sweet night of wonders when Arsenal won the League and we poured out onto the streets of Highbury and made our way to the ground, even on that night with a team that included Thomas and Rocastle, with Davis on the touchline, you could hear them chanting those white trash mantras of bile that would not be out of place at a Nuremberg rally.

'*We hate the Tottenham yids, we hate the Tottenham yids.*' You can spot them coming a mile off – in the tattooed jungle everybody turns into a fat fuck at 20. Though they deride the intellectual, they mercilessly punish their flesh and blood with an unforgiving hedonism. Mine's a large pint of biriani and a vat of something yellow. Fill little Wayne's nose bag full of sugar, and a duty-free pack of Silk Cut for the wife.

In fact, here 'it' comes right now. Coo, wot a state, eh, John? Her bottled blonde head wreathed in cigarette smoke – you have to smoke in the tattooed jungle – she totters on her high are-you-free

heels (her concept of glamour is derived from soap operas and prostitutes), her spreading haunches squeezed into robot-mottled denim,
or, when the summer comes to the city, a skimpy mini-skirt made of
the finest man-made fibres. It is then that you notice her remarkable
legs. They are not shaved. They are not waxed. These pins are positively *scalped*. Obviously treated with battery acid, they actually
gleam with hairlessness and she totters on those bald white legs like
some gross travesty of a 'real' woman – *get stuck into that, yew
carnt!*

Call me old-fashioned, but it still shocks me when I see that some
of these women are, in the fashion of merchant seamen, tattooed.
They tattoo everything that moves in these parts. All the men are
tattooed, some of the women and, worst of all, so are some of the
faces. In 40 years time there are going to be all these little old men
with free bus passes and an eagle tattooed on their forehead.

They will be doing it to babies next. And Alsatians. One of the
worst things about these people is that they always act like the dis-
enfranchised, even when they have money. You make a mark on
your body when you feel you can't make a mark on your life.

Many forces have conspired to build this unthinking, brutal tattooed jungle. The death of the grammar schools – those public
schools without the sodomy – resulted in state education relinquish-
ing its role of nurturing bright young working-class kids. And then
there is the betrayal of the ordinary people by the Labour Party – it's
a sobering thought that the last Labour Prime Minister was Jim Cal-
laghan! – and its descent from the natural party of power to a bunch
of secular Mullahs, endlessly arguing about theological fine points
while the country rots, while Thatcher and her suburban pirates run
down the health service and the schools and turn this country into a
land fit for selfish little shits.

But most of all it has been made a barfing reality by the very roots
of our culture. To be born an Englishman – ah, what an easy conceit
that builds in you, what a self-righteous nationalism, a secure xeno-
phobia, what a *pride* in your ignorance. No other people speak so
few languages. No other people – certainly not the Germans, Italians
or French, and not even the multi-ethnic Americans – have an expression that is the equivalent of 'greasy foreign muck'. The noble,
wisecracking savages depicted everywhere from *EastEnders* to *Boys
From the Blackstuff* are exercises in nostalgia who no longer exist.

They have their videos and their turbo-charged Capris, but the
British working class have lost something more valuable. Look at

their faces in footage of cup finals in the Forties and Fifties. You do not have to look through pinko-tinted glasses to see how hopeful and happy and fundamentally *decent* they look, with their suits and their NHS teeth and their heartbreaking rattles. Kids used to stand on orange boxes; now you think long and hard before taking a small child with you to a match.

There was a time when I wanted – more than almost anything – to see England win the World Cup one more time before I died. Now I don't even want us to qualify for the thing. I don't want to see English football supporters in Milan and Rome and Naples and Florence next summer. I am sick of my country being embarrassed by my asshole countrymen.

There was recently a wonderful story about a colonial outpost of the tattooed jungle by Ian Jack. Writing in *Granta*, his article was called 'Gibraltar', and it started out as an investigation into the death of three IRA members at the hands of the SAS and evolved into something more. Jack is neither a Thatcher toady or a Troops Out lefty.

'I write as a Scot,' he said, 'and one with too much of the Protestant in him ever to empathise much with the more recent traditions of Irish republicanism, as well as an ordinary level of human feeling which precludes the understanding of the average IRA bomber. But the longer I spent in Gibraltar, the more difficult it became to prop up a shaky old structure – that lingering belief in what must, for lack of a more exact phrase, be called the virtues of Britishness.'

What is so wrong with this country is that it never questions those virtues, it never doubts itself in its murderous loathing for the other. No other country in the Western world has such a slavish devotion to the concept of military glory – as an SAS officer told the enquiry in Gibraltar, his unit's initials provide a 'sexy headline' for the tabloids. Jack's story was illustrated by a stunningly ugly photograph of a young man on the beach of Gibraltar. Judging by his haircut and his demeanour, he is an off-duty serviceman. He is flamboyantly flexing his muscles and there are baroque, mawkish tattooes all down his muscular limbs. His hair is cropped and, inside his stupid Union Jack swimming trunks, he has a semi-erection. The leer on his face says that he is unbelievably pleased with himself. He brings to mind his spiritual mate – the young wife who displayed her sagging breasts to the Task Force when it was departing for the Falklands, the unknown English Rose who got her tits out for the lads.

Oh patriotic tattooed jungle, how you mock the concept of

freedom, democracy and liberty when you produce this race of mind-less gluttons, how profoundly depressing that the unchained spirit breeds such as you. Especially in the year when communism was finally seen globally as a bankrupt philosophy that carries the seeds of its own destruction, in this year when Mao stands revealed as a liberator of the scale of Hitler and Stalin, how wretched and sad it is that they are dying from the Black Sea to Peking for the kind of rights that we take for granted, for the freedoms that we piss all over.

'In the end you must either allow people liberty or you must shoot them,' wrote William Rees-Mogg. 'If a man claims a vote you must either give him a vote or be prepared to take his life.' The vote, Bill? I'd rather have a can of Tennents.

After the slaughter in China it was a revelation to go down to the Chinese Embassy in Portland Place and witness the protest of the ordinary Chinese people of London. The quiet, angry dignity of their picket across the street from the large silent house where not a Mao-ist stirred was truly moving, awesome in its calm outrage, fuelled by a moral fervour that has been missing from the British for years. As far as I am concerned they should let every last one of the four million residents of Hong Kong into England. It would definitely improve the place, for these are people who seem to aspire to something higher than the coarse delights of the tattooed jungle. In fact if you invert that old racist cliché, the one they used to trot out all the time during the Vietnam War, then it finally turns out to be true.

Life just doesn't mean as much to us as it does to them.

The Polenta Jungle

Arena, March/April 1993

NOBODY LOVES the middle class.

The working class are widely admired for their raw-boned vigour and chirpy, cheeky demeanour. The upper class are hugely revered for their impregnable self-assurance and breezy stoicism. But though both the toffs and the riff-raff have their groupies, absolutely nobody loves the bourgeoisie.

And why should they? Hilaire Belloc – a bourgeois boy if ever there was one – lashed out at that cringing, self-loathing fear of life that is such a distinguishing feature of middle-class existence:

> The people in between
> Looked underdone and harassed
> And out of place and mean
> And horribly embarrassed.

Neither posh nor poor, haughty aristocrat nor honest working man, the bourgeoisie are caught in the no man's land of the British class system. Being middle class means always having to say you're sorry.

In her fine book *Class*, Jilly Cooper suggested that the middle class suffers the way a middle child suffers. 'Everyone makes a huge fuss over the first born and everyone pets and coddles the baby (who, like the working classes, is shored up by the great feather bed of the welfare state),' wrote Cooper. 'But the child in the middle gets the most opprobrium, is often left to fend for itself and ganged up on by the other two.'

Absolutely true, of course – both the nobs and the proles despise the middle class. *Epater les bourgeois* – baiting the middle class – has always been a national pastime, whatever end of the social scale you hail from.

The toffs hate the middle class because they see them as pushy, money-grabbing arrivistes who have 'bought their own furniture' (as opposed to inheriting it). The proles hate the middle class because they stand for all the suburban values – thrift, hard work, high standards of personal hygiene – and because they think the middles look down on them (which of course they do). The uppers hate the middles for being counter jumpers. The workers hate the middles for being snobs.

The upper and the working class have many things in common – dogs, uncomfortable houses, a love of the Union Jack – but above all they have a mutual loathing for the middle class, who are considered despicable whether you are from a council estate or a country estate.

There has always been a secret pact between the upper and working class. George Walker, the great East End boxer, saw his daughter marry the Marquess of Milford Haven – effortlessly, George's grandchildren will be upper class. And back in 1970, Lady Kathleen Pelham-Clinton-Hope, daughter of the Duke of Newcastle, actually married an Underground guard.

'We have heard of the Grenadier Guards and the Coldstream, but the Underground . . .' her mother is reported to have said. But it is reasonable to believe that an Underground guard was more acceptable to the Duchess than a small businessman from the middle class. The bourgeoisie are the real untouchables of the British class system.

'At a dinner party I went to the other day, where most of the people came from the historically privileged classes, a man arrived a little late,' wrote Adam Nicolson, Old Etonian, in *The Spectator*. 'What was it about this man? His clothes? Too clean, too finished in their effect? (You should take, I remember being told at school, ten minutes to notice that a man is well-dressed. Any quicker and he's probably queer.) The way he removed his jacket so soon after arriving, that *faux*-casual gesture betraying unease?'

Soon the late arrival is making all the wrong moves – being a little too eager to be liked, showing too many teeth, asking one woman if she is a model, another how long she has been 'preggers'.

'At these remarks the social spines stiffened and what Auden called "the eyelash barrier", the unbreachable gates of exclusion, closed,' said Nicolson. 'He was out, he was making the wrong signs, his very attempts to be more a part of the place where he found himself were driving him further outwards.'

The intruder was, of course, middle class – the saloon bar bonhomie, fondness for coy abbreviations and wet-palmed need to be liked are all unmistakeable. Nicolson reports that a working class man was at the same dinner and received none of the disdainful looks or raised eyebrows.

You can see why Nicolson and his chums despised the bourgeois intruder – the middle class have a far greater capacity for social embarrassment than either the upper or working class, simply because they are so desperate not to do anything wrong. Although both the proles and the toffs are, in their own unique ways, terrible slobs, there is an ease about both of them. They stick to their private worlds and so they are always at home. The middle class is never at home.

Alastair Little, the chef, has mentioned that even entering a restaurant gives them palpitations. 'From the minute they arrive, you can see it in their body language,' says Little. 'The Germans have a name for it: they call it Threshold Angst.'

The bloody bourgeoisie! Terrified of placing one foot in front of the other in case they get it wrong! Even the great revolutionaries, with their dreams of a world where all men are equal, could find no love in their red, red hearts for the middle class. Marx and Lenin dreamed not of slaughtering the toffs but of overthrowing the middle class. 'The substitution of the proletarian for the bourgeois state is impossible without a violent revolution,' said Vlad.

But if nobody loves the middle class, perhaps it is because they are such an unlovable bunch. The concerns of the middle class are so petty, their dreams so small, their horizons so limited.

What is the great terror of the middle class? It is Getting It Wrong. Nothing so obvious as using the wrong knife but infinitely more subtle giveaways like saying 'pardon?' instead of 'what?', 'toilet' instead of 'lavatory' (the middles usually compromise with 'loo'), 'hello' instead of 'how do you do?' – all those little signals that reveal suburban, bourgeois roots.

The great fear of the middle class is looking middle class.

The middle class covers a huge part of society, of course – but they are united in their denial of being middle class. Have you *heard* Nigel Kennedy talk? To be fair, Nigel's quasi-Cockney accent is no more ludicrous than the cod-posh accents of Edward Heath or Margaret Thatcher – all three are desperate to be something other than what they are. Something other than middle class.

'*Les bourgeois, ce sont les autres,*' quipped Jules Renard – the bourgeois are other people. There is no honour in being middle class, at least not in Europe (it's different in America and Japan). Often middle class teenagers upgrade or downgrade their accents – so it is not uncommon to have a boy who sounds as if he is from Tower Hamlets and a girl who could be from Sloane Square in the same family. Anything to avoid looking middle class.

In *Noblesse Oblige*, Nancy Mitford's U and non-U stood for up-per class and non-upper class. By definition, being non-U – meaning gauche, beyond the pale and Not Our Sort Of People – meant being middle class. In Mitford's unforgiving eyes, it was the worst thing in the world.

Oh, who would be a bourgeois? With their scrimping and saving, their timid infidelities, their emphasis on life lived as part of a couple, their endless round of dinner parties and their complaints about house prices, the middle class whine and dine their way through life.

The dinner party is the central middle class experience – just as a night in the pub is the central working class experience and a week-end in the country is the central upper class experience. But if you have been to one middle class dinner party you have been to a thou-sand. The topics of conversation never vary – careers, property, films (nobody has the time to read books any more), schools – and neither does the food. You can't swing a cat without sending it through a plate of polenta. The middle class turn the country into a Polenta Jungle.

But who exactly *are* the middle class? Unlike the upper and the working class, it is not true that you know them when you see them.

The middle class is by far the broadest stratum in the class struc-ture. Unlike the upper and working class, there is an infinite variety of middle class existence. Being middle class covers suburb and city and country. It covers the Home Counties bank manager and the pony-tailed independent producer and Mr Patel at the corner shop. Very different people. But like the rest of their bourgeois brothers and sisters, they are united by certain fundamental tenets. There is a huge gap between being upper middle class and being lower middle class. But being middle class is a lot like being black, Japanese or pregnant – you either are or you aren't. And if you *are* middle class, then you will share certain values with the rest of your breed.

The middle class are all very serious about their professions. They care what people think. They worry about the future. They work hard. They believe in taking care of themselves. And, always, they want *more* – for themselves, for their children, for their community. There is a restlessness at the core of middle class existence.

Like everyone else, the middle class have been hit by the recession. Often the decline was relative and could be overcome with judicious economies. But in the worst cases, houses have been repossessed, small businesses made bankrupt, the good life quietly cancelled.

But if the fighting spirit of the working class has been fatally weakened by the welfare state (just as the upper class has been fatally weakened by too much in-breeding), the middle class are still capable of getting on their bikes.

'Call a mini-cab in the South-East of England and you will no longer be surprised to be collected and chauffeured by a former stockbroker,' wrote Nicholas Monson, author of *The Nouveaux Pauvres*. 'Attend a drinks party and you won't be astonished if your host, an unemployed architect, starts pressing you to buy costume jewellery. Hire a well-spoken window cleaner who has recently set up in the neighbourhood and you won't be shocked to learn that he is a qualified chartered surveyor.' You would think that this ability to survive and thrive in adverse circumstances would get the middle class a better press. Yet their acquisitive individualism is one of the things that makes them roundly despised. Perhaps because Britain – unlike, say, the United States – is a country where we expect people to know their place. Yet if we believe that the wealth of the developed world was created by men very different from this, then we fool ourselves.

But of course the main reason the middle class are hated is because – while both the aristocracy and the proletariat continue to decline – the rise of the middle class has been inexorable and relentless.

A pre-war social event at an RAF base invited 'Officers and their ladies, warrant officers and their wives, airmen and their women.' That England – paralysed by class and convention – has not completely disappeared. But it is fading fast.

There has not been a member of the upper class as Prime Minister for thirty years. In the Fifties we had three Prime Ministers in a row who went to Eton – Anthony Eden, Harold Macmillan, Alexander Douglas-Home. But since 1964 no PM has even gone to public school.

In the Tory leadership election of 1990, Douglas Hurd, Old Etonian, felt the need to hide his silver spoon under a bushel. His father, who is a peer, he said was only 'a tenant farmer of 500 not particularly good acres'.

Well, stone the crows, Doug, and pass the bleeding fish fingers. The irony is, of course, that Hurd would have almost certainly been a better Prime Minister than Major. But Britain will no longer accept a member of the upper class as its leader – and neither will the Tory Party.

But if potential Conservative leaders have to pass themselves off as more middle class than they are, nobody is actually ready to embrace the bourgeoisie as a role model. John Major dreams not of a country that is middle class but a land that is classless. Will nobody defend the middle class?

'I come from the middle classes,' said Neville Chamberlain, 'and I am proud of the ability, the shrewdness, the industry and providence, the thrift by which they are distinguished.'

Neville had a point – the virtues of the middle class are not very exciting, but they are the backbone – or at least the wallet – of any nation. Genteel, dull, anxious – well, all right! But the middle class also starts the businesses. They read the books. They fill the theatres (watching plays about how awful the middle class are). The arts would collapse without them. And of course they put infinitely more into the welfare state than they ever take out.

So go tell it on the golf course! Sing it from the DIY Superstore! Shout it from the garden centre! The middle class – those two-car lepers of the British class system – have much to recommend them.

There is precious little to admire about either the working class or the upper class. The toffs in *Tatler*, the oiks in the *Sun* – who needs them? Both are distinguished by a distrust of culture, a kneejerk nationalism and bad teeth – no wonder they get on so well.

The discreet charms of the bourgeoisie have been underrated for too long. They are the most cultured class. The hardest working. They believe in the welfare state but are aware of its corrupting nature. Yes, there are many things to despise about the middle class. But, unlike the nobs and the riff-raff, they do not know their place. They believe in self-improvement.

And you have to admire that. Don't you?

Ultimately the middle class are entitled to echo the bewildered sentiments of the Michael Douglas character in *Falling Down*.

'How did *I* become the bad guy?'

Street Trash

Beggars of Britain

Arena, September/October 1991

P UNK BEGGARS, DRUNK BEGGARS, beggars with babies. Beggars in shell suits and beggars in rags. Beggars stinking of cheap lager with snot on their chin and a mangy mutt on the end of a piece of string. Lots of them.

And gipsy beggars who try to stuff a ratty flower into your button hole with some sentimental line – 'For the children,' coos some obese hag. Old beggars too shagged out to beg, young beggars who look like they could run a four-minute mile if they ever made it up off their fannies. Beggars in King's Cross, beggars in Covent Garden, beggars on the street where you live. All kinds of beggars everywhere in this city, and they will be with us forever now. They have no shame. Because begging is no longer taboo.

I think that my father would rather have seen us go hungry than have to go out there and ponce for our supper. I think that the old man, may he rest peacefully, would have preferred to rob, cheat or watch us wither with malnutrition before standing on a street corner with a Uriah Heep look in his eye asking for a hand-out. He would have been happier seeing us sleeping in a shoebox full of shit than he would have been *begging*.

The fact is that my father's generation was incapable of begging. The children they raised were also incapable of begging. There were standards that were not negotiable. There were certain lines you never crossed; there were taboos. Respect the elderly. Don't rat on your friends. Never hit a woman. Never stand on a street corner with snot on your chin and a dog on the end of a piece of string asking passers-by if they have any change. Of all the taboos, *don't beg* was the greatest of all. You could sleep with your sister before you went begging.

Somewhere between then and now, between our childhood and our thirties, all the old taboos disappeared. But taboos are good, taboos are the no-go areas that mark the parameters of society's moral code. When taboos fall, civilisation is built on dangerously shifting sands.

Liberals would blame the fall of the begging taboo on the let-the-bloody-orphans-take-care-of-themselves ethics of Thatcherism. Conservatives would blame the hey-you-guys-let's-catch-crabs permissiveness of the '60s. What is certain is that violence against women, children and the wrinklies is at an all-time high; and that begging is suddenly shame-free, an acceptable way to make a living. It is now quite all right to earn a crust with the crumbs you can ponce from strangers. Begging is a vocation. Soon beggars will have agents and accountants who will write off the food for their dogs-on-a-rope against tax. How low can you go? The British have become a nation of nappy-wearers.

In that underrated comedy classic *American Psycho*, Patrick Bateman is plagued by beggars at every turn. In the exchanges between Bateman and the beggars, Bret Easton Ellis reveals that he is really an old softie at heart. The beggars are invariably homeless and hungry and deserving of sympathy, easily reduced to tears of shame and regret. Meanwhile, the American Psycho himself is an archetype of right-wing heartlessness, saying things to the cry-baby beggars like, 'Listen – do you think it's fair to take money from people who *do* have jobs? Who *do* work?' just before he slices out their eyeballs with a platinum Am Ex card.

The most unrealistic thing about the beggars in *American Psycho* is their shame. It is quite believable that they are outside every restaurant. It is perfectly credible that they inspire nausea and disgust in Bateman. What smacks of pure invention, however, are the tears of self-loathing that course down their cheeks whenever Bateman gives them a stern look. I never saw a beggar yet who would recognise guilt if it bit him on his unwashed ass. In real life – over here and over there – beggars have no shame. Their whole schtick is a transference of guilt. Shame is meant to be in the eye of the beholder. Twenty years ago – *five years ago!* – the beggar might have felt guilty. Now it's the *beggee* who's meant to feel bad. Well, I'm sorry, but any liberal guilt I might feel about brushing past yet another beggar – and there are so many of the bastards – has long been overwhelmed by compassion fatigue.

Now that begging is an acceptable career option it is worth considering a few tips from poncing masterclass. Place yourself somewhere the public can't miss you, say outside a West End theatre or at the foot of some tube station steps. Consider the use of props – a child is good, a baby even better, though you would be surprised at the well of compassion you plumb when you have some flea-bitten mongrel at your side. Signs are fine. Knock out ones that say, 'Please give generously – No home, no job, no shame' or 'Take pity – Mohawk with run in tights' or 'Dog on a rope to support'. Make eye contact and be persistant, friendly – don't be too specific. Ask the beggees for 'loose change', rather than money for a cup of coffee or money to catch the bus to the Job Centre. Everybody knows you are going to piss it away.

You can always sing a little song or do a little dance, but a true beggar frowns on these gimmicks. Busking is begging with music (give me money because I am entertaining you) just as mugging is begging with menace (give me money or I will fill your face in). But begging purists want you to give them money because – what? Because you are better off than they are? Because life has dealt them a bad hand?

Well, I don't buy it. I don't believe that the people begging are the unluckiest people in town. They are merely the people with the least pride, dignity, self-respect – all the intangibles that hold the human spirit together. It's strange, but I don't recall ever seeing a black beggar in London, or a Hong Kong Chinese beggar or an Indian beggar. I must have seen hundreds, thousands of beggars in this town, and they have all been white trash. But when you look at the sick-making state of the white working class – all the men turning into fat fucks at 20, all the girls turning into their mothers a year later – what possible hope could there be for the next rung down on the caste system? If the people with jobs have the aesthetic beauty and intellectual ability of a cow pat, what chance is there for the people without a job? Though of course by now begging *is* a job – the newest profession.

I used to give, I used to give generously. These people disgusted me, but still I gave. I was appalled, but I felt sorry for them – and they knew it! Oh, they could spot old muggins a mile off! It was feeding frenzy time at the zoo when I came down the road! I was a soft touch – I thought it was the correct emotional response. In a way, my concern has simply been exhausted. So sorry, *no change!* Ponce your next bruise-blue can of Vomit Brew from some other sucker. There's just *too many* of them. But it goes beyond mere compassion fatigue. I think I have grown to truly hate them.

I hate the way they make a beautiful city ugly, the way they shuffle about in a lager haze first thing in the morning – booze is a bigger factor than bad luck in the begging world – and I hate it that my son came home one day saying he had given his tube fare to a man who really really needed it. I wish he could grow up thinking all men are brothers. But it is hard to think of a man as your brother when he has a brain addled by alcohol, snot on his chin and a dog on a rope. Then every man feels like an only child.

Begging defaces the city, degrades the spirit. It dehumanises you as well as them; it brutalises us all. You learn to walk past these people, you have to, and it makes it easier to turn away from the truly needy. These professional leeches, big strapping lads some of them, harden your heart, put callouses on your soul. They make every cry for help seem like junk mail.

In Africa you see beggars with deformed legs crawling, literally crawling, by the side of the road. In Africa you see old men with their eyes turned a horrible milky blue by river blindness being led around by their grandchildren. You see sights that make you feel like weeping – you see beggars with every excuse for begging. But London isn't the Third World. It just smells that way.

In America they have beggars who are suffering from AIDS – that's probably a couple of years away for us – which begs the question, what's so special about AIDS? Of course it's terrible, all terminal, all tragic. Because there is no social network to take care of these people, you say. Because the medical services can't cope. Well, you can believe that if you want. Or you can believe that begging is like eating human flesh, being cruel to animals or pushing your granny while she's shaving – something that no-one in the developed world should ever do, under any circumstances. The virus that we are truly blighted by is the one that attacks the human spirit. It is reflected in the general degeneracy of life in our capital, in the pathetically unctuous faces of all these healthy grown men whose best friend is a dog on a piece of string.

But it may not be very long before we look back on the good old days when the only beggars we had to contend with were gipsies, punks and drunks. The new hard times are not a northern, working-class, trouble-at-mill thing this time around. This time the recession has hit the middle class – it's wonderful, it's never been so easy to hail a black cab – and now that the last taboo is gone, how long before you are asked for loose change by a Channel 4 commissioning editor or a *South Bank Show* researcher, or an editor at Random House? How long before you look into the face of a beggar on Old Compton Street and realise – the horror, the horror – that you have had *lunch* with this person?

The taboos are coming down, and so are all the borders. The other day I saw a family of East Europeans jabbering away in some Slavic dialect. You wouldn't believe these people. The woman was wearing a little Porsche badge on clothes so synthetic they were a fire hazard. If you think that Thatcher has made us a nation of nappy wearers, then wait till you get a load of the paragons of dependency that Marx and Lenin have produced. The opening up of Europe creates all sorts of possibilities for the begging industry.

We owe it to ourselves to walk past them, metaphorically gobbing in the grubby palms of their outstretched hands, chanting our protest against a world that is forever changing for the worst. No change, we say, no change. Just say no change.

Gender Benders

Why women shouldn't drink (too) much

Arena, November 1993

WHY SHOULD A WOMAN NEVER get drunk? Because being drunk makes you loud, obnoxious, sentimental, self-pitying and stupid. And of course most women are like that when they are completely sober.

There are some things in this world that women do better than men. Shopping, weeping hysterically and cleaning up around the house – women do all these things brilliantly and we should go down the pub and let them get on with it.

But one of the things that women should leave to men is gettting drunk. Being drunk is like having a moustache. It looks good on a man and terrible on a woman.

Drunkenness does not suit all men, of course. After two cocktails, a few beers and half a bottle of Chardonnay, most men do not become better people. In fact, they are far more likely to become troglodytes who swear eternal friendship one minute and threaten to punch your face in the next. But while some men make bad drunks, *all* women are bad drunks.

The dark side of drunkenness is raised voices, casual violence, crazy laughter, unwise sex – it makes a man look like a fool. But it makes a woman look insane.

There are some men – the urbane, the sophisticated, the lovers of life – who can handle getting drunk. After a hard day at the office, a little bacchanalian excess actually improves a few of us. After the pressures and stress of the working world, with a few drinks inside us we become more relaxed, more open and more talkative. But did you ever meet a woman who needed to become more talkative? Too much drink tends to remove a woman's dignity, pride and underpants – usually in that order.

And alcohol is powerful stuff. It can bring you down. Sometimes you have a few glasses of vino and soon you are pondering the very nature of existence. This kind of philosophical, moody introspection does not suit women. Because they are intuitive rather than cerebral creatures, it makes them sad and bitter. It makes them think too much – and that is not what they are best at.

After a few drinks, a man will say something like, 'If God really exists, then why does He allow so much suffering in the world?' But a drunken woman is far more likely to say, 'My mother warned me about you and she was absolutely right, you filthy bastard!'

Drink tends to emphasise all that is unpleasant about a woman. If she is a bit of a slut, then getting drunk will find her offering a blow job to the wine waiter. If she is over-emotional, then getting drunk will find her overturning tables, throwing plates and cutting up your clothes with a pair of shearing scissors. If she has a rather melancholy personality, then getting drunk will make her suicidal. Drink is poison to the female heart. No matter what her personality is like, it will be made much worse by drinking alcohol.

Some men look wonderful when they are drunk. I have a friend who, when he is really smashed, leans back in his chair, develops this glassy look in his eyes and gets this little secret smile playing around the corners of his mouth. About two minutes later he usually falls off his chair but in that short time before he disappears he is a charming and delightful companion.

But his girlfriend drinks just as much as he does and it doesn't do anything for her. She suddenly develops this uncontrollable urge to discuss French cinema. As you can imagine, this completely spoils the evening.

There are approximately 10 million wonderful women in the world. But not one of them is made more interesting, more attractive or more loveable when she is drunk. It doesn't matter if she is a high-powered career woman with a university degree or a suburban *hausfrau* with a gold ankle chain, drink brings out the worst in her. There is something sluttish about a pissed female. A drunken woman seems – and tends to act – like a waterfront strumpet. And I don't feel like discussing French cinema with her. I feel like selling her to a couple of sailors.

And though some men are made more charming, extrovert and garrulous by drink, in all honesty alcohol usually just makes us behave badly too. We try to get total strangers to go to bed with us, we get into arguments with their boyfriends, we piss out of the windows of trains. OK, we have all done it. *But there is not a woman alive who looks good trying to piss out of the window of a train.*

There are men who get drunk and become sentimental, depressed and incoherent. It certainly doesn't look good on them. But it looks far worse on a woman. And if a man wants a sentimental, depressed and incoherent woman, he can always stay at home with his wife.

Drinking is a man's world. Pubs, bars, clubs – these are the hunting grounds of the male of the species. It's good that women are there but if they are talking too loudly, making fools of themselves and making stupid jokes – if they are drunk – then it spoils the fun. Who wants women to act exactly the same as us? Who is wearing the trousers around here? Who is paying for the drinks? OK, OK – so the modern woman pays her way. But heterosexuality is a celebration of differences. A drunken woman acts like a bad imitation of a man.

Alcohol is a powerful drug and nobody can truly predict the effect it is going to have. After the third bottle of sweet dessert wine, there is just no telling how you are going to feel. The roulette wheel of intoxication – you never know where it is going to take you. You never know if you are going to spend all evening laughing, or get into a fight with a policeman or wake up naked in an alley tied to a lamppost only a few postal districts from where your friends have hidden your clothes. And no woman should ever be that out of control. I am with Camille Paglia on this one – it's too dangerous for women. We are equal but different.

I am not advocating that women should abstain from alcohol. Far from it! Women should all be able to drink a little bit. Like knowing how to massage and sew buttons and change the wheel on a car, drinking in moderation is one of those skills that every woman should have – just as a man should know how to cook, take care of babies and operate the washing machine without a phone call to his mother.

Women should be able to take a sip of spritzer or even – on very special occasions – a small glass of white wine. Because there is nothing worse than going out for dinner with a woman, ordering a bottle of wine and then having to drink it all yourself. When a man goes out with a woman who doesn't drink at all, he always gets far drunker than he intended to.

But the trouble is that women either drink too little or too much. They either can't smell a barmaid's apron without getting completely drunk or else they don't know when to stop. When a woman starts ordering aperitifs, a second bottle of wine and a cognac, you should immediately throw away her telephone number. She will be boring to talk to and equally boring in bed. Drink is *not* an aphrodisiac, not for any of us. Drink is not like having Spanish Fly – it is more like having hermetically sealed pyjamas.

Although when we were teenagers we tried to get local girls drunk so that we could stick it in them, there is actually little joy to be had from making love to a drunken female. We only did it when we were teenagers because there was no other kind available. But in bed a drunken woman is either completely inert, laying there like a dead fish, or else she goes to the other extreme and imagines she is in a remake of *Fatal Attraction*, bouncing around on top of the dishwasher until she starts turning green and asks you, 'Quick – where's the bathroom?' Either way, you are not really fucking her. You are only fucking some drunk.

But if there is one thing uglier than a drunken woman then it is a woman with a hangover. A hangover – the dry mouth, sore eyes, bilious stomach, throbbing head, sinking exhaustion and stinking self-loathing – is bad enough when it is happening to you. When it is happening to the woman you are waking up with, it is even worse. Who wants to wake up with someone who looks as bad as you do?

So why do they do it? Why do modern women – friends, colleagues, lovers – try to drink like men? Why can't they stick to a couple of small spritzers and a packet of pork scratchings? Because they have grown up being taught by the shrill vixens of feminism that men and women are the same. Anything we can do, they can do too. But this is bullshit. Men and women are equal but we are most certainly not the same. When women look good with moustaches and pissing out of train windows, that's when I'll be ready to do some serious drinking with them.

It is time for all men to admit that we disapprove of drunken women. In his heart, no man wants to be around a stumbling woman who slurs her words, laughs too much, talks too loud, flirts with anything that moves, throws up in the taxi on the way home and then sinks into a deep depression. No man wants to go out with a bore or go to bed with a dead fish. No man wants a drunken woman.

They make you ashamed, disgusted and embarrassed. Even more importantly, they make you spill your drink.

Hippy Nouveau

Space cadets and cosmic ninnies

Arena, December 1992/January 1993

E VERYONE WHO GREW UP IN THE LATE '60s and early '70s was touched by hippy culture. Even if you sported a number two crop, Ben Sherman and white Sta-Prests, you were part of it. In those days everybody – apart from the most Neanderthal peanuts, who were almost always called Steve – was a surrogate freak, an honorary head. At the cusp of the '60s and '70s, everybody had at least a little hippy blood.

As a teenage skinhead, I smoked my first joint listening to 'Riders On The Storm' just after Jim Morrison took his last bath. I knew my way around the second Led Zeppelin album as well as any trench-coated, acid-fazed hairy (who, of course, only a few summers ago had been some fresh-faced kid who played football with you in the park until it was too dark to see the ball).

And although I copped my first feel of where life begins from some reluctant, hard-faced skinhead girl in a butcher's doorway, naturally I would have infinitely preferred to be inside the Afghan of some gentle hippy chick with a beatific grin and a willing way.

True, a lot of hippy culture was trash. Drug-addled, pretentious and dull as only the cosmically-inclined can be. No culture which makes required reading of *The Lord of the Rings*, *Zen and the Art of Motorcycle Maintenance* and *Jonathan Livingstone Seagull* can be all good. What the fuck does a bloody seagull know about anything?

But there is no denying that the hippies had a rich and noble culture. Hippy had the best music, the prettiest girls, the most noble ideals. What indeed is so funny about peace, love and understanding?

Punks, of course, made great sport of baiting the hippies (who had anyway pretty much disappeared from the streets by the summer of 1976), but they shared a lot in common. Both lived an existence of bohemian squalor which consisted of dreaming of a better world, taking far too many drugs and – in those innocent days – fucking almost anything that moved. And of course the original hippies were a recent folk memory for the punks. In my crumbling Crouch End bedsit, you could still smell the whiff of a thousand joss sticks.

It was not hippy that punks objected to so much as corporate rock. John Rotten was a big fan of Neil Young and Captain Beefheart. Hell, who wasn't? Well, me for a start – but you take my point. Half of the punk antipathy for hippies was rhetoric and half of it was class animosity. If you came from a working-class background then *everybody you knew* was a skin. You have to drop an awful lot of acid to overcome that kind of peer pressure.

But it did not really matter if you didn't grow your hair down to your ass, wear a kaftan and call your dad 'man'. You were part of hippy anyway, it was the dominant culture, its influence was everywhere. Dances with freaks – those were the days.

And now they are back. Changed, certainly, but with those faraway eyes, that aura of sartorial neglect and that cavalier disregard for personal hygiene that only a hippy can muster.

I look at Nirvana's Kurt Cobain (not to mention his lovely wife) and I see an unreconstructed hippy, albeit one who wouldn't have landed a job as a Led Zeppelin roadie. I read the latest bulletin from techno-pagan sound system Spiral Tribe – 'the mismanagement, manipulation, corruption and stupidity of the self-appointed power freaks who consider themselves in control of our planet has not gone unnoticed. As a network of global communications technology grows it spans continents as well as penetrating deep within the invisible micro dimensions of the newly explored electrical circuitry' – and it strikes me as being pure, unadulterated hippy babbling. A Spiral Tribe missive always begs the question – what the fuck are you going on about? I thought they just played records in fields.

I hear The Orb talking about UFOs, I note The Shamen going on about 'The Archaic Revival' and their 'shamanic theory', I can't fail to miss all the New Age travellers queueing up at some rural post office for their state benefits and I say to myself – this is hippy culture with all the good stuff taken out. Where are the pretty girls? The great music? The noble ideals? This isn't hippy – this is hippy nouveau.

Hippy nouveau shares many of the buzzwords of real hippy. Progressive, tribal, psychedelic – all these are deployed, often in the same sentence.

'Let's say you go to an underground party and it's really progressive and very tribal and very sophisticated and very psychedelic,' The Shamen's Mr C recently suggested. 'There's definitely a telepathic community formed in which everyone does experience many different feelings together as a whole unit. At the end of the night you get everyone talking about the same thing, the same comments on the party.'

Heavy! Hippy nouveau discovers the profound in the ordinary and has an unflagging belief in cosmic concidence. OK, the old-style hippies could be intellectually flatulent too, but at least they had a sense of playfulness about them. I always thought it was sweet how in the early '70s hippies would smoke dope (which they disgustingly called 'shit') and watch *The Muppets*. They knew how to have fun. One of the things I object to most strongly about hippy nouveau is that its practitioners are such po-faced bastards.

The grunge rockers of America can reasonably be considered part of hippy nouveau. Crap clothes, crap hair, crap drugs, been a while since they made the acquaintance of a bar of soap – yes, these people are hippy nouveau all right.

But it is the young people (or not so young – Alex Paterson of The Orb is only a few years younger than a wizened veteran like myself) of our own islands that are at the vanguard of hippy nouveau. And curiously, in Britain it is not rock music that has given them a home but dance culture. Disco merchants have never been so full of themselves.

Spiral Tribe, The Orb, The Shamen – these are very different groups. Respectively, they are the Grateful Dead, Pink Floyd and Slade of the '90s. But they are all hippy nouveau because they are all cosmic ninnies, they all believe in the infinite possibilities that can be glimpsed just above the city skyline, they are all quite happy to sing through their sphincter about the boundless cosmos.

They witter on about the sanctity of tribal culture, a coming new age and – titter ye not – making contact with aliens. And they are all the product of a bankrupt culture that is exhausted by chemical excess.

Ecstasy has meant as much to the current generation of wild youth as The Sex Pistols did to mine. For three years in the late '70s, I got my roughage from amphetamine sulphate (a high-fibre drug – and always has been). For us punks – and the real hippies before us – drugs were an integral part of our lifestyle. For the rave generation, it has been more than that. Ecstasy has given them a reason to be alive.

But no generation can rave forever. There comes a time when the madness has to stop. Sooner or later the wild rhythms of youth must be put aside and replaced with something more mellow. Your dancing shoes are traded in for carpet slippers. You put down the Ecstasy and pick up the Bovril. And you buy a copy of The Orb's new compact disc. Hippy nouveau is the last refuge of the shagged out.

When Lionel Richie's greatest hits package 'Back To Front' was knocked off the top of the album charts after nearly two months, it was the signal that the generation who have been raving to house, techno and other souped-up dance rhythms since 1987 – the happy hoofers who have metamorphosed into nouveau hippies – were finally starting to feel their age.

Because the record that replaced the lilting love songs of Lionel was 'U.F.Orb' by The Orb, 74 minutes of ambient house. Dance music for when the dancing has to stop. It has a quiet, hypnotic beauty. You don't need to be an exhausted raver to like The Orb. I haven't been taking Ecstasy and looning about in an open field next to the M25 for the last five years, but I can understand where The Orb are coming from.

This is the ultimate easy-listening music. I am quite taken with it. The Orb would be likeable if they were not so full of shit.

The Orb are an odd couple – a balding, 32-year-old ex-Killing Joke roadie and public schoolboy called Alex Paterson and a 23-year-old ex-studio engineer called Thrash. These boys have a definite cosmic perspective. They are into secret visits from alien life forms, the mystic power of prehistoric stones and altering their consciousness (sometimes it is so altered that their punctuality goes right out the window).

Their track 'The Blue Room' tells the story of Hangar 18 at the Wright-Patterson US Air Force base in Ohio. The Orb insist that this is the secret location where the American government keeps all the UFOs and extraterrestials that it has captured over the years. The Orb sent faxes to Wright-Patterson demanding more information. The Americans faxed back that they didn't know what The Orb were talking about. Well, they would, wouldn't they? Make mine a large conspiracy theory, man.

I was actually going to meet the boys. I was looking forward to discussing their music and associated topics, such as alien life forms and the high price of Rizlas. Alas, the guys got bad vibes from my astoundingly successful film *The Tattooed Jungle* and cancelled our tryst at the last minute.

It is not like hippies to be so gutless. Consider John and Yoko enduring the jeering mass media for the sake of peace. Staying in bed for a week, eating chocolate cake in a bag – they had a lot of nerve. Ah, but The Orb are cod hippy. Fake hippy. Hippy nouveau.

There is a lack of moral courage about these cosmic twerps. The most startling thing about The Shamen's 'Ebeneezer Goode' was the way the group belatedly denied it had anything to do with drugs. They even rather improbably suggested that 'Veras' was rhyming slang for 'gins' rather than 'skins'. Hendrix would never have denied that 'Purple Haze' was about artificial stimulants. Gutless hippy nouveau bastards!

Like the psychedelic pop groups that evolved from the hippy underground, The Shamen take the culture that produced them and make it cute for the masses. That's fine by me – I always preferred The Monkees to the Grateful Dead. What stops me finding them cute is that they are such paragons of hippy nouveau. Witness the last track on their CD 'Boss Drum' where an American psychedelic ex-pert called Terence McKenna rambles on about life, the universe and nothing, accompanied by the musical farts of The Shamen.

'Human history,' Tel suggests, 'represents such a radical break with the natural systems of biological organisation that preceded it that it must be the response to a kind of attractor or dwell-point that lies ahead.'

This garbled message of imminent revelation is echoed elsewhere by the wild-eyed boys of hippy nouveau.

'The earth is re-connected,' say Spiral Tribe. 'The signal is ready to be sent.'

'The clouds are flying in time with the birds!' gasp The Orb.

Beam me out of here, Scottie! Hippy nouveau is now the dominant strain of what we used to call youth culture. These babbling space cadets wandering fields with their head full of cosmic drivel are what we have come to. Truly, we can sink no lower. And no, I *don't* have any bloody Veras.

Caught In the Act

Hard core

Elle, February 1987

THIS IS SOHO'S DEAD ZONE – the middle of the afternoon, when even the longest of lunches has ended, down a narrow back alley where the square mile still looks as seedy as it did 30 years ago. This is not the *Soho nouveau* that has been getting celebratory spreads in all the glossies for the past couple of years. This is old-style Soho. Shadowy basements. Steep staircases. Stale sweat, cigarette smoke and girls, girls, girls. This is the hard core.

The shabby backstreet is bathed in rain and neon; it looks like life imitating a B-movie. John Pluck strides down it purposefully. He is slight, wiry, 40-ish – he looks like a cheerful Tom Bell. Pluck is wearing a white collar and tie, a smart two-piece suit, and you would take him for a middle-aged, middle management executive if he were not carrying that crowbar under his arm. This is a raid. Pluck is accompanied by a small team of plain clothes officers, young men and women in their 20s who are all in their street clothes. ('Dress is casual,' I'm advised by the Met. 'But not too casual.') This is the porn squad who operate out of West End Central in Savile Row, crossing the prim sweep of Regent Street to dig out the dirt in the lurid heart of the city.

We enter a book store where, even at this hour, a good number of book lovers are perusing the covers of Cellophane-wrapped periodicals with titles such as *Kingsize*, *Shaft*, *Shiny*, *TV Mistresses*, *Black Masters*, *White Slaves* (for porn gourmets who hate women *and* blacks – a large market) and, of course, *New Cunts* (subtlety is not one of hard core's strong points).

'Gentlemen!' says Inspector Pluck happily to the haggard young sleazeballs behind the counter. 'Would you mind closing your premises?'

When the shop's clientele – respectable-looking, menopause-age males – suddenly realise what is happening, they hastily shove the copy of *Kingsize* back on the shelf and scramble for the door. As one of the shop assistants is locking up, a man with a club foot tries to get in. For a few seconds it is pure farce, the porn merchant trying to keep the man with the club foot out of the store, the limping man on the street trying to force his way into the middle of a police raid. I momentarily have my preconceived notions confirmed by the presence of the man with the club foot – the cripple who needs pornography because he can't have a normal relationship. But most porn users look a lot more normal that that.

The door is finally locked. While one officer takes statements from the shopkeepers, others start taking down titles from one of the shelves. Just one of the shelves because most of the books in here are ragged paperbacks that have been bought wholesale from jumble sales and now gather dust. The law demands that sex shops have a licence which costs over £12,000, so many stores try to keep up the pretence of being in the same business as W. H. Smith.

But on one shelf there is the shrink-wrapped real thing. It is a numbed and numbing pageant of violated flesh.

D. H. Lawrence called pornography 'the attempt to insult sex, to do the dirt on it', and in this pantheon of porn, the cruel and the grotesque have pride of place. Of all the glossy sordid images that Pluck's men loaded into sacks, the two I remember most clearly are the old women in *80 Plus* (the title refers to chest measurement, though by the end of the day a magazine for men who like octogenarians would not have surprised me) and the young girl with five men pushing themselves into her face. Those two images sum up hard core's passion for the circus freak show, the grossly bizarre, and its need always to go one step further. Those who say that pornography has its place and try to say where they would draw the line are missing the point. You can't draw the line because pornography crosses all the lines. That is what it is about. You see a picture of a woman and two men in the act of fellatio and you know that somewhere there is the image of a woman doing the same thing with *three* men. It makes your heart sick after a while.

But what exactly are we looking for? That which is obscene. And what is obscene? According to the law – specifically the Obscene Publications Act – that which is likely to corrupt and deprave. This is, of course, open to infinite interpretation and one of the problems that Pluck and his people face is the often whimsical nature of the law. The guidelines are the erect penis, the vulva that is pulled open – *something happening*. Some hard core publishers try to avoid depicting penetration by having ludicrous red stars placed on the point of entry.

In one magazine there is a black and white picture of a smiling young woman whose vulva is not being pulled open, though it appears to be somewhat ajar.

'Now that,' says Pluck, pointing, 'that is a grey area.'

Outside, the street lights of Soho are coming on. We meet up with some more of Pluck's people who were on another raid. Raids are always simultaneous and designed to keep the sleaze merchants on the jump. They might not see John Pluck and his crowbar for a month and then they could see him every day for a week.

Back at West End Central the sacks full of hard core are dumped on the floor. One young cop manfully swings his catch over his shoulder before emptying it on the lino.

'Oh, Nigel,' a WPC smirks, 'you are so *macho*.'

Pluck's team are an incredibly likeable, decent crowd. Hand-picked volunteers, they work on the porn squad for six months before going back to uniform. There are two reasons for this. One is that after this length of time their faces are becoming too well known for plain clothes operations and the other is that there is only so much hard core that a man – or woman – can take. Hard core has a brutalising effect on everyone who comes into contact with it. At West End Central they do not have a patronising, Mary Whitehouse view of hard core – that it will not corrupt me, but it could easily corrupt you. Officers are back to their units after six months and before that if their work affects their sex drive – either way.

'They are only allowed to watch a maximum of four hours in the viewing room a day,' Inspector Pluck says. 'Four hours of fast forward hard core is enough for anyone.' Two small TV sets flicker with prosaic obscenity. An officer sits in front of each screen, filling out a report (the bureaucracy of controlling hard core, where every numb spasm has to be recorded, filed and ultimately reported to the Crown Prosecution Service, is a surreal mountain of red tape).

'Buggery there ... dildo and buggery ... ejaculation ... good actress, this one ...'

'Nice eyes, she's got,' says a WPC. 'And nice teeth. That makes a change.'

These videos cost around £40 (the 'magazines' around £8). Hard core is big business and has its own film industry, the same thespians turning up again and again, though Dick Rambo (probably not his real name) is unlikely ever to turn up at the Academy Awards.

We are viewing a ménage à trash called *Colour Climax*, featuring two sullen black men and one melodramatically ecstatic white woman, when one of Pluck's young team kindly breaks open a Bounty bar and holds it out to the photographer and me. 'Not right now, thanks,' we tell him in unison, averting our eyes from *Colour Climax*.

Ten years ago there were more than 200 retail outlets dealing in pornography in Soho. Today there are fewer than 20. This 90 per cent reduction has been brought about by the combined efforts of Westminster City Council, the Soho Society (the association of local residents) and the efforts of men like John Pluck. Even more striking than the fact that Soho has been reclaimed for the residents and the revellers is the *type* of pornography that is now on sale. For all its squirming banality it is relatively mild compared with the kind of hard core that was around 10 years ago.

Most of the grimy goods we seized will be charged under section three of the Obscene Publications Act. If eventually a jury of 12 just persons find it to be obscene, then it will be forfeited and, at a secret incinerator in north London in the presence of a senior police officer, burned.

If convicted under section two of the Act, the pornographers don't merely watch their obscene goods go up in smoke, they go to jail. Section two means a prison sentence rather than mere forfeiture.

What is the sickest thing you can imagine? Section two material can top that ... John Pluck has a sealed blue box used for training purposes that contains things no one should ever see, the graphic inventions of the most diseased regions of the human psyche. There is a scrotum being nailed to the floor in the blue box ... I could not look at that. But I saw all the stomach-churning sex splattered with urine, blood and faeces, I saw the animals with humans, and I saw the child.

She was a fair-haired girl of around eight years old and the room she was in was sparsely furnished and full of shadows. You never saw the man's face, but you saw the face of the eight-year-old girl.

When I was out of West End Central and walking through the shoppers on Regent Street, I worked out that there were only three possible reactions to hard core. Firstly, you can argue the case that any form of censorship is a slippery slope to tread, that we should all have freedom of expression – the free country argument.

Secondly, it could be said that, though repugnant to most people on both a moral and aesthetic level, pornography acts as a safety valve for society's basest instincts and, in a world after AIDS, it is necessary, even valuable and important.

Thirdly and finally, you can believe that something as brutal and brutalising as hard core should be wiped from the face of the city. This is *Taxi Driver's* Travis Bickle's view, the wish that a rain would come and wash the scum from the streets, and if I wanted to convince someone that this was the only view that made any kind of sense, then I would try to tell them about the face of that eight-year-old girl.

Night is falling in Soho now. In Groucho's they will be sinking the first of the evening's cocktails, in Brewer Street and Walkers Court they will be replacing the material we seized, and up at West End Central John Pluck and his young team will be wading through a soul-numbing expanse of paperwork.

I think about that eight-year-old girl and I wonder if she is Dutch or American or English – this stuff comes from all over the civilised world – and if those pictures were taken 10 or 15 years ago, or if it was only a matter of months. I wonder if she is thousands of miles away and grown up now, or if she is still a little kid, living in some shabby London street a few tube stops away. I wonder about the men that took her to that sparse room of shadows, and most of all I wonder what it has cost her.

Culture

Amis' Monsters

Elle, June 1987

O N A COLD, BLUE AFTERNOON in West London, Martin Amis is rolling another cigarette in the first-floor flat where he works and talking about the day when he'd have to get into his car, drive the mile to his home and kill his wife and two young sons. Nuclear weapons, Amis will tell you, are starting to make him sick.

'Suppose I survive,' he writes in the introduction to his new collection of short stories, *Einstein's Monsters*. 'I shall be obliged (and it's the last thing I'll feel like doing) to retrace that long mile home . . . I must find my wife and children and I must kill them.

'What am I to do with thoughts like these? What is anyone to do with thoughts like these?'

'It's what you would have to do, isn't it,' he tells me. '*Inversion* is a constant theme in nuclear weapons. Everything is turned on its head.

'The stories in *Einstein's Monsters* are hunches about nuclear weapons. The glimpses we usually get of post-nuclear, post-holocaust life are taken from the Blitz – images of struggle, making the best of it, doing what you can for the injured and elderly – but it would not be like that. Everything would invert and, if you can imagine some kind of cockroach life that would be left for people, I think it might be perfectly natural to *torture* your children.

'All values would be gone. These grotesque and atrocious things you read in the tabloids about the rape of 90-year-old women – those are little *previews* of what life would be like.'

Einstein's Monsters is a work of black brilliance, the result of one of our finest writer's obsession with the final subject. The book consists of five short stories and a long, polemical essay (in which Amis attributes the roots of his obsession to becoming a father and reading Jonathan Schell's *The Fate of the Earth*, a shocking and detailed account of the effects of nuclear war). Three of the stories are sick, shrewd guesses about life after nuclear war – a global concentration camp with the sky on fire. The other two are set in the present, for, as well as the weapons themselves, *Einstein's Monsters* refers to the people living in the shadow of the bomb.

Amis thinks we are getting worse. We can remind him of the butchers' aprons worn by Hitler and Stalin, the slaughter of Indians in North and South America, all this historical unpleasantness, but he remains convinced that we have never sunk this low before.

'Yeah, it's been rough,' he says lightly. The serious frown he tends to wear on TV and in photographs is replaced by a wry smile in real life, even though he thinks that real life is getting ranker by the minute. He believes that you don't even have to press the button – people are already contaminated by the very existence of nuclear weapons.

'Every day there is more loss of innocence and more roughing-up of the planet and of human life,' he says. 'You can draw a line at 1955 – when the arsenals grew to a certain level and the actual existence of the world was threatened – and say that everyone who lived after that time is completely different to those who lived before.

'It would be extraordinary if the most important evolutionary difference there's ever been on the planet did not have profound effects on us all. Nuclear weapons have taken away the idea of the future as something we care about. Yes, the nuclear deterrent has lasted for 40 years – but can it last to the death of the sun?'

Amis is married to American art historian Antonia Phillips. They have two children, Jacob, two, and Louis, one. His fascination with nuclear weapons started when Jacob was on the way and the writer had hard evidence that he had a stake in the future. This fascination grew into an obsession. No, even that does not say it – *addiction* is nearer the mark. 'Nuclear weapons *are* addictive,' he says. '*They* can't give up these weapons and once you get interested in a subject like this, then every other issue looks *tiny* next to it.' (As someone who is in love with the power of print, Amis invariably puts the key words of his conversation into italics.)

His work in progress, a novel called *London Fields*, will be set in 1999 against an apocalyptic backdrop of nuclear crisis.

When the *Guardian* was sounding out various writers to see how they felt AIDS was going to affect the novel, Amis offered the view that the disease was possibly radiogenic, caused by freak atmospheric conditions over Africa brought on by the testing of – you guessed it. It has to be said that Amis bringing nuclear weapons into the debate about sex-death looked just a little, well, *wiggy*.

His addiction shows no sign of receding, so this nuke habit is going to have to be added to the three things that people always say about him: (a) that he is a very tiny man (b) with a very big talent (c) who hates women with a vengeance.

We'll take them one at a time. Sure (a), Amis *is* pretty small – around five feet six, I guess – but he is nowhere near the dwarf league, the midget status, the pygmy size that green-eyed legend makes him out to be (the jealous chorus line has sawn him off at the knees).

Definitely (b), his novel *Money* fulfilled the massive promise Amis had shown over the previous 10 years with *The Rachel Papers*, *Other People* and the dazzling *Success*, confirming his status as the smirking champ of British fiction.

Money was the perfect expression of his art, which is black comedy carved out of things that just aren't funny. The cutting edge of his work is all the fizzing greed and sweating panic of the late twentieth century, and in *Money*'s sub-hero (Amis' characters are much lower down the scale than anti-heroes) he created his most vivid protagonist, the cash-hungry, porn gourmet John Self.

'When I meet a man,' he says, making his voice go dead common as he does his impersonation of John Self, 'I think – will I fight it? And when I meet a woman I think – will I fuck it?'

This is as good a place as any to discuss the accusation (c) that Martin is a misogynist, a charge that is also much levelled at Martin's Booker-winning papa, Kingsley.

'All of John Self's depravities and anti-female feelings always rebound horribly on himself,' says Amis *fils*. 'Like when he tries to rape his girlfriend, Selina. She doesn't get hurt. The first time he gets kneed in the balls, the second time he gets elbowed in the face. And *even then* he considers having another crack at it.'

We laugh, shamefaced. It is infinitely more accurate to say that Amis understands men rather than Amis hates women. He knows exactly what a bunch of haggard masturbators we are . . .

'My wife asserts that *Money* is a book that even a feminist would be satisfied with,' Amis says, perhaps taking his affinity with sisterhood a little too far. 'Uncharitable, terrible thoughts reflect on the thinker. I would stand by that book and say that a woman who considers it an attack is not reading it properly.'

But come on, Martin – what would John Self have to say about the Greenham Common women? I reckon that he would probably start off by talking about 'their jungly tropical armpits' . . .

'Does one want to go to bed with a Greenham woman?' Amis asks himself with a knowing little smirk. Then the sliver of John Self-ism inside him subsides: 'I *admire* the Greenham women!'

Amis will be 38 this summer. His face is long and bony, handsome in a horsy sort of way, and he has a bulging, baby's brow. He has had – as one of his characters might say – a major rug rethink in recent years and the old, dirty blond, floppy choir-boy locks have now been shorn to something a lot more sensible. His middle-class English accent is occasionally invaded by a burst of American drawl ('The academic year 1959–60 I spent as a 10-year-old resident of Princeton, New Jersey,' he writes in the introduction to *The Moronic Inferno*, his collection of journalism on America and Americans. 'I was the only boy in the school – the only male in the city – who wore shorts.').

He mentions his father *a lot*, bringing the old man into the conversation more often than the interviewer does, and he wears a green corduroy suit. You don't see many of *them* these days. Charming and sharp, he smokes to stay sane (rolling his own to keep down consumption) and plays tennis to keep fit. Apparently, when it's really hard, he does both at the same time.

His work flat is, like Amis himself, compact and well-kept, and lined with books. On the side of the building, the only detached house on a white terraced street, there is a KEEP OUT DANGER sign and rust-choked burglar alarms. Inside it looks like the residence of a modestly heeled, alcoholic student instead of the studio of a writer who does not drink nearly as much as he used to.

'I took LSD three or four times, ditto cocaine more than three or four times, never heroin, smoked dope, but alcohol was the one because there are no dope shops,' he says. Alcohol always plays a demonic part in Amisland. Drink is a sexual Chernobyl in his books and it has a particularly devastating effect on working-class counter jumpers like John Self in *Money* or Terry Service (also known as 'Terence' and 'Tel' – Amis is blindingly attuned to the nuances of class) in *Success*.

Amis is the yobbo laureate. Surprising, really, because you are quite posh, Martin. Do you think you would have been very different if you had had a fishfinger childhood?

'I *did* have a fishfinger childhood! I'm *not* posh! My dad's dad was a clerk in Colman's mustard – lower-middle-class pinstripe – born in Clapham. My mother's family were odder – on her side there was a self-made Victorian millionaire who gave his money away and became a missionary. We were very poor until I was a teenager.

So I certainly don't feel posh. I once asked my father, "Dad, are we *nouveau riche*?" And he said, "Very *nouveau* . . . and not very *riche*" . . .'

Are you a closet yob?

'It's an element of my nature and my past,' he says. 'You take an element of your nature and you imagine what sort of state you would be in if that was the *only* part of your nature. I had a yobbish teenage in that it was a totally frivolous, hedonistic street life.'

Though he is one of a tiny, almost non-existent tribe of second generation writers, Amis' background is more nomadic than academic. He was brought up in America, Britain and Spain, attending more than a dozen schools. He was kicked out of a grammar school in Battersea when he was 14 and then went to a series of crammers. By the time he was 16 his parents had divorced and he was managing one O-level every year. Then he went to a boarding school where he got hooked on literature (before that he was a big Harold Robbins fan) and ended up with a first in English at Oxford, not to mention the desire to take over the family firm.

He came late to literature and has the kind of passion for books and writers that you expect to find in the self-educated who almost missed out on the printed world completely. Amis is righteously ecstatic in the presence of the work of his heroes – Saul Bellow, Nabokov – and coolly acidic when confronted by the overblown and overrated. Because he reviews books as well as writing them, it can all get very incestuous at times. Burgess praises Amis, Amis praises Burgess. Amis nails Norman Mailer, 'for 30 years the cosseted superbrat of American letters,' and – yah boo sucks, Amis minor – Mailer calls him 'a little wimp, a pretty boy with a poisonous personality'. Sometimes it seems that Amis is a gallstone caught deep in the innards of the literary establishment.

'It doesn't *feel* like a literary establishment,' he says. 'It just feels like a lot of people beavering away by themselves. You might well get some literary editor who goes to parties all the time, who gives some lady biographer an easy ride though the book is not very good, but it is all *very* woolly stuff. You can't have rackets because when you write you are absolutely alone – unless you are a plagiarist.'

The mention of plagiarism reminds me of the accusation that Amis had been guilty of phrase theft himself. The accusation was made by John Self in *Money* (Self narrates the book, Amis appears in a cameo role), who reports that the writer was once 'caught with his fingers in the word till.'

'Self got it wrong,' Amis smiles. 'What happened was that *I* was ripped off. An American guy whose novel had done very well – he now writes scripts for TV – had taken 20 or 30 chunks, word for word, from *The Rachel Papers*. I wrote a piece about it and there was a terrific scandal, it all got out of hand. Anyway, John Self hears about the plagiarism thing and naturally *assumes* that Martin Amis is the culprit!'

You see how twisted he is? He makes up vicious rumours about himself and *then* he sprays them, sadistically unchallenged, on the lavatory walls of his own novels. This is what people like most about his work – he is outrageously, ineffably funny. The man is a stand-up novelist.

Not that there are too many tears of mirth when Amis is scribbling in the huge monastic ledger that lays open on his desk. 'The two great ingredients of writing are solitude and anxiety,' he says. 'Some days you have a good day and you write a lot, maybe 1,000 words, and you think it's really good. Then you set that against all the days you didn't do anything and just felt like shit and thought you would never get any further. But when you are finishing a book you get a real attack of anxiety and the anxiety is somehow commensurate with what you've taken on.

'If you finish a book and have no anxiety at all then I don't think you're on to anything. But I felt *terrible* when I was finishing *Money*, almost literally sick, *gagging* with anxiety. Sometimes you hand in a book to your publisher and you expect that by the time you get home there will be a white van and a few psychiatric nurses waiting to put you in a strait-jacket and take you off.'

If the laughter in his work has been black in the past, then from here on in it looks like getting positively funereal. There is, for example, a character in one of the *Einstein's Monsters* stories who, nuked to a state of calm insanity in which he convinces himself that he is immortal, imagines: 'On one occasion – when there was nobody around – I teased out a lone handjob for an entire summer.'

Elsewhere in the same story Amis is not playing for laughs. Though he claims that the only purpose of the stories is to give 'various kinds of complicated pleasure', he also wants to make your stomach shiver at the thought of the next war, the final war, the very last word in wars. 'Recently I have started staying out in the daylight,' he writes. 'Ah, what the hell. And so, I notice, have the human beings. We wail and dance and shake our heads. We crackle with cancers, we fizz with synergisms, under the furious and birdless sky.'

'*Mad Max* is by far the best guess about the post-apocalyptic world in that it is so crazy and barbaric and *inverted*,' he tells me. 'That is how it is going to be.'

Minus Tina Turner, Martin . . .

'With a bit of luck you might get Tina as well,' he smirks.

And so we take our leave of Martin Amis, standing on the edge of the abyss, howling at the end of the world. But now and then he thinks of the hair, legs and teeth of Tina Turner or something just like them and then his sombre Doomsday countenance cracks into that familiar, fleshy smile.

At Lunch With Jonathan Ross

Not waving but dining

Arena, May/June 1987

E XACTLY ONE YEAR AGO the pilot of *The Last Resort* was produced. This dry run featured Fanny Craddock, Cynthia Payne and an anthropologist called Nigel Barley who talked about a tribe who practise full penis circumcision.

'They skin the dick for its entire length,' grimaces Jonathan Ross. 'Really gross.'

The tone of the show was set . . .

One year after that dick-skinning debut, *The Last Resort* is the subject of rave reviews and high ratings and its 26-year-old host is the smirking champ of the British chat show.

The first time I met him, four years ago now, Jonathan Ross was a junior researcher on *Loose Talk*, the chat show as disaster movie. Jonathan was the one who slipped nervous guests a drink during the commercial break. Jonathan was the one who had to explain to Tom Waits that the show's budget didn't quite run to cutlery as the singer forlornly clutched some soggy cod and chips in the bacchanalian hospitality room.

Today Jonathan and I are having lunch in the understated elegance of The Red Fort, a mere cocktail's throw up Dean Street from Groucho's. We call for Kingfishers – 'The king of beers,' Jonathan gallantly tells our host – and I ask him how he made that jump across the chasm of dreams from apprentice media brat to the Johnny Carson of Camden Town (the first home of baby Ross).

'We – me and Alan Mark, my partner and best friend – realised that the only way you can make money in TV in this country is by owning shows,' Ross says. 'You have to own the shows you work on. Channel 4, especially Mike Bolland, deserve a lot of credit – they saw a gap in the market and were supportive enough and sharp enough to think we had a good idea there. When they said they were interested we went in to see them once a week and said this is what we would put in, that is what we would leave out, this would work and this wouldn't . . .'

That must have taken a lot of power lunches, Jonathan. 'We used to take chocolate biscuits or a cake along to our meetings! We could give them to the people at Channel 4 and say, thanks for meeting us, there's your bribe, now give us £45,000 to do a pilot. Eventually they said – fair enough . . .'

The Last Resort takes a corny old recipe, all those staple diets of show business like chat, variety, songs and sketches and turns them into what Derek Jameson would call cracking good indoor entertainment. No definitive interviews but never a dull moment either. There is a lot of hard graft and inspired thinking behind *The Last Resort* and in Jonathan Ross the show has a front man who is totally lacking in the crawling conceit of most TV presenters. He is a charming motor mouth who – unlike a lot of television people who save up their good points for the moments they are getting paid for – is even more engaging in the flesh than on the screen, where he tends to smirk and look both shifty and pleased with himself. 'I sometimes look very smug,' he confesses as the Kingfishers begin to loosen his tongue. Ross fizzes with ambition and yet he is no mean-spirited careerist. A lot of people in his position, caught in the first full glare of fame, would be up for nothing but Perrier and small talk, Badoit and bullshit – but Jonathan Ross is young enough to still enjoy indiscretions and getting Kingfishered.

'When I started the series,' Jonathan says with that winning voice that can't quite decide if it wants to have a speech impediment, 'they said – let's face it, you're pale and unattractive. Go down to the sunbed and at least you'll be tanned and unattractive. So I went down to the sunbed and I'm lying there under the blue lights and the artificial heat and I'm thinking – what kind of a pop star uses a place like *this*? And when I came out George Michael was getting dressed . . .'

He's very *golden*, isn't he?

'He's *tandooried*.' Jonathan says. 'Which brings us back to the menu . . .'

The Red Fort, where Jonathan sometimes comes with his mother, is as far upmarket as an Indian restaurant goes. Elegantly bossed by Amin Ali, the Labour-voting food fan who left the co-operative The Last Days of the Raj to open up shop a few years ago, The Red Fort boasts a calm luxury, a menu made to make your mouth swoon and a service that is almost loving.

Jonathan orders Paneer Pakoras, cottage cheese deep fried in spiced gram flour, while I go for the Momo, minced meat and spices wrapped up in small pastry envelopes and served in a volatile sauce, the nearest that the Indian kitchen gets to Dim Sum.

Through mouthfuls of nirvana we reflect on the great chat show moments of all time which inevitably are all of a confrontational nature. My vote goes to the night that Emu attacked Michael Parkinson – it was controversial, it was meaningless and at least one of the combatants was a glove puppet.

'It sums up the medium,' Jonathan nods, while choosing the Parkinson-Muhammed Ali bout as his own personal favourite. 'It was a classic moment and everyone remembers it – like the *Blue Peter* elephant shitting in the studio.'

Sometimes it seems that working on Channel 4 is like being an Alfred Marks temp – you're here today and tomorrow God knows where you are, shows seem to get decommissioned all the time.

'This is the first time that I've worked on a show where they have recommissioned us,' Jonathan says, 'where they actually want us to come back and do it again.' But now that it is clear that Channel 4 will not be pushing him, Ross has decided to jump. 'I'm going to do two series of this and then do something else – a film show about directors like Russ Meyer, Cronenberg, Carpenter, David Lynch, Corman – all these *obsessive* filmmakers.'

It must be difficult keeping the IBA quiet when you have an audience who are baying for blood and guts.

'If we don't get at least one violent drunken punch-up on this show then I'm sure we will have let a lot of people down. Let's hope it's not the night we have Tyson on. I would have thought that our staple audience are pissheads just back from the pub . . .'

And of course the IBA and the mob might have different views about a circus sleazeball who swallows a ball of string, punctures a small hole in his stomach and then slowly pulls the string out, streaked with pale blood and milky guts. How could he *do* that?

'It was *obviously* a trick!'

It was?

'A brilliantly done magic trick!' Jonathan says. 'He had a false stomach made out of latex. They used to do it in Houdini's time with animal skin over the stomach.' *The Last Resort* was getting a lot of heat from the IBA about the stunt but Jonathan Ross, rabble soother, was unrepentant. 'It's what *I* would want to see for five minutes . . .'

By the time our main course arrives, the Kingfishers are flowing like a burst pipe and I am tapping my foot to Jonathan's cover version of 'Last Christmas'.

'*Last Christmas I gave you my heart. The very next day – you gave it away* . . . their farewell concert was one of the greatest shows I've ever seen. I was there, singing along with all the greats, doing the hand movements. George Michael – now there's someone who seems to have some problem resolving his own sexuality. Which way to go? He can't resolve it. He doesn't know which way to go but he knows it's all there if he wants it.'

We have both ordered from the Fort's exceptional list of poultry dishes. Jonathan has chosen the Malai, diced chicken with dried nuts and cream, while I have the Makhani, spiced chicken cooked in the clay oven and served in a sauce that is rich and wild. There is also a light Basmati rice, Aloo Gobi as a vegetable dish and, best of all, a Peshwari nan, stuffed with almonds. This is possibly the finest Indian food in town – only the lush Hawelli in Hampstead and the spartan Shalamar in the East End even come close.

Jonathan talks with mixed feelings about the people who are now just notches on his cue card. Berkoff and Peter Cook were good, Wendy Richards and Malcolm MacLaren were various shades of nightmare. He talks with infectious enthusiasm about people he would love to lure to *The Last Resort* – 'Mailer! I'd kill for Mailer! He could have the whole fucking . . . he could host it if he wanted' – and I think of the younger Jonathan Ross, the post-punk researcher standing in the shadowy wings of *Loose Talk* and *Solid Soul* watching the Friday night action on Channel 4 and thinking, 'Christ, I can do that.' The suits he was wearing then were from Robot rather than the Armani, Boss and Gaultier numbers he wears big today, but he is still righteously ecstatic talking about the things he loves ('*Pale Fire* is the best book *ever* written.') and he still takes the medium that has made him a household smirk very lightly indeed.

'TV is trivia and the chat show is the most basic form of TV,' he says. 'It's a really stupid way to make a living.'

We order Kulfi, the Red Fort's gorgeous but brick-hard home-made ice cream and scorning convention, another brace of King-fishers. As is customary at the end of these Soho summits we then get out our little books and exchange a few telephone numbers. I get an Attenborough – the one that squats among the monkeys – and Adam Ant for the Amis that I have, which I guess is fair exchange.

'My partner and I went to America last November,' Jonathan says. 'We went to the William Morris agency and told them we were doing a chat show in England and we would like to bring some Americans over. And they said – so how *is* TV in England? Is it popular these days? And we said, yeah, we've got sound, we've got colour now ... in terms of the size of what they are doing we are just so unimportant. We think we are so important and yet we are just this piss poor little island ...'

I heard that Johnny Carson likes it that the *Tonight* show never took off in England so that he can come over and watch Wimbledon without being bothered ...

'I know how he feels,' Jonathan says. 'It's exactly like me and the rest of the world. No, I *don't* want to be big in America, Australia or Japan. I want to have somewhere to go at the weekend.'

The Strangeness of Comfort

Ian McEwan

Arena, November/December 1987

U NDER A WISPY BEATLE CUT that is now etched with silver, a frown passes across Ian McEwan's watchful mandarin face. He is considering all those people who think he is a sick man. 'I have this troubled streak in me,' he says finally. 'It happens less now but I would become possessed by, say, the deadpan voice narrating *Butterflies*.'

Butterflies was his short story about a very young girl who gets violated and killed down by the canal. '*It took a long time*,' recounts the charmer who narrates the story, '*pumping it all out into my hand*.'

'I would become possessed by that voice and take immense *pleasure* in getting it right,' McEwan says in his soft, classless, rootless voice. 'It is what Graham Greene called the chip of ice. You *don't care*. In that sense all writers are sickos.'

But no other writer has charted the blackest, most diseased regions of the human psyche as brilliantly and with such relish as Ian McEwan. He has been sending dispatches from the dark side for more than 10 years now. His two collections of short stories (*First Love, Last Rites* and *In Between The Sheets*) and his first two short novels (*The Cement Garden* and *The Comfort Of Strangers*), all of them with taut, horrific plotlines hewn in McEwan's sparse, gleaming prose, have made him one of the very few British writers trusted by both public and critics ('Genius' – *The Times*, is one of McEwan's more restrained reviews).

In the past his work has dealt with themes that run the gamut of debauchery and degradation. He has built his career on tales of suspense, mystery and imagination splattered with blood, vomit and semen. But paradoxically these stories have been told in the most concise, pristine, gem-hard prose imaginable. At his best McEwan has matched even the work of Martin Amis, the smirking champ of British fiction.

Children in particular have had a tough time in his work. They have been fucked, murdered and been made to throw up at the most inappropriate moments. More than one of the poor little mites has cross-dressed. Women too have been forced to sniff the short end of Ian McEwan's spiteful stick.

There is a Nabokovian voice he does very well, full of laconic decadence and cultured, fastidious malice, and McEwan seems to enjoy making the rich and sophisticated do unspeakably low deeds. There is the man who owns the famous forgery of a Rodin sculpture who shares his bed with a storeroom dummy (*Dead as They Come*). And the diplomat's son who plays master-slave games so enthusiastically that his wife ends up a cripple (*The Comfort of Strangers*).

Every one of his readers has his favourite McEwan moment, when Ian has sunk lower than you would have dreamed possible. For my money the purest Black Mac moment is in *Psychopolis* where the man and the girl are eating dinner in a restaurant in Los Angeles. The man is telling the girl that she is the best thing that ever happened to him, that he loves her so and that he would do anything for her, anything at all. So the girl tells him what she would like him to do.

'I want you to urinate in your pants, now. Go on now! Quick! Do it now before you have time to think about it.'

And he does. And he sits there in a puddle of piss staring at his dream girl. And then she tells him that the middle-aged couple who just walked into the restaurant are her parents and she calls them over to meet him . . .

McEwan's first collection of short stories won the Somerset Maugham Award in 1976 and his second novel was shortlisted for the Booker Prize in 1981. He has enjoyed even more early success than Martin Amis, but as McEwan enters his 40th year it seems his future could be considerably less golden than his past.

Many of the promising young British novelists of the last 10 years are in the middle of a crucial change of life. McEwan, Amis, Julian Barnes, Peter Ackroyd, Timothy Mo – all of them are coming up to or just passing their 40th birthdays. You cannot go on being 'promising' and 'young' forever – not even in publishing. It is time to deliver.

Amis considerably upped the ante with his triumphant study of a porn gourmet, *Money*, while Mo, Ackroyd and Barnes have enjoyed more modest success with, respectively, *An Insular Possession*, *Chatterton* and *Staring at the Sun*. But Ian McEwan, most lavishly-praised word-brat of this insular set, with whom not even Kingsley's boy could live in the '70s, *that* Ian McEwan has published a novel, *The Child in Time*, which even his staunchest supporters are finding difficult to admire.

It was time for McEwan to prove that, for all the austere beauty of his prose, he was not merely a talent which has horror and cheap thrills at its foundation. He has done himself little good with *The Child in Time*. Even before its official publication date dissenting voices were wondering if the book proved that McEwan was a major talent who had lost his way or a minor talent that has for a long time been vastly overrated.

'Tries to be sensitive and clever,' *Vogue* said of the book. 'Just ends up being vague and wet.'

'*The Child in Time* operates on various levels of achievement,' said the *Literary Review*. 'Which is a fancy way of saying that it is uneven and not very well constructed.'

The Child in Time attempts to prove to the world that Ian McEwan is more than the thinking man's Stephen King, more than the Roald Dahl of the heavyweight lit set.

In the background of *Butterflies*, as the young girl is being slaughtered by the canal, a gang of young boys are roasting a live cat over a fire, just to rub your nose in it, you understand, to show there is absolutely no hope for mankind. But with *The Child in Time*, Black Mac discovers that this can be a wonderful world. Incredibly, at times he is positively *cloying*.

Set in a post-Thatcher, authoritarian England of the near future, *The Child in Time* is the story of Stephen Lewis, an author of children's books who is conscripted onto a government commission to help create a definitive childcare handbook, which will be the blueprint for bringing up the next generation. It is a liberal nightmare – Victorian values choreographed by Orwell.

Stephen daydreams his way through endless committee meetings, forever haunted by the kidnapping of his three-year-old daughter Kate, who was silently snatched from her father's side during a trip to the supermarket. The loss of the child has wrecked his marriage because neither Stephen nor his wife can come to terms with the tragedy. McEwan glumly charts the disintegration of their union. Meanwhile Stephen's best friend Charles betrays him by secretly drawing up an alternative government childcare handbook, the one the rotters planned to use all along. Charles then betrays himself by quitting politics, London and adult life and moving out to the

country where his wife becomes his mother and he reverts to a ma-
cabre conkers-and-bogies childhood, dressing up in short trousers,
carrying a catapult, building a treehouse and talking like Just William.

Stephen is eventually reconciled to his estranged wife, the bovine,
hammock-breasted Julie, and though the kidnapped Kate is never
brought back, the book ends with the woman giving birth. It is a
madly ecstatic rather than a happy ending, and while it would be
wrong to knock McEwan for being overwhelmed by the sight of a
child being born, I have to confess that I found his mawkish eulogies
to milk-gorged tits a little hard to stomach.

Parts of the book – especially the moment Kate disappears and the
description of Stephen paralysed by grief, struck so numb by a des-
pairing inertia that all he can do is watch game shows – are McEwan
at the height of his powers. But such moments are few and far between. You have to search out the good things in *The Child in Time*
whereas in McEwan's past work there was no fat, no gristle, not a
steely phrase wasted. Though only a shade over 200 pages, *The Child
in Time* is almost twice the size of McEwan's other novels and he
seems lost in all that space. Despite the rare times when he shows
himself still capable of tightening the muscles around your throat, the
overall impression is clumsy and hifalutin'. The work is shot through
with reflections, thoughts and little lectures on the nature of childhood and time.

The longtime McEwan fan will no doubt second Paul Taylor's
final judgement in the *Literary Review* – 'He should stick to being
Ian McEwan' – but the chances are that *The Child in Time* is a fairly
accurate reflection of what middle-period McEwan is going to look
like, just as *Einstein's Monsters* revealed where Martin Amis is going
to be for the foreseeable future.

Both writers are changed men, and it is having children that has
changed them. Fatherhood has made these former *enfants terribles*
concerned for the world – though it is a concern that can sometimes
sound like special pleading – and it has humanised their voices. Neither McEwan nor Amis are the haggard masturbators they were in
their 20s, lapping up the black side of life like maggots inside a body
bag, though so far Amis has certainly incorporated this new found
humanism into his work more ably than McEwan. Has all this personal joy (McEwan and his wife have two small sons) dulled the
cutting edge of his work? Has Ian McEwan gone soft?

'Well, this would be the very romantic view of literature that
through *suffering* . . .'

I don't mean you have to be tortured and starving in a *garret*.

'If you say having children is a positive thing in your life then you mean it in its totality,' McEwan says. 'It brings out things in you that for a man come out reluctantly; degrees of tenderness, the experience of serving someone else – something you don't do if you are living alone and running around town. A lot of things about having children are quite difficult and you have to cheer yourself up, tell yourself you are being extended and that you would not be without this love affair with this child. You become sensitised – towards tenderness *and* anxiety. You become a kind of hostage to life.'

I meet up with Ian McEwan in the ritzy Bloomsbury offices of Jonathan Cape. We are in a very small room that is stacked high with cardboard boxes full of copies of *The Child in Time*, spiderishly autographed. McEwan is soon on the phone with the director of *Sour Sweet*, the Timothy Mo novel that is soon to be a minor motion picture, its screenplay written by McEwan. It seems there is a problem with the film's budget and McEwan is being consulted on how to keep down costs while maintaining the movie's artistic integrity.

'I suggest we cut the stunt and the scene with the Buddha,' he murmurs into the telephone.

All these guys do *something else*. Amis interviews writers who are older than he is, Julian Barnes had his post-Clive James TV column in the *Observer* for years, Mr Mo works for a boxing magazine and, most lucrative of all, McEwan writes for the screen, both large and small. His teleplays like *The Imitation Game* and *Solid Geometry* (notoriously banned by the BBC in 1979 for featuring a large penis preserved in a jar of milky liquid) and the screenplay for *The Ploughman's Lunch* have done as much to enhance his reputation as his books.

There is a copy of the *Literary Review* on the desk in front of him. I feel a little sorry for him. He has the bruised authority and hurt pride of a monarch who has survived a messy coup attempt.

'At least it is well written,' he says, tapping the *Review*.

I really *enjoyed* all that sensationalist stuff you used to write. Have you come to look down on your past work?

'No, I enjoy that stuff too,' he says in his neutral '60s voice, an accent untouched by the taint of class or emotion. 'But my sense of what is extraordinary has extended to something I saw. It is an extraordinary thing to see one human being coming out of another, it is as bizarre a thing as I ever clapped eyes on . . .'

I guess I know what he means but I still think it's a raw deal (for him as well as the rest of us) that McEwan lets his joy and wonder at the process of procreation turn his steel to mush, his icy sagacity to clumsy pretension. I wonder aloud if he has been a little *too* lavishly praised over the years and if the adoration of the critics hasn't made him overreach himself. McEwan thinks not.

'It is too drawn out a process, writing a novel is such a long haul and, in the end, the critics cancel each other out. The reality is a quiet room and what you can do.'

If McEwan has doubts about his latest novel then he is keeping them well hidden. For more than 10 years people have been telling him how impossibly hot he is and now that they are saying he has fallen flat on his fleshy, expressionless face, he just doesn't believe them.

'In a way *The Child in Time* feels like my first novel because it is the first time I have ever used the freedom allowed by the form of a novel to expand, use different strands and have a more complicated structure.'

But it is not only different in structural terms.

'The world it describes is bleak and menacing but it hangs on to a flimsy kind of optimism. I see it as a continuation, there are many things in the book that I was writing about even when I was writing short stories – children and the degree of control exercised over them by adults. The child that is within you. The idea of regression and – again – the sense of *threat* that I feel and expressed in various ways.'

But it is so strange to see you this reverential about children. In the past, the world you have had them inhabit has been a global concentration camp . . .

'Well, the child in the book gets stolen, which is in many ways the worst thing I can think of. But I am more concerned with the child within us and the deal *it* gets. I'm concerned with our relationships with the total accumulation of our lives and what we deny when we get older and more pompous.'

The things you have put kids through in your work have made people wonder about your moral health.

His shrewd, blind eyes glisten with mild bewilderment.

'Someone once wrote '*The idea of being Ian McEwan's child is absolutely chilling*'. I thought, I could get offended by that. But life's too short. If you write first person narratives you run into this problem. Actors don't get it. Nobody goes up to Jonathan Pryce and says, you fucking murderer, I saw you in *Macbeth* last night, you should be locked up – you *and* your wife . . .'

In *Solid Geometry* the man says to his wife, 'You don't even have the blessing of an unhappy childhood.' Do you think that maybe an unhappy childhood is good preparation for life because it is *not* all trips to the seaside and R. White's lemonade out there, but dog eat dog and cat eat mouse?

'No, I think a happy childhood is a much better preparation for the world – we can argue about definitions but I mean being secure and loved which means you are able to love, and I would count an unhappy childhood one where you were neglected, abused, unloved, fucked around – and you become the kind of person who does those things as an adult and contributes to the world's unhappiness rather than partaking in its happiness. But I actually think that a happy childhood is quite a rare thing. A lot of us are walking around with bruises.'

There seems to have been a lot of dislocated love in McEwan's own childhood. It is probably no coincidence that he is at his heart-thumping best when writing about loss and grief. He was born in the barracks town of Aldershot where his soldier father was stationed. His father was posted overseas to Africa and the Far East – this was in the '50s, when the sun was setting on the British Empire, but very slowly – and young Ian sometimes travelled to these far away, exotic bases but often did not.

His mother, a Scot like his dad, had two children from a previous marriage but they were much older than Ian so he grew up as a kind of hemmed-in only child. Once he hid behind the sofa when his father came home on leave, not recognising him. Another time he came down the stairs piping, 'Please, I want to be a girl,' just like the youngest boy in *The Cement Garden*, who wants to be a girl because girls don't fight and get hurt.

The Armed Forces made McEwan a painfully class-conscious child (lower middle, he says, explaining that his dad only joined up to escape the dole), and he did not enjoy those army-occupied beaches where the children of the ranks, like him, were segregated from the gilded offspring of the officers.

Mediocre at boarding school, his brain only woke up after he had read literature at Sussex University and gone on to take a post-graduate course at the University of East Anglia. He started writing here when he was part of Professor Malcolm 'The History Man' Bradbury's writing programme. Someone on the same course remembers McEwan as manipulative and calculating, setting out even then to be a rich and famous Great Writer. The suggestion clearly upsets McEwan much more than criticisms of his latest book.

'When I was at UEA I certainly didn't have any clear idea that I was going to be a writer,' he says, this most mild-mannered of men turning suddenly heated. He quickly comes off the boil. 'If I had wanted to get rich and famous then writing short stories and sending them to *Transatlantic Review* would not have been a very clever way to start. I was really just enjoying myself at UEA. There was a lot of experimenting with drugs – which is an absurd thing to say, they were just consumed – and it excited me to be writing into the night, no matter how badly. I had no clear sense of wanting to be a writer. That only happened when I *came back* and was yearning for some stability.'

Where Ian McEwan came back from was the hippy trail to Katmandu. He had bought a magic bus in Amsterdam and headed for the North West Frontier. It was 1972. 'Psychotropic drugs,' he has written, 'were consumed in large quantities.'

Three years later when *First Love, Last Rites* was published to ecstatic reviews, McEwan was already living modestly on what his short stories earned. In the early '80s the writer moved from the ascetic squalor of his South London pad to the lusher pastures of Oxford. Today he lives in a spacious house with his wife Penny Allen, an alternative healer, Penny's two teenage daughters from a previous marriage and the couple's two young sons, William and Gregory. McEwan was present at both births and 18 months ago he delivered his youngest son himself. McEwan seems to be happier now than he has ever been.

But what is Ian McEwan *for*?

'I would like – it sounds pompous – I would like to make people feel more alive. I am a closet moralist with a puritan streak that I am finding harder to control as I get older. Not that I am pointing the way to better behaviour but I would like to make people . . . more alert to whatever is within them.'

And just how good is Ian McEwan? Did he peak 10 years ago or is the best yet to come? My view is that it is too early to put his name down for a place in history but writing his obituary is also a little premature. As the Bard said – it's not over till it's over . . .

'Posterity? I only think about it when I am in my cups.'

Your friend Martin Amis told me that it is the only thing that matters. Being read after you are dead. And he was serious.

'Martin did an interview where he talked about how much

posterity means to him and the article had a very witty cartoon with Martin hanging off London Bridge, staring into the Thames, and the reflection he was getting back was Shakespeare.' McEwan laughs out loud. 'But I am not sure that the final judgement belongs to the future . . .'

And so we take our leave of Ian McEwan. Tonight he is staying with Amis in Westbourne Park and tomorrow he will go home to Oxford where there is a light that never goes out. I hope that he comes back.

'Horrific things are a *lot* more interesting than nice things,' he says. 'You paint the world black to find out what is good. It is like Portia's line – I'm paraphrasing – about the candle in the darkness and how far that little candle throws its beam, so shines a good deed in a wicked world. It is immensely satisfying for a writer like me to light that one candle.'

But you have taken so long to get your matches out, Ian.

'But they were always in my back pocket,' he says, and seals it with an adjective. 'Rattling.'

Jerry Built

Jerry Hall

Elle, November 1988

'**M**R JAGGER has just left the building.'
It is first thing on a big blue Monday morning in Kensington and I am standing on the doorstep of a discreetly swank apartment, getting no response to prolonged ringing of the doorbell. Two paint-splattered workmen pause from their task of carrying a plank into the apartment next door and tell me that the wild man of rock and I have just missed each other.

'Mr Jagger just this moment left the building. You just missed him.'

'In fact I am not here to see Mr Jagger. I am expected by . . . Miss Jerry,' I say, sounding rather like the old black maid in *Gone With The Wind*.

They assure me that Miss Hall should still be at home and I stand on the secret threshold to Jerryland, ringing the bell until I eventually find myself having a dislocated conversation through the letterbox with an outrageously voluptuous Texan accent.

Jerry is shocked to find me on her doorstep. At first she thinks I am what she calls 'a car from *Elle*', arriving without warning to whisk her off to some glossy modelling assignment that she knows nothing about. I assure her that I am in fact the man from *Elle*, arriving as planned to probe her inner psyche.

It is all a bit tense. I shudder inwardly at all those recent *Jerry Quits Mick* fabrications in the tabloids, which cannot have inspired the prairie rose to feel much affection for the press. But she eventually opens the door and lets me inside.

We face each other in the hall, Jerry in a long golden dressing gown, and though the unkind say she can look a little equine in photographs, in the perfect, lightly toasted flesh, she is pure feline. Cheetah. Panther. Jerry.

'Ah do not usually *give* interviews in mah *home*,' she says coolly, the frosty note in that lush drawl making her sound like Scarlett O'Hara in imperious mode. 'Suh,' I expect her to say, 'what is the *meaning* of this imposition? Ah suspect, suh, that you are a scoundrel and a Yankee.' Actually she says, 'You may wait in the *drawing room*.'

One of the smiling hired hands takes me through while Miss Jerry flounces off to get dressed. I sit in a comfortable room with huge Schiaparelli-pink chairs and a coffee table groaning under the weight of art books and Sotheby's catalogues. The room leads through to a gleaming dining room with a polished 12-seater table bearing two huge candelabra. In the room I'm in there is a guitar case and a big fat ghetto blaster in the corner – Mick's equivalent of pipe and slippers. I would like to tell you about the photographs and the paintings on the wall but I can't – I promised Jerry. Sorry. It is between us.

When she comes back, Jerry is transformed, the Southern charm no longer on hold. Shucks, it turns out that Jerry is bone tired after being up with her feverish kids all night and plumb forgot about our little pow wow. Now that she remembers she is nice as pie and twice as sweet. She gives me that dazzling, slightly goofy smile and it is like being winked at by God. Frankly, you can see why Jagger is her devoted love vassal.

She arranges those long Jerry limbs in an armchair and tosses her hair, which goes on for ever. Jerry is cool inside a simple cream number. She is gloriously barefoot and the nails on the Jerry toes have been painted ruby red. A thin gold chain swathes one ankle. She looks like a slave girl out of Chanel. She punctuates almost every sentence with an explosion of laughter and I can exclusively reveal that Jerry and her slightly wizened beau have no immediate plans for separation or marriage.

'It's the "m" word,' she says. 'Oh-oh, we mustn't mention the "m" word. Ah *do* thank that people kin spend a lifetime together, even in these days. Ah thank the main thing it takes is honesty. *Umf!*' (That is Jerry laughing.) 'Ah *always* tell the truth – though it often gits me into trouble. Umf-umf-umf!'

The career that Jerry built is currently pushing out in several new directions at once. She finds it impossible to give up modelling ('Ah never turn down good jobs – ah always thank it would be awful if one day ah had to go back and work at Dairy Queen,' she says, though it is unlikely she will ever have to go back to making banana splits at that Texan ice-cream parlour), and she's hiring out her lovely face to sell products from Bovril to Bentley, as well as appearing in an American stage production of the 1956 Marilyn Monroe movie *Bus Stop* (Jerry plays the tart with the heart – and hair – of gold, natch) and designing her own range of luxurious swimwear.

'There are 57 swimsuits and ah designed all of them,' she says, and I silently gasp at how deftly she has steered the conversation around to her watery wares. She really is a murderously good businesswoman and, as she semi-jokingly points out, under that dumb blonde exterior lives an incredibly smart brunette. 'They are *very* glamorous.' The two key words in Jerryspeak, which come up over and over again, are glamour and fun. Glamour and *fahn*.

'Ah have used a lot of new materials that have just come out – like this waterproof lace and velvet. They are cut high at the front.' She traces a long index finger around the upper curve of her hip. 'And very low at the back. So your bottom doesn't hang out – for good exits and thangs. The tops are like cocktail dresses and there are skirts and pants to go over them. Ah spend a lot of time in Mustique and there people wear swimsuits all day long. You kin wear *ma* swimsuits and not feel so completely naked. They are for . . .' – there is an ad man's glint in those big, Caribbean-coloured eyes – '. . . swimwear living.'

The coconut milk of the swimwear lifestyle turned sour on Jerry early last year when she was wrongly accused of possessing 20 pounds of marijuana in Barbados. Although the trumped-up charges were finally dropped, for a while she faced the prospect of spending years inside a primitive cell. She says the incident was a living nightmare, but brought her and Jagger even closer together.

'Mick was furious and I was in a complete state of shock. He was *so sweet*. Ah thank the whole thang started out as a mistake and then they did not want to rectify it.'

Is that because – though she is light years away from Marianne and Anita Pallenberg and Bianca and there will be no drug overdoses or painful obscurity or frustrated ambitions for *her* – the world still regards Jerry as a Rolling Stones woman? And that means drugs?

'The Rolling Stones don't *take* drugs any more – they cain't!' Jerry roars with laughter. 'They're *too old!* It was all 25 years ago. If you take drugs that long and consistently, then you *dah!* That's jest the way it is – you cain't take drugs for ever. Now they are all *getting on*, with *small kids*, trying to get it *together*, and they are not taking drugs. But people can never believe it and the Stones don't want to show this good image – it's not rock and roll! But Mick went through a phone book that he had from the '60s and half the people in it were dead. It was really . . . terrible. Now he doesn't even have coffee or alcohol or cigarettes. Ah have the odd glass of wine, ah smoke and drink coffee and he thanks ah'm rilly *baaad!*'

Jerry Hall has always been a clean-living girl – an obedient child of this yoghurt-eating age. She tells me about her wild days of dancing on Paris tables with her frisky friend Grace Jones and says that, if she threw up between shoots on a job the next day, it would only be because she had eaten a bad oyster. But even her wild days were pretty tame – most men were too intimidated by her Amazonian presence to get close.

'Ah thank sometimes men are intimidated by me. Ah remember when ah was single – before ah lived with Mick or Bryan – ah was living on ma own and not many guys would ask me out. Only rilly very confident guys would – who tend to be rich and famous! A lot of times when people want to write bad things about me they call me . . . a *gold-digger*.' She makes this rather quaint expression sound like a cheap, cocaine-sniffing tramp. 'They said that about Robert Sangster and then this other guy.'

Sangster is the horse-breeding tycoon who Jerry had a brief fling with in 1982. The other guy is believed to be Lord David Ogilvy, who was much more recent grist for the rumour mill. 'Mean things. It's not true because ah make ma *own* money.' Obviously true – she *has* to be making much more than Mick these days. 'No guy has *ever* given me money – and ah am sure ah *would* go out with someone who *wasn't* rich and famous.'

The door opens and two beautiful, but slightly sickly seraphim pad in. Both have white blonde curls spilling down to their little shoulders and – you can't help but notice – very full-lipped sensuous mouths that reach out in permanent fleshy pouts as if to kiss the whole planet. Elizabeth Scarlett, four, climbs behind her mother and attempts to insert her head down the back of the armchair. James, three, toys in mute wonder with the metre-long golden curtain of his mama's hair.

Despite those brief intermissions, Jerry has been with her prancing paramour for 11 years now – 'Ah'm 32, so that's more than a *thurd* of ma *lahf!*' – and you get the impression that family is even more important to her than glamour and *fahn*.

She comes from a big brood herself with three sisters (Jerry Faye has a twin sister called Terry Jaye) who grew up with their romantic mother (who saw *Gone with the Wind* 16 times) and their roaring father (who drove trucks carrying toxic waste that splashed his face with acid) in Mesquite, Texas. It could be a Raymond Carver short story, full of bad luck and too much booze, fist fights in the kitchen and love under siege. While her friends pinned The Beatles and the Stones to their bedroom walls, Jerry took her lead from her mother and became obsessed with the pristine glamour of old Hollywood.

'Ah was tall and skinny and awkward – always trying to look smaller – slumping down, always wearing woolly tights to make my legs look thicker, doing all sorts of stoopid thangs to make myself look shorter and fatter. Ah was looking in the mirror when ah was about 14 and ah thought – maybe ah rilly *am* purty and people just haven't noticed yet.'

Unlike most of us, Jerry lost her virginity to a cowboy. He was part Indian (Jerry has some Indian blood herself) and worked the local rodeo. He had deflowered Jerry's friend the week before he arrived at Jerry's jeans and, though he had very little to boast about (you could not boil an egg in the time that he laboured over Jerry and her friend), he bragged about it to all his cowpoke pals, so that the girls' lives were hell and their names were mud.

When you hear about all the rotten things that happened to Jerry down in the badlands of her early life, you can see how she worked up the nerve to head off to Paris when she was just 16. And the rest, as they say, is industry.

'Ah believe you can change your destiny,' she says, 'by wanting something and going for it. That's more powerful than luck or beauty. That's what our mother taught us.'

Another thing Mama told Jerry was that a woman can hold her man by being a maid in the living room, a cook in the kitchen and a whore in the bedroom. Jerry told Mama she would hire the first two.

'Ah am so happy here in London,' Jerry exults. 'Ah thank England is sooo civilised and all the buildings are sooo old and everythang. People here are sooo polite – where *ah* come from, in the South of America, people are polite, too. In New York they are not polite at all. And John Lennon's death made it a scary and unpleasant place to be . . .'

Later this year, Jerry, whose passport has always said 'Model/Actess', hopes to be wowing theatre audiences in London with her witty and languid performance as Cheri in *Bus Stop*.

'It is over 30 years old but there are sooo many good messages in it still.'

Like what, Jerry?

'Lahk ... Cheri rilly wants respect. And she believes that you should not keep lurve locked in your heart.' A frown passes across the lovely Jerry face. 'Ah cain't remember *all* the messages,' she says a little impatiently, and then a memory illuminates the big blue Jerry eyes. 'And *lurve* is the best thang in the *world*,' she says. '*Umf!*'

The Life of Bailey

Arena, March/April 1988

TEN DAYS AFTER HIS 50th birthday, David Bailey is sitting in a wintry loft and telling me how his working habits have changed over the years. 'When I was younger I was more easily diverted,' he says in his Leytonstone Mandarin accent. 'Especially by women. Fashion photography is the best way in the world to get laid. I can't think of a better job.'

Musicians do okay.

'Oh no, it's different for musicians. A lot of the women who chase musicians are pretty ropey.'

And that face – a debauched cherub, a battered seraphim – cracks with mirth and his studio, this beautiful acre of light and space, echoes with his raucous laughter.

What about your motivation? Has that changed?

'That doesn't change,' he says. 'Everybody likes a bit of adulation, sex and money. Although for me the adulation is not such a driving force – I far prefer the sex and money.'

But you have had more than your fair share of both – why do you keep going? Do you still have something to prove to the world? 'I still have something to prove to myself,' says Bailey (everybody calls him simply Bailey – his wife, his staff, even his two and a half year old daughter calls him Bailey).

Down in the small toilet below the studio you get some idea of what he has proved already. The walls are covered with studies of Jean Shrimpton, Catherine Deneuve, Marie Helvin. There are awards from Greenpeace, the anti-fur lobby and the advertising industry (Bailey is a Capitalist Green – he has a left wing heart and a right wing wallet). There is a gold disc of Alice Cooper's slimy masterpiece, 'Billion Dollar Babies'. A collage of tabloid headlines shriek about Bailey's banned TV documentary on his pal Andy Warhol. There is even a certificate – awarded in the early '70s, when it was becoming clear that there was far more to Bailey than the click-

click-baby-baby image projected in the '60s – naming him a Fellow of the conservative Royal Photographic Society.

In this little lavatorial museum you get some idea of what has made David Bailey – above Weber, Newton, Cartier-Bresson, Avedon, all of them – the most famous photographer alive.

Initially it was a career built on taking the pink chiffon out of fashion photography and replacing it with sex. Later, after the break up with his great partner and muse the Shrimp ('Nobody could touch her,' he once told me as the sunlight was dying over Primrose Hill), he began to build up the huge evocative body of portrait work – from the Krays to Man Ray to Michael Caine, from John and Paul to Polanski and Tate – that were later published in his books *Box of Pin Ups, Goodbye Baby and Amen* and that wonderful greatest hits package, *Black and White Memories*.

As time has gone by, his fashion photography has become portraiture and his portraits have become historical document. It is a career that has drawn its strength from blurring all the lines – between his private and professional life, between merchandise and art, between reportage and protest (his photographs of the Boat People and, more recently, on the Ethiopian-Sudan border for Band Aid, have a heart-thumping resonance that straight journalism can never match).

Like all great artists, this one is motivated by sex and money and . . . something else.

'It is his unfathomable energy and sense of wonder that keeps Bailey at the top,' Brian Clarke writes in the introduction to *Trouble and Strife*, Bailey's erotic record of the fantasy and reality of his third wife, the twinkle-eyed Marie Helvin. 'He never relaxes, never rests on his laurels.'

Upstairs in the studio, Bailey's fourth and probably final wife is watching a tape of a fashion show on a huge Sony TV screen. Fresh faced, impossibly thin and a beauty of the Anglo-Roman school, Catherine Dyer is a former model (he has been married to three models and one actress) who works for *Vogue* as fashion editor. She is the mother of Bailey's two children, young Paloma and baby Fenton. Bailey's professional association with Catherine has never received the coverage that was accorded to his liaisons with Shrimpton, Deneuve, Helvin or Penelope Tree, but many of the photographs he took of her in the early '80s – in Cornwall for *Harpers & Queen*, in Scotland for Italian *Vogue* – are memorable, and some of them are unforgettable. It is inconceivable that Bailey could love a woman and not take her photograph, claiming what he calls his 'ransom against time'. Catherine squirms excitedly on the sofa, staring wide-eyed at the big Sony.

'I've got a girl for you, Bailey,' she says. 'I can't believe she has never made it. The only problem is – she's a bit old.'

'How old?'

'30.'

'That's okay,' Bailey says magnanimously. 'I'm looking for a 30 year old. Get her over.'

Mr and Mrs Bailey sit on the sofa holding hands. It's dead sweet – after a few years of marriage and a couple of kids, they are still swooning over each other as if they were courting. Apart from the happy couple, a little furniture and some state of the art technology, Bailey's studio is almost empty. There is an exotic bird squawking in the corner (bird-watching is one of his lifelong passions – people used to think that David Bailey being into bird-watching was some kind of put-on), a neatly stacked metre of CDs by some giant black speakers (everything from Willie Nelson to Wagner, more Ella Fitzgerald than anything else, and the new solo CD by the best man at Bailey's second wedding, Mick Jagger) and, casually stacked on the floor, a pile of awards from the advertising industry.

Bailey has always been a jobbing photographer, taking on work for the money, the experience and – not immune from the dark insecurities of the freelance life – to feel wanted. In the past he has always mixed it up, dividing his time between commissioned work and the projects he took on unpaid and for himself. But that has changed. Over the last couple of years, apart from his work for *Vogue* and some big fashion shoots, almost all of the work he has taken on has been commercials commissioned by advertising agencies.

'I don't take stills any more,' he says, a little too casual. 'I made 27 commercials last year. Already this year is looking the same. Advertising people tend to like you to win prizes. And over the last two years, I have won all the prizes.'

Didn't turning 50 make you feel that time was running out? Didn't it make you wonder how much time you have left?

'I wonder how much time I have left every night,' he says.

Then I can't believe that you are going to spend the rest of your life making commercials. It doesn't add up.

'As John Lennon said – life is what happens to you when you are busy making other plans.'

It still doesn't make sense. Bailey has built a career on moving to somewhere else when all the big, smart money told him to stay where he was. It doesn't tally that he would spend his last decade or two making superior TV commercials.

'I like the aggravation of commercials,' he says. 'I like dealing with 50 people. It's much *lonelier* doing stills. You get tremendous experience with a moving camera doing commercials. You use more *technique* in 30 seconds than most feature directors use in three or four films. And I want to make films now. I did documentaries before and I don't want to do them again. I want to direct features. Yes, it is research doing commercials. But everything is research. Life is research.'

Now *that* makes sense.

'You have to do everything well – everything sounds so corny when you talk about it – but you should never be *too* happy with anything. I love the story of Lartigue and Brassai: Lartigue never wanted to see Brassai because he always talked about the past and Lartigue wanted to look forward to the future – this is when they were both over 85!!'

Is that why Lartigue was such a great photographer?

'That's why Lartigue lived to be 96.'

David Royston Bailey was born on the second day of 1938 in the East End street next to the one where Alfred Hitchcock made his debut. Bert and Glad Bailey's only son – he has one sister – had a childhood that bears a remarkable resemblance to that other pint-sized stud, Frank Sinatra. Both were adored and pampered only sons growing up in a tough, working class neighbourhood. Both were dressed up in clothes that belied their parents' income, baby prole dandies who enjoyed their finery while not always relishing the attention it brought them.

'What chance have you got in a punch up in East Ham when you are wearing sandals?' Bailey later complained.

If Francis Albert escaped his drab environment in the radio, then Bailey – growing up amid the bomb sites, ration cards and prissy austerity of post-war England – lost himself in the movies, sitting gaping at Hollywood from the 1/9s at least six times every week. For a child born and bred in the grey, exhausted streets of mid-century Albion, the effects were shattering. 'Bailey became determined to somehow lead a glamorous life himself,' says Martin Harrison, a close friend and Bailey's best biographer.

A big fan of Mitchum, Bogart and Astaire, Bailey was also a great admirer of Walt Disney's natural history documentaries and, his interest in bird-watching awakened by bike rides out to Epping Forest, his first photographic subject was a small brown sparrow in the back garden of Leytonstone. The snap failed to come out and resulted in Bailey for several years believing that his visa out of the East End was going to be the trumpet he picked up in his teens. But when he first left England to do his National Service at the age of 18, cameras were in cheap and plentiful supply in Singapore and Bailey's interest in photography was reawakened. The army was meant to make a man of you – but it made David Bailey a photographer. Four of these earliest photographs – a Malayan landscape, a self-portrait in his barracks, a moody jazz man silhouetted against a Singapore sky – appear in *Black and White Memories* and show that his eye was there all along.

'Some things are pre-ordained,' he says. 'I never went to school very much – I don't believe in rules or any kind of authority. But I believe in destiny.'

His hunger to be a professional photographer heightened by an Henri Cartier-Bresson picture of four heavily veiled women on a hillside, Bailey served the briefest of apprenticeships with John French ('Everyone thought we were having an affair,' Bailey has said. 'But in fact, though we were very fond of each other, we never got it together') and struck out on his own. In 1960 he was offered a contract by John Parsons, the Art Director of *Vogue*. Five years later he photographed an entire issue of that magazine and he had become the person he was meant to be: the cool eye at the heart of the '60s hurricane. The best historical records of those times all catch glimpses of Bailey's smirking shadow, never still for very long, but always where he should be.

'The spring of '63 I met a just-married beauty called Jane Holzer,' Andy Warhol writes in *Popism*. 'Nicky Haslam took me to a dinner at her Park Avenue apartment. David Bailey was there and he had brought the lead singer of a rock and roll group called The Rolling Stones that was then playing the Northern cities of England. Bailey and Mick were both wearing boots by Anello and David, the dance shoemakers in London.'

Tom Wolfe reported the thoughts of Baby Jane Holzer in his story, *The Girl of the Year*: 'They're all young and they're taking over. It's like a whole revolution. I mean, it's *exciting*. They are all from the lower classes, East End sort-of-thing. There's nobody exciting from the upper classes anymore, except for Nicole and Alec Londonderry. They are all young, it's a whole new thing. It's not The Beatles. Bailey says The Beatles are passé, because now everybody's mum pats The Beatles on the head.'

In many ways Bailey was the ultimate '60s celebrity – Jean Shrimpton was his lover, Andy and Mick his friends, la belle Deneuve was his wife, everybody who was anybody was his subject – The Who to Bardot to Snowdon, Bill Brandt to Mia Farrow to Oliver Reed – and of course when Reggie Kray walked down the aisle, the wedding photographer was Bailey.

There was a doubt – even in his own mind for a while – that he could avoid the black hole of the '70s that swallowed up Herman's Hermits, Bobby Moore and Simon Dee. 'I went through a period of accepting any work that was offered to me,' he says.'After that first flush has worn off you think, my God, this is the last one. In the late '60s I got a bit nervous. I did too many jobs that . . . were not right. I did them for the money, for all sorts of reasons – sometimes I did them to feel wanted. Careers are a bit like restaurants, aren't they? They are either a quick flash in the pan, or they are there forever.'

There is some debate as to whether the consistently high profile that Bailey has had for more than a quarter of a century has been a help or a hindrance to his career. It has certainly rubbed a lot of people up the wrong way, and it is not uncommon for critics to identify Bailey with the haggard young masturbator taking pictures and getting his leg over in Antonioni's swinging London epic *Blow Up* rather than the dazzling body of work that he has built up over a period of nearly 30 years.

Nancy Hall-Duncan (a woman with a double-barrelled name and a single-barrelled brain) says in her *History of Fashion Photography*, 'Bailey's photography was subordinated to his lifestyle.' The charge is clearly nonsense because, while Bailey has stepped out with many of the great lookers of his time, he has also built a lifetime's portfolio that stands – from the austere beauty of his portraits to the heartbreaking despatches from the Sudan – as one of the most vivid and astute records of what it was like to be alive in the second half of the twentieth century.

But the celebrity must also have had its uses? It must have got you work which got you money which bought you freedom? 'Actually it can scare people off. They think – oh, he is going to be difficult, or a prima donna, or very expensive. All those things that are not particularly true – or I don't *think* they are.'

Ah, the *working* Bailey. Today it is a working lunch – Catherine has gone off to a restaurant but Bailey and I eat roast beef and smoked salmon sandwiches in the studio and the man is charm incarnate. There are reports that when the working lunch is over and Bailey is back behind his camera, he can be a less enchanting character than he is in conversation. George Melly said in *Revolt Into Style* that Bailey was, 'uneducated but sophisticated, elegant but a bit grubby, arbitrary yet rigid,' while Martin Harrison has written, 'he is capable of switching from great charm to great arrogance, from sensitivity to selfishness.'

Cecil Beaton, photographed by Bailey for *Vogue* in the '60s, caught him in a sunny mood (and made him sound almost *exactly* like the David Hemmings character in *Blow Up*). 'He has this fantastic charm and energy and directness,' remembered Beaton. 'While he was taking his pictures he kept up a continuous stream of encouragement. *Marvellous, darling, super-super, a bit to the left, chief, that way, doll, great, marvellous.* Absolutely non-stop and at the end of the sitting one felt really exhilarated.'

So is it all true?

'Oh, I think I'm really easy to *live* with – working, I might turn round and call someone a stupid cunt, but five minutes later I have completely forgotten it.'

Maybe they remember it all their lives.

'Maybe they do – but that's their problem and not mine.'

Bailey is laughing his mad, hiccoughing laugh – but he means every word of it. 'I hate mediocrity. I don't mind people making mistakes but I hate stupidity. In the end, common sense is more use to you than talent. Matisse and Picasso had a lot of common sense. A year in Picasso's life was like another painter's entire career – he pre-empted everything that came after him. He chopped every other painter's balls off. A lot of common sense . . .'

You said to me once that you didn't get involved with fashion photography because you were amused by the little pleat at the back of the frock but because it combined the two things you care about most – photography and women. You said the same thing to someone else but said it combined photography, women and money. How important is the money to you?

'It's very important to me because it means I can afford to say no to things. Money means freedom. And all the things I've got going – offices, the studio, staff – are quite expensive. I have enormous overheads.'

Do you have regular meetings with accountants? Are you *that* into it? 'Not regular, no. I don't know what I'm worth, not even approximately.' Bailey pours a little scalding coffee into his lap. 'Shit, it makes me nervous talking about money . . .'

Do you still have your place in Primrose Hill? 'Yes, but I have just bought an incredible, huge house right on Dartmoor. Hugh Hudson found it for me. He said I have found this really depressing, Gothic house – it will suit your personality perfectly! He said, it is only ten minutes from me *by horse*. That hooked me.'

Why don't you go down there and relax?

'What am I going to do if I relax? I have this enormous guilt problem – if I'm not working, I feel as though I am wasting my life. It is the work ethic of a protestant, working class background. And it is more than that – it is an obsession, a compulsion. I wouldn't know how to relax . . .'

David Bailey is an ambitious, avaricious man who has the vision of an artist and the artisan's faith in hard work. Early success, which could have ruined him, made him restless and strong. He has a pretty good idea of when he can exploit his fame for all it is worth and when he should retreat from it. His confidence is real enough but so is the need to prove to himself – again and again and again – that it is not unfounded. He has been around for all of our lives and yet he acts as if he is just getting warmed up. He is probably guilty of most of the things people accuse him of and has no doubt made more than his fair share of photographer's assistants and wafer-thin models leave the studio in tears. But that cannot take anything away from his very real and considerable talent, which is to record, in images of spartan gloss, the times we live in.

I ask him how much gets through to him – what was going through his head and heart when, say, he was taking photographs for the Band Aid book, *Imagine*?

'The ironic thing is, in a situation like that, you are thinking purely about your own survival. Photographing under those conditions you are thinking about your safety – you have to. You think – my God, don't let me get dysentry, not here. Or – when are we going to get a drink that isn't cow piss?'

Bailey was on a cargo plane to the Sudan days after being approached by Kevin Jenden, director of Band Aid. The eerie power of the photographs Bailey took in the Sudan came from the fact that the numbing, familiar images of famine were recorded next to those of hope – the starving child was portrayed next to the curious, smiling, even laughing child. And the fact that the children could live – one bright and alive, the other a cadaver from the concentration camp – in the same border region made the plight of the famine victims more obscene. Bailey humanized the tragedy – leaving little room for a smug sentimentality that could be stroked with a credit card donation, and plenty of room for anger. Down on the Sudanese-Ethiopian border, Bailey took photographs that, in the words of William Golding, 'could keep you awake at night and make you feel as though you will stay awake forever.'

'I tried to mix it up to show that it wasn't completely hopeless. And in a way we were a kind of pantomime. The kids loved playing with the cameras and the flashes. Because kids don't know. They don't know they are dying. You have to confront the *unreality* of the situation. There are so many that you can't take it all in. And you know that when you come back tomorrow, the children you took photographs of today will be dead.'

This is what David Bailey does, what any great photographer – any artist – does. If there is a secret to his success, it is this. He brings something alive and keeps its essence alive forever. He keeps it alive for us to celebrate and to remember but mostly for us to mourn. His work endures, and much of it has an added resonance as the years pass – Sharon Tate's body and face, John Lennon's hair and eyes – the people slip away but the photographs remain always . . . a ransom against time, as time goes by.

'The secret of my success? Oh, there's a Rosebud somewhere.'

Some lost totem from a happier time? A little snow sledge?

'Oh, Rosebud wasn't a sledge,' Bailey says. 'It was the name of the pussy of Citizen Kane's mistress.'

Muhammad Ali

Arena, Winter 1989/90

THE LANGUAGE OF SPORT is the language of hysterical hyperbole. A goal just before halftime is 'a disaster', a stumble on the home straight is 'a tragedy'. But even in this world of extravagant exaggeration, when George Foreman called Muhammad Ali 'probably one of the greatest men of all time' he got it just about right.

Talent and integrity, courage and glamour were never embodied so perfectly in one man. From the total eclipse of Sonny Liston through the classic battles with Foreman, Smoking Joe Frazier and Ken Norton, right up to the night he won the heavyweight championship of the world for an unprecedented third time, my generation grew up marvelling at the genius of Muhammad Ali.

Working-class families who distrusted anyone without skin the colour of yesterday's porridge lost their hearts to the young fighter from Kentucky, and racism in this damp little corner of the world would never come quite so easily again. He changed his given name to something strange and foreign, he cut up Henry Cooper – and we still loved him. He saved his sport – for too long the province of lumbering ex-cons and their corrupt handlers – and then he transcended it. And even when he lost – against Leon Spinks or Larry Holmes or the US draft board – he did so with dignity; you were always proud of him.

Muhammad Ali was in London recently with George Foreman and Joe Frazier to promote a video called *Champions Forever*, a stirring 90-minute reminder of heavyweight boxing's glory days, those years in the '60s and '70s when the fight game had never had it so good; when the cruellest sport seemed exhilarating, important, magical; the good old days before it was swamped by the brutal tedium of Iron Mike.

Frazier and Foreman were both great fighters, fierce men who didn't know how to retreat, but the media drones who poured into the new Arena stadium in London's docklands were there for Ali. He is 47 now and fighting the terrible fog of Parkinson's Disease. His speech is quiet and sometimes slurred, but he is still Muhammad Ali – you still knew that you were in the presence of greatness.

'Time passes so quickly,' he said quietly. 'It is 27 years since I fought Henry Cooper, 27 years.' He shook his still-handsome head. 'Time passes so quickly.'

If he has been diminished by the passing years and the sad rags of growing older – well, who isn't? George Foreman calls him 'Champ' without irony and when you briefly meet him, that's what you call him too.

The words of his third wife describe him well: 'A warm, affectionate, quiet and serious man.' But the words of Budd Schulberg describe him best: 'Muhammad Ali – loser and still champion.'

The Swinging Septuagenarian

Frank Sinatra at the London Arena

The Daily Telegraph, 6 July 1990

THE SWINGING septuagenarian comes from a time when men were men and women were broads, dames and tomatoes. At the London Arena, Frank Sinatra washed away the years and made it all live again. Bathed in a blue light, emerging from a shroud of cigarette smoke, Sinatra swaggered like a boxer, shoulders rolling inside a tailored tux, crooning his whiskey-soaked lullabies.

He was slimmer than he has been, tanned a light tandoori, hair a metallic white crop. His pipes were in great shape, the odd moment of breathlessness only adding an edge of vulnerability to that rich, perfect voice. He did all the things that Sinatra should – he sat slumped on a bar stool, he danced with himself, he changed all the words. 'She never bothers with some bum she hates,' he asserted in 'The Lady Is A Tramp', 'that's why the chick is a champ.' He oozed Rat Pack hipness, he came on like the coolest man on the planet. 'Weatherwise, it's such a groovy day.'

Mentioning a film he made with Rita Hayworth, the oldest kid on the block started to bark. He picked up a glass of Jack Daniel's and snarled at it: 'You killed my old man but I'll get even with you.' He made like a clown but sang like a dream; he captured a mood and held it in his voice.

There were songs that are as much a part of him as those blazing blue eyes – 'A Foggy Day In London Town', 'You Make Me Feel So Young', 'Mac the Knife' – and others that he made his own, including an incredible version of 'For Once In My Life'.

The man whose acting won an Oscar played out his life before us. He sang of dinner with an angel, breakfast with the blues. He belted out 'Strangers In The Night' and 'What Now My Love', tales of love's first flush and its dying throes. He mocked his 74 years: 'For those of you who have never seen me before – I hope you get another chance.'

He wrapped up the show with the epic set-pieces, a moody 'My Way', Frank playing the Hamlet of Las Vegas, and a barnstorming 'New York, New York', the perfect, life-affirming end to a summer night when Sinatra yet again proved himself the supreme master of the American song, night and day, now and forever.

Art Without Shame

Jeff Koons

The Daily Telegraph, 4 April 1992

WHEN I INTERVIEWED Jeff Koons and his wife they were very much in love. One week later they were preparing for divorce. Not long after that they were back in each other's arms. Every stumble and fall on their path of true love was recorded by the mass media. Mr and Mrs Koons are the Liz Taylor and Richard Burton of the art world.

Now 37, Jeff Koons long ago made enough money from his art never to need to work again. But he is as prolific – and as controversial – as ever. His critics call him a charlatan. His friends hail him as the last great artist of the 20th century. What few people seem to accept is that he might be exactly what he appears to be.

'Art lacks glamour,' says Koons in his calm, persuasive monotone. 'Art lacks charisma. Art is up for grabs.'

His wife smiles at him adoringly, her mouth as red as Snow White's. As they cross the lobby of the Langham Hilton, Mr and Mrs Koons scarcely warrant a second glance from the assembled tourists, despite Mrs Koons's shocking pink dress, platinum-blonde coiffure and orange eyebrows.

But 24 hours earlier, a flock of shrieking paparazzi had tailed them all over London; because 40-year-old Mrs Koons, née Ilona Staller, is the former Italian parliamentarian and porn star Cicciolina (variously translated as 'the dumpling', 'the plump one' and 'little pinchable one'), while her husband is the most talked-about artist since Andy Warhol.

'Ilona and I have a clippings service,' says Koons. 'They send stories about us from all over the world and they charge $1.25 a clipping. And it costs up to $8,000 every month.'

But Jeff Koons can afford it. His 1988 exhibition was staged simultaneously at identical shows in New York, Chicago and Cologne (Koons made 18 pieces in triplicate) and it quickly sold out, grossing $5 million, despite one critic denouncing the work as 'a recycling of kitsch taste for jaded sophisticates'.

The exhibition consisted of giant ceramic sculptures featuring the likes of a white Michael Jackson cuddling his pet chimp, a girl in a bathtub being surprised by a periscope, and a menagerie of smiling bears, penguins, puppies and pigs. It was the flotsam and jetsam of every seaside gift shop, the debris of 10 million suburban mantelpieces, but blown up to epic proportions, made mythic and crafted by European artisans' to Koons's instructions. The exhibition was called Banality.

'I was trying to remove the guilt and shame of the bourgeoisie,' says Koons. 'I believe that I have never worked with kitsch. What they mistake for kitsch is our past. I try to make art that is open to a large group of people.'

But now the charges against Koons of dubious taste have been joined by accusations of sensationalism and obscenity. His latest exhibition is Made in Heaven, a Kama Sutra of paintings and sculptures, starring Jeff and his muse Ilona, that mix the trappings of romance – flowers, butterflies, lots of baby pink and bridal white – with what one critic called 'the most hard-core images in contemporary art'.

When Made in Heaven appeared at New York's Sonnabend Gallery last year, the crowds broke all records for an exhibition in a commercial gallery. And they were not all smut-seeking window-shoppers. Prices for Koons's work start at $65,000 (and went up to $250,000 at the Banality show), but there are plenty of takers. Charles Saatchi has 15 Koonses.

Koons's admirers compare him to Salvador Dali. Others are less impressed. 'Jeff Koons has provided one last pathetic gasp of the sort of self-promoting hype and sensationalism that characterised the worst of the '80s,' raged Michael Kimmelman in the New York Times, while Robert Hughes of Time called Koons 'the starry-eyed opportunist *par excellence*'.

Koons sees himself as a direct descendant of the Baroque – 'Bernini and stuff like that' – a florid exuberance in revolt against all élitism, emotional coldness and stuffed shirts.

He is certainly all that, but I see him as the new Jasper Johns – that great transformer of icons – with sex, shopping and the detritus of the suburbs in place of John's targets, beer cans and flags.

Koons's work teaches you to see, or at least to look again. The marketing of the man should not blind us to the fact that he is a great artist, unafraid of engaging mass culture. He is also a lot of fun. Koons himself remains sanguine in the face of all the bitter debate.

'Ilona and I are the new Adam and Eve,' he tells me. Before or after the Fall? 'After the Fall, but accepting our past without guilt and shame,' he says, in a soft, hypnotic drone.

'Eez very beautiful, no?' smiles Cicciolina.

It is a little after breakfast and the Koons have just walked into their first scandal of the day. His advertisement for the Hayward Gallery's Doubletake show has just been vetoed by London Underground.

'I tried to produce something that was very beautiful, very generous and very warm; that showed the family life I have with my wife,' says Koons, a little hurt. Entitled *At Home with the Koons*, it shows a trio of puppies in the foreground while, modestly veiled by the lovable little hounds, the middle regions of Jeff and Ilona are engaged in the intimate act that is known as, well, doggie-fashion.

But a furore like this is bread and butter to the Koons. He is a media manipulator of genius, so adept at the mechanics of mass communication that he pauses mid-sentence when he sees that my cassette recorder has run out of tape, waiting patiently until I have inserted a new cassette before carrying on with what he was saying from *exactly* where he stopped. I have never seen anyone else do that.

Aware of the importance the Koonses place on the media, I show Ilona a copy of *The Daily Telegraph*. 'Eez very beautiful,' she purrs approvingly.

She is in the early stages of pregnancy, her belly gently swelling inside her pink dress, and she tells me with obvious delight that she is expecting a summer bambino. 'Luna if eet's a girl,' she says.

'And Kitsch if it's a boy,' says Jeff. 'To me our child is my most important work, a biological sculpture. We look forward, more than anything, to being able to have a family and a family life. We look forward to seeing the world anew and to trying to build a life that is as beautiful as possible for our children. We would like to have five. You know, the most fertile image I can imagine is Ilona standing next to a Bavarian cow.'

'Hee-hee-hee!' laughs Cicciolina. 'Very beautiful, no?'

Though cynics would see their union as a match made in a PR's wildest dream, there is no doubting that their intentions towards each other are honourable.

But Ilona's alter-ego remains a bone of contention between them. He accepts her porno past but demands from her a virtuous future. A few days after lovingly comparing his wife to a Bavarian cow, he issued divorce proceedings because Ilona was playing footsy with the

Italian Love Party, a coalition of pornographers – 'terrible men, like pimps,' Koons told me – seeking publicity for their tawdry wares. They later kissed and made up when Ilona renounced her Love Party tendencies.

It was the second time they had broken up and been reconciled. Jeff's attitude to Cicciolina can be shockingly normal – in a predictable male way.

Ilona Staller moved to Italy when she was 17 and you would imagine that more than 20 years as a star of blue screen and stage – she had an act with a tame snake that caused concern among Italian animal-rights organisations – would have left her a little world-weary.

Even when she was a politician she let potential voters fondle her breasts on the hustings (her politics are a sexually-liberated shade of Green: she is in favour of love hotels and the environment). But if she can't stop being Cicciolina, it seems unlikely that she will last as Mrs Koons. In the early days of their engagement, she volunteered to sleep with Saddam Hussein if he would release the hostages. In a fit of jealousy, Koons broke off their engagement. But Saddam did not return her calls, the hostages stayed where they were and Jeff and Ilona were married in her native Budapest last summer.

Ilona seems to have won Jeff's heart by embodying an American adolescent boy's fantasy of dirty sex. But the reason he loves her is the reason she is hard to hold. The little pinchable one will find it hard to settle down to housewife piety.

Koons is clearly crazy about the woman. During our interview, he is constantly trying to show her how lovable he is. I ask him about his days as a commodities broker on Wall Street – Koons spent his days as a struggling artist working on Wall Street rather than starving in a garret – and he directed his answer to Ilona, because the anecdote shows the charming, apple-pie side of his nature.

'This is great, Ilona,' he says, leaning forward, 'because when I was working on Wall Street trying to get someone to risk his money on cotton, I would say, "Bob, how can you get hurt by cotton? Cotton is soft and fluffy!".'

Mrs Koons smiles dutifully.

Ilona lives in Munich with her husband because US Immigration regards her as an undesirable. But she is a genuinely sweet, almost child-like woman, constantly saying things like, 'Ah, zee snow in Munich eez so beautiful. You like snow?'

Koons says that it is exactly this childlike aspect that makes her vulnerable to the tacky mandarins of the porn industry, whom Koons loathes, despite the mountain of mad flesh in Made in Heaven.

'I initially made contact with Ilona because I wanted to be a porn star as well as an art star. For me Ilona is one of the world's great artists. She has no guilt. No shame.'

Intimacies soon followed and, because they did not share a common language in those early days, the words of love that they shared over breakfast had to pass through a translator. 'Our hormonal aspects fit together perfectly,' says Koons with his beatific grin. 'We find beauty in the most simple things.'

If he is tormented by demons, he keeps them well hidden. He has an unshakeable self-confidence, which no doubt dates back to when he sold his first paintings at nine years old, these early Koonses going for hundreds of dollars in Henry J. Koons Interiors, his father's furniture store in a small town in Pennsylvania. 'I was very loved as a child,' says Koons.

If the ghost of Elvis is in his haircut, then the spirit of Colonel Tom Parker, the King's flamboyant manager, is in his rhetoric. 'I was always a very good salesman,' says Koons. 'I was always the top broker at any firm I worked for on Wall Street and before that I sold memberships at the Museum of Modern Art. I doubled their membership list. I enjoy sales. The market is the greatest critic.'

Made in Heaven will be at London's Anthony D'Offay Gallery in September. Koons is creating new sculptures for the show, but the work will follow the general thrust of Made in Heaven in New York, which poses two central questions to the unconverted. Is it pornography? And is it art?

Koons has no doubt. 'To me pornography is an activity which alienates one from life,' he says. 'And this work does absolutely the opposite.'

One week after our chat Jeff hit Ilona with divorce proceedings and everyone in the art world crowed that they had always known it wouldn't last. I called Koons at his home in Munich during what turned out to be a temporary separation. He sounded like a man who was trying to be brave after his marriage had just fallen apart. There was real sadness in his voice. It did not surprise me. Jeff Koons is for real.

Lifting the Loincloth

Phillip Schofield

The Daily Telegraph, 16 January 1992

WAS PHILLIP SCHOFIELD man enough to fill Jason Donovan's loincloth? Could the smirking Valentino of children's television, previously best known for his in-depth interviews with Gordon the Gopher (*Going Live*'s stupendously useless glove puppet), really pull it off as male lead in Tim Rice and Andrew Lloyd Webber's biblical romp, *Joseph and the Amazing Technicolor Dreamcoat*?

The predominately nubile audience in the London Palladium were in no doubt. As soon as Schofield appeared in his white mini-dress – very popular among the young men of ancient Canaan – the little girls squealed with delight. By the time Jacob's favourite son had evened the score with his jealous brothers, there was not a dry seat in the house.

You had to feel a little sorry for Joseph's brothers. They were portrayed as a yobbish bunch, prone to casual violence and drunken wenching. Chelsea supporters transposed to the Promised Land. They paw Joseph's dreamcoat, give him a kicking in the desert and eventually sell him to slave traders. You feel that if there was a football special in Canaan, then these boys would smash it up.

Still, they are infinitely preferable to Schofield's Joseph, an insufferable prig with a politician's smile and a brown, wavy wig that might best be described as early Elsie Tanner.

Schofield handled his role with all the assured charm of a game show host. His voice was strong and true on the low notes and only took a tea break on those difficult high notes. 'Children of Israel are never *alone*!' he shrieked, and we feared that a hernia might be lurking beneath his white mini-skirt (it is possible that the real reason Joseph's brothers disliked him was because he refused to wear anything but women's clothing).

Cynics who came expecting a disaster of Titanic proportions found only a pastel-coloured dinghy with a few leaks in it. True, the dance steps were rheumatic, Schofield's smug grin began to grate after a while and, as his outfits became skimpier, the ageing heart throb (30 on April Fool's Day) revealed an unappetising body, the top half running to flab and the bottom half all bony.

He brought little sense of tragedy to the role – when Joseph languishes miserably in an Egyptian dungeon Schofield plays it as though he has had his BMW clamped – and those knobbly knees didn't help. Schofield's Joseph was more Twiglet than Hamlet. But he has all the cloying charisma of a male Doris Day. Butter wouldn't melt in his loincloth.

Jason Donovan's Joseph had been blond, bemused and beefy – the biblical hero as dazed beach bum. Schofield's Joe was a prissier creature, poncing around in his Technicolor coat like John Hurt mincing in front of a mirror in *The Naked Civil Servant*. The flirtatious smile, the cow-like eyes and the permanent-wave wig combined to make him look like the girl in the perfume commercial who makes complete strangers go crazy. Children of Israel just can't help acting on impulse.

But, before the standing ovation had ended, the girls were swarming around the backstage door like flying insects around a custard doughnut. They say Schofield has been asked to take on the role permanently. Smart man, that Andrew Lloyd Webber.

The Songsmith Who Made Sinatra Great

Sammy Cahn

The Daily Telegraph, 28 January 1993

ANY MAN WHO CAN write the line 'If you could use some exotic booze there's a bar in far Bombay' is obviously touched by genius. Sammy Cahn, the writer of those words – from Sinatra's 'Come Fly With Me' – died last week aged 79 and a part of old-style showbusiness died with him.

The tributes to Cahn have been warm but have tended to underestimate his worth. 'Cahn belongs near the top of the B group,' said Benny Green, rating him well below the likes of Cole Porter and George Gershwin.

But I have before me a copy of Sinatra's *Twenty Golden Greats*. Here is the greatest saloon-bar singer of all time singing the work of the best songwriters of the pre-Lennon and McCartney era. The record includes two songs by Cole Porter, two by Johnny Mercer and one by Rodgers and Hart. But there are no fewer than seven songs co-written by Sammy Cahn – 'Love Is The Tender Trap', 'It's Very Nice To Go Trav'ling', 'Three Coins In A Fountain', 'High Hopes', 'Come Fly With Me', 'All The Way' and 'Love And Marriage'. Seven songs out of 20! On Sinatra's greatest hits!

It is no exaggeration to say that Sammy Cahn defined the Sinatra persona of the '50s: the cocky insouciance, the bruised romanticism, the existential cool, the off-beat humour. Of course, all these qualities were there in Sinatra anyway. But through Cahn's songs they were magnified, made mythic, transformed into something epic.

Cahn wrote lyrics so inventive that he was nominated for an Oscar 30 times (he won four). When asked if the words or the music came first he replied: 'Neither – the telephone call.' He was an artist masquerading as an artisan.

Sinatra's great Capitol recordings of the '50s are unimaginable without the contribution of Sammy Cahn – as unimaginable as they would be without the arrangements of Nelson Riddle. Cahn songs like 'It's Very Nice To Go Trav'ling' with a line like, 'Your heart starts singing when you're homeward winging 'cross the foam' would have been memorable in the hands of any good singer. Sung by Sinatra in his prime, they were unforgettable.

Cahn (born Samuel Cohen on New York's Lower East Side) couldn't sing for toffee – he had a voice like 'a vain duck with a hangover', he said – but he wrote like a dream.

There was a goofy quality about some of his songs. 'High Hopes', 'Love And Marriage' and Dean Martin's 'Relax-Ay-Voo' were all knockabout stuff. But Cahn was capable of a beautiful unabashed romanticism. In 'All The Way' his promises of undying love – 'Through all the good and lean years and all the inbetween years, come what may' – made words of seduction sound like wedding vows. A generation of baby boomers were conceived to this music.

And it wasn't all fairytale romance. There were also the saloon-bar songs of bleak despair like 'When No One Cares', 'Only The Lonely' and 'Guess I'll Hang My Tears Out To Dry'.

Despite all the slapstick humour, Cahn – like Sinatra – had a strong melancholy streak.

Cahn wrote songs with Jule Styne, Jimmy Van Heusen and Axel Stordahl – but his enduring partnership was with Sinatra. It is not too much to say that Sinatra, the grand old master of the American song, would have had a lesser career without Sammy. To his eternal credit, Sinatra himself appreciates the debt he owes to men like Cahn, and in his shows he never fails to credit the writers before every song. Cahn and his peers were the last of the old school of songwriters. Less than 10 years after all those great Sinatra recordings on Capitol, Lennon and McCartney came along and placed a time bomb in Tin Pan Alley.

After John and Paul, the norm would be for singers also to be songwriters. Inevitably, they rarely write them like they used to.

Cahn's great achievement is that out of all the songs he wrote, there are dozens that will live for as long as music is used to win a lover, to lift the spirit or to nurse a broken heart. Frank Sinatra's voice was one of the most expressive instruments of the 20th century. The songs of Sammy Cahn gave it life.

Alex Through the Looking Glass

A Clockwork Orange

Empire, December 1993

O NLY ONE CHARACTER DIES IN *A Clockwork Orange*. Early on in Kubrick's lost masterpiece, Alex DeLarge, the teen with a taste for rape, murder and Beethoven, makes his last appearance in classic droog chic – white shirt, braces and trousers, black bowler hat, right eye framed by a spider's web of heavily mascaraed false lashes – when he bungles a burglary and smashes in a middle-aged woman's skull with a sculpture shaped like a giant cock. And though the film is littered with battered and abused bodies (and another victim eventually expires quietly off-camera), the woman who Alex kills in his valedictory appearance as a Droog is *A Clockwork Orange*'s only onscreen fatality.

By any cinematic standards this is a very modest death toll. For a work with the lurid reputation of *A Clockwork Orange*, one killing seems a remarkably low body count. Yet, even now, it remains a supremely shocking film. There are countless films more violent than *A Clockwork Orange*. But there is not one that even comes *close* to matching its inflammatory power.

There's a chilling conviction about the sex and violence in *A Clockwork Orange*. Conceived by the novelist Anthony Burgess as a fable about man's choice between good and evil, when the film appeared in 1971 it was seen by some young hotheads – not to mention the majority of judges, policemen and tabloid editors – as a thesis on how good it feels to be bad. *A Clockwork Orange* was big box office and even bigger news, and was blamed for inspiring a plague of teenage violence from every pulpit and soapbox in the land.

The hysteria eventually became too much for Stanley Kubrick, who told Warner Bros that he no longer wanted *A Clockwork Orange* to be distributed in the UK, the country the American director has made his home.

In the deafening furore around the film, hardly anyone noticed that Kubrick never went on record to explain this decision. Did he pull *A Clockwork Orange* because he was sick of seeing his film carry the can for society's problems? Or because he thought that perhaps it really was responsible for inciting violence among some confused souls? Or because he was frightened to be seen as the man responsible for creating what one judge called 'that wicked film'? The honest answer is that we do not know, although sources close to Kubrick claim that he was profoundly disturbed by the reaction the film received in this country.

So *A Clockwork Orange* disappeared into a black hole and has remained there ever since. But beyond the hysteria of the tabloid headlines, here was the greatest film ever made in Britain – a giddy cocktail of stark brutality, slapstick comedy and futuristic nightmare. It is a dazzling social prophecy (Alex is eventually brainwashed by a weak government attempting to stay in power by taking a tough stand on law and order). It is brilliant social satire (Alex and his Droogs sip milk spiked with hallucinogenics, sporting uniforms – the lone girlie eyelashes, the gentleman's bowler hat – that are both celebrations and satire of every British youth cult from Teds to Punk). And, for all its horrors, *A Clockwork Orange* is frequently achingly funny (the leading man has Marty Feldman's eyes). Yet there is no denying that the film also has a touch of evil about it. What made *A Clockwork Orange* subversive was that it seems to rejoice in its dirty deeds. This is a film completely lacking in what screenwriting guru Robert McKee calls 'the centre of goodness'. There is no moral redemption at the heart of *A Clockwork Orange*. The 15-year-old hero has the choice between good and evil. Emphatically, he chooses evil.

When Alex and his Droogs rape a woman, the camera lingers on her face in leering close-up, as if it is the next in line. When a rival gang is beaten to bloody pulp, it is to the exhilarating strains of Rossini's 'The Thieving Magpie' (classical music is all over the sound-track, a classy counterpoint to all the GBH). And when Alex puts the boot into a man whose home he has invaded, it is while he is doing a tap dance and crooning Gene Kelly's 'Singin' In The Rain'.

And yet you can't help liking him. Alex (Malcolm McDowell in the performance of a lifetime) is one of cinema's most seductive heroes – articulate, witty, whispering his amoral philosophy in a breezy voice-over, calling the audience 'my brothers'. Alex rapes, murders and crushes testicles. And we want to be his friend.

A Clockwork Orange cruelly exposes the old liberal line about great cinema making us realise the horror of violence. *A Clockwork Orange* put forward a strong case for the symphonic beauty of violence, the glamour of evil. There are scenes where the violence is as choreographed as anything in *West Side Story*. But then Kubrick subverts the theatricality with a sudden close-up of a bottle being shoved in someone's face. Naturally, the boys in the back row of the late show lapped it up. *A Clockwork Orange* may have drawn the art house crowd in the rest of the world; in this country it attracted the lads, the mob, the masses.

The film had been running in London's West End for over a year when Kubrick pulled the plug. *A Clockwork Orange*'s steady ascent to mythic status in this country over the last 20 years often makes us overlook its initial commercial impact. In its day it was *huge*.

The director withdrew his film from distribution only in Britain. Here you can't buy it on video or see it at the cinema. But in the United States you can buy it on LaserDisc. In Paris it is still playing to packed houses. In fact in the rest of the world *A Clockwork Orange* is as fêted as *Citizen Kane* and as easily available as *Home Alone* 2. Only in Britain is it censored by the man who made it.

And so, of course, the dark legend continues to grow. *A Clockwork Orange* is the mainstream film that descended to the underground. In London – 22 years after it was released – there is at least one video rental store that displays a sign saying, 'No: We do not have *A Clockwork Orange*.'

What is it with Britain and *A Clockwork Orange*? This country and *A Clockwork Orange* have always had a special relationship. Perhaps understandably so – the clothes, language and drugs of Alex and his friends were directly inspired by the emergence of the early British youth cults. The rest of the world consider it a serious film by one of the greatest directors of the last 30 years. But here it has been demonised, portrayed as a danger to society and made a scapegoat for all our ills. The Fleet Street clippings of 20 years ago are full of cases of rape, murder and mayhem where it was pointed out that the defendants had seen *A Clockwork Orange* – as if that explained everything.

'We must stamp out this horrible trend which has been inspired by this wretched film,' said Judge Desmond Bailey, sending a 16-year-old boy to borstal for beating up a younger boy while wearing white overalls and a black bowler hat. 'We appreciate that what you did was inspired by that wicked film, but that does not mean you are not blameworthy.'

It is, of course, impossible to say how much violence was inspired by *A Clockwork Orange*. Certainly a few terrible crimes were committed with Kubrick's symphony of violence ringing in the heads of the perpetrators (in Lancashire in 1973, for example, a 17-year-old Dutch girl was raped by a gang chanting 'Singin' In The Rain') but whether these crimes would have been committed without the prompting of *A Clockwork Orange* is another question. The critics of *A Clockwork Orange* have acted as though the film introduced evil into the world.

Anthony Burgess was a teacher in Malaya and Borneo from 1954 to 1960. During World War II his wife had been raped in London by four American deserters. When he returned to Britain there were still Teddy Boys on the streets, and later he and his wife witnessed the first battle between Mods and Rockers on the Brighton seafront. It is said that the expatriate who returns home after a long absence sees his country with the eyes of a time-traveller. *A Clockwork Orange* was set in the future, but in young Alex every British youth who ever wore the uniform of a teenage tribe could glimpse his own reflection. I was in my mid-teens 20 years ago and me and all my friends felt that here was a film about us. What a triumph for a British film!

The major difference between Burgess' novel and Kubrick's film is that in the book the reader was screened from the unfolding horrors by the barrier of language. Alex narrates his tale in Nadsat – Burgess' brilliant combination of Cockney rhyming slang and corrupted Russian (the book was written in 1962 when it still seemed as if the Reds could win the Cold War). So we hear that Alex and his three Droogs start the evening by tolchocking some starry veck, indulge in lashings of the old ultraviolence and then subject a devotchka with horror-show groodies to the old in-out. But in the film, although the Nadsat is still there and although it is all as stylised as *Blade Runner*, you see the victims' faces and hear their screams.

'A film,' noted Burgess, 'is not made of words.' When people talk of *A Clockwork Orange* they usually think of the mayhem in the film's first 15 minutes. But beatings, rape and murder are only the start of our story. Alex quickly winds up in jail after killing the woman with the XXL-phallic sculpture, where he volunteers to be brainwashed so that every thought of violence literally makes him sick. He does not want to be good. He wants to be *free*.

So with his eyes clipped open, Alex is pumped full of the appropriate medication and forced to watch scenes of Nazis marching and

Droogs gang-banging while his beloved classical music plays in the background. This results in an ironic side effect to his treatment that he really objects to – not only can't he stand the thought of hurting someone, he also can't bear to listen to 'lovely, lovely Ludwig'.

The transformation of Alex from free-thinking psycho to politically correct robot forms the basis of both Burgess' novel and Kubrick's film. At the climax of the film he is brainwashed back to his old rotten ways by a government facing a storm of bad publicity for its authoritarian measures.

Alex ends *A Clockwork Orange* triumphant, fantasising about some of the old in-out.

'I was cured all right!' he rejoices.

But for most of the film, Alex is a prisoner. And although *A Clockwork Orange* is relentlessly amoral, he gets more punishment for his crimes than any villain ever did. He is beaten in the cells by the police (including a young Steven Berkoff), he is subjected to radical aversion therapy, he is assaulted by his former victims and nearly drowned in a water trough by his former friends. Despite the Droog rampant you always see in stills, for most of the film Alex is in civvies, whimpering and crying and wiping snot from his nose. Alex is only part of a gang at the start – for most of the action he is horribly alone. But when the film was released, all anyone seemed to notice was the old ultraviolence in the first 15 minutes.

It was this part of the film that made the judges and tabloid editors foam at the mouth. And it was the opening scenes of Alex on the rampage with his Droogs that touched a peculiarly resonant chord in British adolescents. *A Clockwork Orange* is the most tribal of films. The violence is ritualised, the dress code is rigorous, the cult is king. It seems appropriate that it should have become the ultimate cult film.

More than two decades after its release, *A Clockwork Orange* still seems like the most controversial film of the last 30 years. How tame the fuss around *Reservoir Dogs* seems next to the uproar caused by *A Clockwork Orange*! How paltry is the impact of *Hard Boiled* next to Kubrick's bloody rhapsody! What an anti-climax are the antics of all the big screen tough guys after a night on the tiles with little Alex!

The film continues to inspire great passions. Even now *A Clockwork Orange* is unfairly held up in some quarters as a byword for contemporary violence. That was one of the reasons why I wanted to make a documentary about it for Channel 4's arts series *Without*

Walls, looking beyond the hysteria and hyperbole that has surrounded the film and hopefully shedding light on its dark legend. Because the documentary used clips from *A Clockwork Orange*, Warner Bros brought and were granted an injunction preventing Channel 4 screening the programme, though the injunction was overturned by the Court of Appeal. Channel 4 argued that our use of clips was justified under Section 30 of the 1988 Copyright Act which allows the use of extracts for legitimate review and criticism. The programme was eventually transmitted three weeks later than planned. It was called 'Forbidden Fruit'. What else *could* it be called? *A Clockwork Orange* remains British cinema's missing masterpiece.

And yet, just a ferry ride away, they are selling videotapes of *A Clockwork Orange* at the giant record megastore FNCA Musique at Place de la Bastille, Paris. And funnily enough, there are no reports of copycat violence.

Time to reconsider, Mr Kubrick, brother?

Jung Chang

The Daily Telegraph, 28 February 1994

'For many years I had nightmares every night,' says Jung Chang. 'For years the fear was quite terrible. The dreams were all violent, all horrible and I often screamed in my sleep. But Britain is a wonderful place and since I came here I have met nothing but generosity and kindness. And in such a gentle place your nerves gradually relax.'

Not many of us would think of Britain as a gentle place. But then not many of us could begin our family history with the sentence, 'At the age of fifteen my grandmother became the concubine of a warlord general.'

Jung Chang's *Wild Swans* became the bestselling book of 1993 by combining the intimacy of personal memoir with a massive historical sweep. It is the story of three generations of Chinese women – Yu-fang, who fled life as a concubine when her warlord general was on his death bed. Bao Qin, her daughter, an idealistic young Communist who saw her husband hounded into madness during the Cultural Revolution. And Bao Qin's daughter, Jung Chang herself, who was a Red Guard at fourteen, exiled to the foothills of the Himalayas during the Cultural Revolution and finally left China to study in England in 1978.

But *Wild Swans* is more than a real-life family saga. It is also the story of what happened in the twentieth century to one quarter of the world's population. As Chang's calm, measured prose leads us through the terror and suffering that was inflicted on her family, we glimpse the terror and suffering that was inflicted on millions of lives. *Wild Swans* begins with the footbinding, concubines and warlords of feudal China, advances to the horrors of Japanese occupation and Civil War and then, with the coming of Mao, it all gets infinitely worse. The story left critics dumbfounded with admiration. '*Wild Swans* made me feel like a five-year-old,' said Martin Amis. The critical acclaim has been matched by a commercial success that shows no sign of abating.

In Britain, paperback sales of *Wild Swans* are fast approaching one million. And not only is the book still the number one non-fiction bestseller, it is outselling the book in second place by almost four copies to one. The number one bestseller of last year is well placed to become the number one bestseller of this year.

And *Wild Swans* is a global success. When I produce my wife's Japanese edition to be autographed, Chang proudly tells me that the book has sold one million copies in Japan in hardback.

'My mother is now constantly visited by Japanese tourists!' cries Jung (pronounced 'Yung'). 'She has changed since I wrote the book. She is now very much at ease with herself and the past. Now she finds understanding not only in her daughter but in millions of readers all over the world.'

It is difficult to recognise the happy, sophisticated woman Chang is today as the solemn young Red Guard seen posing in Tiananmen Square in *Wild Swans*. As a girl, Chang loved to be alone with her poetry and books. But China during the Cultural Revolution was the worst place in the world to have such solitary tastes.

'In Britain people leave you alone if you want to be left alone,' she says in her perfect English. 'That's a tremendous emancipation for me. When I first came here some foreign students would say that the British were cold but I found that reserve just right for me. People are very warm here. They don't impose on you but if you have problems, they are always there. That's just ideal for me.'

Jung Chang was born in the Sichuan province of China in 1952, the daughter of high-ranking, highly principled Communists who found themselves denounced as class traitors during the Cultural Revolution. Her mother was paraded through the streets with a derogatory placard around her neck, jailed and finally sent to a distant camp. Jung's father, Wang Yu, was literally driven out of his mind by persecution (he died in 1975).

In a world where vicious beatings and pubic humiliation were a daily occurrence, Chang's parents became old almost overnight. What is unforgettable about *Wild Swans* is the courage and humanity they both showed in the face of institutionalised brutality.

'My mother and my father were both very principled but in different ways,' Jung says. 'My father was very single-minded and had his idea of personal integrity. He refused to write any confessions during the Cultural Revolution. But when my mother was asked to write confessions saying she was a capitalist roader, she would do it. It was only when she was asked to denounce my father that she refused. She wouldn't denounce him because she knew that it would kill him.'

Chang's father is the most tragic figure in *Wild Swans*. After devoting his life to China, this stubborn, self-educated man is forced to burn his beloved books in obedience to Mao's mindless edict, 'The more books you read, the more stupid you become.' And though he could be maddening to live with – 'This baby has bulging eyes,' were his first words on seeing Jung as a baby – his wife never stopped loving him.

Chang says that leaving China for England was like coming to another planet. At first she could not even understand the signs on lavatory doors.

'I had no idea why the little figure in trousers was supposed to be a man,' she smiles. 'Because that's exactly what women looked like in China.'

China was not easy to leave behind. Taken dancing in Leicester Square, she demanded to go home after noticing some men staring at her. She thought they were spies for the Chinese authorities. Her companion assured her that they were staring because she was – and remains – a gobsmackingly beautiful woman. Even as you sit discussing economic reform in modern China, you can't help remembering that when she was a teenager a young admirer wrote her a love letter in blood.

Chang studied at York University (where she became the first person from China to receive a doctorate from a British university) and later taught at the School of Oriental and African Studies, London University. She started *Wild Swans* in 1988 after a visit from her mother, who began talking about her life in a way that she had never done before.

'The first story my mother told me was how she and my father walked from Manchuria to Sichuan (a distance of over a thousand miles). My father was entitled to a horse or a jeep, whichever was available, but my mother had to walk because she was new to the revolution.'

Chang's mother was pregnant and miscarried during the march.

'My father's behaviour, in a Chinese context, was only to be admired,' says Jung. 'But when my mother saw that I understood how she felt, she was thrilled. Writing the book has definitely brought us closer together.'

There was a deep bond between Chang and her grandmother and the brave, vivacious former concubine's death is one of the most moving passages in *Wild Swans*. During the collective madness of the Cultural Revolution, Yu-fang, with her love of beauty and collection of jewellery, was as cruelly isolated as her grand-daughter.

'One of my biggest regrets is that I am not able to take my grand-mother shopping in London,' says Chang, her chunky gold earrings glinting in the W11 sunlight. 'Because my mother *is* a revolutionary. She doesn't *like* shopping! She goes into a shop, buys what she wants and leaves. But I can imagine how my grandmother would enjoy all the beautiful window displays and what great pleasure they would give her.'

Chang married historian Jon Halliday when she finished *Wild Swans* in 1991, fulfilling a prophecy made on the banks of the Yangtze that she would one day marry a foreign barbarian. Halliday is a very distinguished-looking barbarian who works on the ground floor of their Notting Hill house while Chang occupies the top floor. More than the writing of *Wild Swans*, Chang credits Halliday with helping her to exorcise the demons of the past. And even after Ti-ananmen Square, she remains optimistic about China's future.

'Under Deng Xiaoping, the Chinese people have a better life than at any time this century,' she says. 'And in a way more freedom. After Tiananmen Square, people were asked to denounce each other, but very few did. The country has changed so much that it was impossible not to carry on with the liberalisation. But there is still one area that is very tightly controlled – publishing.'

Wild Swans has a strange status in China. There is no problem taking the Chinese translation of the book in from Hong Kong while Chang comes and goes freely, visiting her mother and researching her next book, a biography of Mao. But the censors have not allowed *Wild Swans* to be published.

'People can say most things today but it is different to get your words published,' Chang says. 'But a lot of publishers are trying to find a way for *Wild Swans* to appear. They are suggesting if we make certain cuts, would the censors allow it – it's complex be-cause the situation is changing all the time. When I was in China in September there were several books published about sexuality and they were enormous bestsellers. Two months later the books were banned. No one is quite certain how far they can go. Or how far they want to go.'

Wild Swans ends with Jung Chang on the plane to London. 'I was eager to embrace the world,' she concludes. Sixteen years later, almost all of the world has embraced her family's story. If *Wild Swans* were to be embraced by her homeland, then that reallywould give her heartbreaking book a happy ending.

Among the Soccerati

Not previously published; written June 1994

THESE SHOULD BE dog days for British football. In the United States the World Cup is being played without the participation of England, Scotland, Wales or Northern Ireland. Closer to home Manchester United, the double-winning colossus of English football, were knocked out of the European Cup by a bunch of Turkish artisans. And yet in England this year, gates were up for the eighth season running – the longest period of growth in the 106-year history of the Football League – with the season's total of over 21 million through the turnstiles the biggest for 14 years. More importantly, the boys back home feel good about our football.

'It's utter stupidity that England are not in the World Cup,' says one commentator. 'Everybody knows that we are certainly among the top twenty-four nations in the world. But I don't blame Graham Taylor for failing to get us there. I blame the men who made him England's manager.'

'The fact that England are not in the World Cup is just an historical coincidence,' said another commentator. 'Domestic football is far more exciting than it was ten years ago.'

Who are these advocates for domestic football? Saint and Greavsie? Big Ron Atkinson and Jimmy Hill? In fact, respectively, they are Melvyn Bragg – broadcaster, novelist, Arsenal supporter – and Bill Buford – author, editor of the literary magazine *Granta* and Manchester United fan. Football is not merely more popular than it has ever been before. Suddenly, it is intellectually respectable.

There was something shaming about being a football fan in the '80s, the decade when the problems that had blighted the game for years – hooliganism, unsegregated fans, ancient terraces and fences that penned in the crowds like cattle – finally resulted in tragedy.

But even as the bodies piled up at Bradford (40 fans killed in a fire), Heysel (41 Italians crushed during a riot) and Hillsborough (96 Liverpool supporters crushed on the terraces), you knew that you would not – could not – stop loving this game, even if it seemed you would have to keep quiet about it in polite society. Decent people, it was believed, were not football fans. But now that has all changed. And our secret love's no secret any more.

Ian Hamilton, the poet and biographer, has just published his reflections on Paul Gascoigne, *Gazza Italia*, expanding on his long essay in *Granta*, 'Gazza Agonistes'. Benedict Mason's new opera, *Playing Away*, is the tale of Terry Bond, an ageing footballer. And BBC2 recently celebrated the start of the cricket season by broadcasting *Goal TV*, an entire evening's worth of football programming. Football is no longer the love that dare not speak its name. Now it is the passion that is shouted from the rooftops.

You can take football anywhere these days. John Major is the first Prime Minister to come out as a football fan (Chelsea) since Harold Wilson. But there is a crucial difference. In 1966 England were the kings of the footballing world. In 1994 we have an almost Third World status. And yet English football continues to boom, as gloriously self-contained as French cinema. Now *there*'s a hi-falutin' comparison you couldn't have got away with ten years ago!

How did we get from Heysel and Hillsborough to Gazza on the cover of *Granta* and 'Fantasy Football'? Melvyn Bragg sees the decline of hooliganism as a major factor in the sport's rehabilitation.

'I was one of the middle-aged men who had broken with the habit of going to football for ten, fifteen years,' he says. 'I returned when it felt reasonably safe. Then when you start going again you find you are keener than you ever were. Now I feel ludicrously involved.'

Bill Buford, whose book *Among the Thugs* was the result of spending eight years running with Manchester United hooligans (quite a feat for someone born in Baton Rouge, Louisiana), also cites the decline of football's riot culture as a reason for its renaissance.

'Violence was hip in the '70s and '80s,' says Buford. 'That is no longer the case, although there is still trouble and the violent fans come out of the woodwork for the big games. But something snapped after Hillsborough. The fans reclaimed the game. After Hillsborough there was the rise of the fanzines and the supporters' clubs, a celebration of the game that culminated in the 1990 World Cup and a series of serious books about football.'

There were great football books before the '90s but the game's library seemed pitifully modest compared to the acres of print devoted to cricket and boxing. But 1992 saw the publication of *Fever*

Pitch, Nick Hornby's critically acclaimed, commercially triumphant confession of his *amour fou* for Arsenal.

'I have measured out my life in Arsenal fixtures, and any event of any significance has a footballing shadow,' wrote Hornby. 'When did my first real love affair end? The day after a disappointing 2–2 draw at home to Coventry.'

Hornby's touching, funny, endlessly engaging account of a fan's life showed the world that football supporters were not all Cro-Magnon psychopaths. And it showed publishers that a football book could be a bestseller. *Fever Pitch* has sold 30,000 in hardback and 190,000 in paperback. Suddenly the world of books is taking football very seriously indeed.

'Publishers had taken the view that people who go to football are idiots and therefore they published idiotic books,' says Hornby. 'And then – incredibly! – no one wanted to buy them. So they gave up publishing football books altogether. But I did think *Fever Pitch* would sell when I was writing it. There was a market. The fanzines were doing very well. I was meeting people all over the place who went to football a lot and read a lot but had never read any books about football. Now there's an overreaction and now everyone's publishing anything about football they can get their hands on.'

Après 'Fever Pitch', *le déluge*. Flick through most publishers' catalogues for the coming months and you will see the obligatory football title. Hornby himself edited an anthology called *My Favourite Year*, containing football writing by Roddy Doyle, D. J. Taylor and other literary bods. But why weren't they writing about football ten years ago?

'Football has crossed the same threshold that music crossed in the '60s or that television crossed when Clive James and Julian Barnes were writing about it in the '80s,' says Bill Buford. 'These people have always been football fans but there was a sudden realisation that it was acceptable subject matter. And shared culture is an incredibly rich thing to write about.'

Nick Hornby is convinced that nobody is climbing on a football bandwagon. 'I have yet to meet this mythical person who didn't like football through the '70s and '80s and suddenly started to like it in the '90s when it was cool. These mythical people who used to play golf and now they've suddenly decided that they're Arsenal supporters. Someone like D. J. Taylor – who is a very studious, bookish man – is football mad. He was going to Norwich when he was seven or eight. But no one ever thought to ask him if he was interested in writing about football.'

Hornby maintains that football's change of fortune is largely generational. 'There are all these people in their thirties who grew up with the 1966 World Cup, the Manchester United team of Best, Law and Charlton, the Arsenal double side – and suddenly they are in the position to spout off about it. Football hasn't changed as much as the people who work in the media.'

'Writers felt a degree of self-consciousness in the past,' says Melvyn Bragg, who recently covered the European Cup Winners Cup Final for the *Sunday Express*. 'It was as if writing about football would look as though you were trying to show off your common touch.'

'Also masculinity has become a lot more self-analytical,' says Nick Hornby. 'Partly because people employ male writers to talk about it. Women commission men to talk about what it means to be a man. And football is a part of this.'

'The football ground is a place where men feel things more intensely and a far greater range of emotions than probably anywhere else in their life,' says Bill Buford. 'Much more feeling goes into this arena than, say, the relationship with their wives. And this very important experience has been discovered and that's the reason for the great excitement.'

But one man who is unimpressed by the torrents of new football writing is Hunter Davies, whose 1972 book about Spurs, *The Glory Game*, was the first truly great book on football's reading list.

'I suspect that all the people currently writing about football were weeds and wimps who never got a game of football at school,' says Davies. 'They might love football but they never played for the school team. That's my theory. They are like East European refugees trying to integrate themselves with an alien culture – in this case the working class.'

'It's no longer a working class game,' Melvyn Bragg says firmly. 'I have to pay nearly £500 each for our season tickets in the Upper East Stand at Highbury. And I meet all sorts of upper middle class people who are *seriously* interested in football.'

'Anyone who thinks it is only *The Late Show* crowd who go to football should sit there when Arsenal are playing West Ham,' says Nick Hornby. 'Even if there are a lot of middle class people they don't make much noise in a crowd of thirty thousand.'

But when did it all change? When was football's theatre of hate replaced by this field of dreams? Many see the turning point as the 1990 World Cup, when Pavarotti sang 'Nessun Dorma' and 30 million people watched Gazza weep, the emotional double whammy that helped humanise the game after years of rotten publicity.

'England went out there as no-hope yobs and played Germany off the pitch,' says Bragg. 'Gascoigne's tears made you realise how much it *mattered*.'

'Footballers have learned how to conduct themselves,' says Hunter Davies. 'Gary Lineker is the Queen Mother of football.'

But if the last World Cup was when football was truly rehabilitated, the seeds of the current revival were sown much earlier, in the horrors of the '80s. Football got better because it had hit bottom and could hardly get any worse.

And although the game has changed, it hasn't changed completely. Football still has an untamed, feral heart and despite some of the finest minds in the country flocking to football matches, and despite the all-seater stadia, segregated fans and Sky Sumo wrestlers at halftime, you can still sometimes catch a glimpse of the bad old days.

When Arsenal played Manchester United at Highbury late last season, the sending off of Eric Cantona, the flamboyant Frenchman, sparked a ferocious fight up in the expensive seats where my son and I were sitting. Two Arsenal supporters set about one United fan, clearing one of those sickening gaps in the crowd that always signalled that blood was being spilled. The United fan went down but the beating continued. No police came. No steward came. It went on and on. The thing you notice about football violence is that it is always horribly unfair.

'But they are all pretty old,' says Nick Hornby of the surviving football hooligans. 'They are all thirty-five and forty-year-old beer boys. I haven't seen any kids involved in anything for years. Football violence is worse in almost every other European country. You don't see it on the old large scale. You can't, not with seats.'

And it's true. Football might occasionally still provoke scenes that you very rarely see in the auditorium of the National Theatre. But the horrors of the '80s are unthinkable today. Football has boldly reinvented itself and stands revealed as what it has always been – the beautiful game, the ballet of the working man, the greatest sport in the world.

This social acceptability of football is no passing fad. Football is loved because it deserves to be loved. Our national game is facing a bright future and nothing can wipe the smile off its face. At least not unless the Argies or the Krauts win the World Cup.